Słownik idiomów

amerykańskich

dla Polaków

Słownik idiomów

amerykańskich

dla Polaków

Essential American Idioms for Polish Speakers

Richard A. Spears, Ph.D.
Ewa Niezgoda, Polish Editor

Printed on recyclable paper

NTC Publishing Group
Lincolnwood, Illinois USA

Library of Congress Cataloging-in-Publication Data

Spears, Richard A.
    Słownik idiomów amerykańskich dla Polaków = Essential American idioms
for Polish speakers / Richard A. Spears ; Ewa Niezgoda, Polish editor.
      p.   cm.
    ISBN 0-8442-4207-1 (paper)
    1. English language—Conversation and phrase books—Polish.
2. English language—United States—Idioms.   3. Americanisms.
I. Niezgoda, Ewa.   II. Title.
PE1129.S6S64   1997
428.3491851—dc21 *2. Polish Language*   97-15349
                                      CIP

TO THE USER

Every language has phrases that cannot be understood literally. Even if you know the meanings of all the words in such a phrase and you understand the grammar completely, the total meaning of the phrase may still be confusing. English has many thousands of such idiomatic expressions. This dictionary is a selection of the most frequently encountered idiomatic expressions found in everyday American English. The collection is small enough to serve as a useful study guide for learners, and large enough to serve as a reference for daily use.

The phrases in the dictionary come from many sources. Many have been collected from newspapers and magazines. Others have come from existing dictionaries and reference books. Students studying English as a second or foreign language at Northwestern University have also provided many of the entries, and their lists and questions have helped in selecting the particular idiomatic expressions that appear in this book.

Słownik idiomów amerykańskich dla Polaków: Essential American Idioms for Polish Speakers should prove very useful for Polish-speaking people who are learning how to understand idiomatic English.

How to Use This Dictionary

1. Expressions are entered in an alphabetical order that ignores hyphens, spaces, and other punctuation. Each expression is entered in its normal form and word order. Entries that begin with short function words such as *a, an, as, at, be, by, do, for, from, have, in, off, on, out, under,* and *up* appear both in normal word order and in inverted word order, cross-referenced to the normal entry; for example, at the entry **active duty, on** the reader is referred to the entry **on active duty**.

2. A main entry may have one or more alternate forms. The main entry and its alternate forms are printed in **boldface type**, and the alternate forms are preceded by "AND." Two or more alternate forms are separated by a semicolon. Words enclosed in parentheses in any entry form are optional. For example: **break (out) into tears** stands for **break out into tears** and **break into tears**. When entry phrases are referred to in the dictionary, they are printed in *slanted type*.

3. Some of the entry phrases have more than one major sense. These meanings are numbered with boldface numerals. Nubered senses may also have additional forms that are shown in boldface type after the numeral. See, for example, **get something sewed up**.

4. Some entries have additional related forms within the entry. These forms are introduced by "ALSO," and cross-referencing leads the user to each of these embedded entries. See, for example, **get a black eye**.

5. Alternate forms of the definitions are separated by semi-colons, and some definitions are followed by comments or explanations in parentheses. See, for example, **add fuel to the fire**.

6. In some cases where the entry phrase refers to either people or things—as expressed by "**someone or something**"—the numbered senses can be used with people only or things only. In such cases the numbered sense begins with "[with *someone*]" or "[with *something*]." See, for example, **cut someone or something to the bone**.

7. Each entry or sense has at least two examples printed in *italics*.

A

A bird in the hand is worth two in the bush. przysłowie mówiące, że coś, co już masz jest lepsze od czegoś, co dopiero możesz dostać. ❏ *Bill has offered to buy my car for $3,000. Someone else might pay more, but Bill made a good offer, and a bird in the hand is worth two in the bush.* ❏ *I might be able to find a better offer, but a bird in the hand is worth two in the bush.*

according to Hoyle zgodnie z zasadami; zgodnie ze sposobem, w jaki coś się normalnie robi. (Wyrażenie odnosi się do reguł gier; Edmond Hoyle napisał na ten temat książkę. Wyrażenia używa się w odniesieniu do czegoś innego niż gry.) ❏ *That's wrong. According to Hoyle, this is the way to do it.* ❏ *The carpenter said, "This is the way to drive a nail, according to Hoyle."*

a chip off the old block ktoś (zwykle mężczyzna) zachowujący się tak samo jak jego ojciec lub bardzo podobny do ojca (Ojciec to "stary pień"– "an old block".) ❏ *John looks like his father – a real chip off the old block.* ❏ *Bill Jones, Jr., is a chip off the old block. He's a banker just like his father.*

act high-and-mighty zachowywać się dumnie i władczo; zachowywać się wyniośle. ❏ *Why does the doctor always have to act so high-and-mighty?* ❏ *If Sally wouldn't act so high-and-mighty, she'd have more friends.*

Actions speak louder than words. przysłowie mówiące, że lepiej coś zrobić, by rozwiązać problem niż tylko o tym mówić. ❏ *Mary kept promising to get a job. John finally looked her in the eye and said, "Actions speak louder than words!"* ❏ *After listening to the senator promising to cut federal spending, Ann wrote a simple note saying, "Actions speak louder than words."*

active duty, on Patrz *on active duty.*

act of God wydarzenie (zwykle wypadek), za który człowiek nie jest odpowiedzialny; żywioł taki jak burza, trzęsienie ziemi czy sztorm. ❑ *My insurance company wouldn't pay for the damage because it was an act of God.* ❑ *The thief tried to convince the judge that the diamonds were in his pocket due to an act of God.*

act one's age zachowywać się w sposób bardziej dojrzały; zachowywać się stosownie do swojego wieku. (Często używane w stosunku do dzieci lub nastolatków.) ❑ *Come on, John, act your age. Stop throwing rocks.* ❑ *Mary! Stop picking on your little brother. Act your age!*

add fuel to the fire AND **add fuel to the flame** pogorszyć sytuację; powiedzieć lub zrobić coś, co jeszcze pogorszy sprawę; jeszcze bardziej rozzłościć kogoś już zagniewanego. ❑ *To spank a crying child just adds fuel to the fire.* ❑ *Bill was shouting angrily, and Bob tried to get him to stop by laughing at him. Of course, that was just adding fuel to the flame.*

add fuel to the flame Patrz poprzednie hasło.

add insult to injury pogorszyć sytuację; jeszcze bardziej urazić kogoś, kogo uczucia już zostały zranione. (Klisza.) ❑ *First, the basement flooded, and then, to add insult to injury, a pipe burst in the kitchen.* ❑ *My car barely started this morning, and to add insult to injury, I got a flat tire in the driveway.*

A fool and his money are soon parted. przysłowie mówiące, że ktoś, kto niemądrze wydaje pieniądze, szybko je traci. (Często mówi się tak o kimś, kto właśnie stracił jakąś kwotę z powodu złego oszacowania czegoś). ❑ *When Bill lost a $400 bet on a horse race, Mary said, "A fool and his money are soon parted."* ❑ *When John bought a cheap used car that fell apart the next day, he said, "Oh, well, a fool and his money are soon parted."*

afraid of one's own shadow ktoś, kogo łatwo przerazić; zawsze przestraszony, nieśmiały lub podejrzliwy. (Nigdy nie używane dosłownie.) ❑ *After Tom was robbed, he was even afraid of his* *own shadow.* ❑ *Jane has always been a shy child. She has been a-fraid of her own shadow since she was three.*

A friend in need is a friend indeed przysłowie mówiące, że prawdziwy przyjaciel to taki, który pomoże ci wtedy, kiedy pomocy potrzebujesz. ❑ *When Bill helped me with geometry, I really learned the meaning of "A friend in need is a friend indeed."* ❑ *"A friend in need is a friend indeed" sounds silly until you need someone very badly.*

against the clock w wyścigu z czasem; w ogromnym pośpiechu, by zrobić coś przed określonym czasem. ❑ *Bill set a new track record, running against the clock. He lost the actual race, however.* ❑ *In a race against the clock, they rushed the special medicine to the hospital.*

air, in the Patrz *in the air.*

air, off the Patrz *off the air.*

air, on the Patrz *on the air.*

air someone's dirty linen in public dyskutować publicznie o prywatnych lub kłopotliwych sprawach, zwłaszcza podczas kłótni. (Ta *bielizna* odnosi się do problemów, porównując je do prześcieradeł, obrusów, lub innej brudnej bielizny.) ❑ *John's mother had asked him repeatedly not to air the family's dirty linen in public.* ❑ *Mr. and Mrs. Johnson are arguing again. Why must they always air their dirty linen in public?*

air, up in the Patrz *up in the air.*

a little bird told me wiadomość z tajnego lub tajemniczego źródła. (Stosowane często jako unik, kiedy nie chcemy powiedzieć, skąd się czegoś dowiedzieliśmy. W niektórych sytuacjach niegrzeczne.) ❑ *" All right," said Mary, " where did you get that information?" John replied, " A little bird told me."* ❑ *A little bird told me where I might find you.*

A little knowledge is a dangerous thing. przysłowie mówiące, że niepełna wiedza może albo wprawić w zakłopotanie, albo wyrządzić krzywdę. ❏ *The doctor said, "Just because you've had a course in first aid, you shouldn't have treated your own illness. A little knowledge is a dangerous thing."* ❏ *John thought he knew how to take care of the garden, but he killed all the flowers. A little knowledge is a dangerous thing.*

all fours, on Patrz *on all fours.*

all in a day's work część tego, czego się oczekuje; typowe lub normalne. ❏ *I don't particularly like to cook, but it's all in a day's work.* ❏ *Putting up with rude customers isn't pleasant, but it's all in a day's work.* ❏ *Cleaning up after other people is all in a day's work for a chambermaid.*

all over but the shouting zdecydowane i ukończone; dzieło zakończone, pozostaje go uczcić. (Rozwinięcie wyrażenia *all over,* które oznacza "zakończone.") ❏ *The last goal was made just as the final whistle sounded. Tom said, "Well, it's all over but the shouting."* ❏ *Tom worked hard in college and graduated last month. When he got his diploma, he said, "It's all over but the shouting."*

All roads lead to Rome. przysłowie mówiące, że istnieje wiele dróg prowadzących do tego samego celu. ❏ *Mary was criticizing the way Jane was planting the flowers. John said, "Never mind, Mary, all roads lead to Rome."* ❏ *Some people learn by doing. Others have to be taught. In the long run, all roads lead to Rome.*

all skin and bones Patrz *nothing but skin and bones.*

All's well that ends well. przysłowie mówiące, że coś, co się dobrze skończyło, było dobre, nawet jeśli po drodze wydarzyło się coś złego. (Jest to tytuł sztuki Szekspira. Obecnie stosowane jako klisza.) ❏ *I'm glad you finally got here, even though your car had a flat tire on the way. Oh, well. All's well that ends well.* ❏ *The groom was late for the wedding, but everything worked out all right. All's well that ends well.*

All that glitters is not gold. przysłowie mówiące, że wiele atrakcyjnych na pierwszy rzut oka rzeczy nie ma żadnej wartości. ❏ *The used car looked fine but didn't run well at all. "Ah, yes,"* *thought Bill, "all that glitters is not gold."* ❏ *When Mary was disappointed about losing Tom, Jane reminded her, "All that glitters is not gold."*

all thumbs bardzo niezgrabny i niezręczny, zwłaszcza jeśli chodzi o sprawne posługiwanie się rękami. (Oznacza to tyle, że czyjeś ręce składają się wyłącznie z kciuków.) ❏ *Poor Bob can't play the piano at all. He's all thumbs.* ❏ *Mary is all thumbs when it comes to gardening.*

all walks of life wszystkie grupy społeczne, ekonomiczne i etniczne. (Wyrażenie utarte. Nie występuje w liczbie pojedynczej lub bez *all*.) ❏ *We saw people there from all walks of life.* ❏ *The people who came to the art exhibit represented all walks of life.*

All work and no play makes Jack a dull boy. przysłowie mówiące, że powinno się nie tylko pracować, ale także wypoczywać. (*Jack* nie odnosi się tutaj do nikogo konkretnego i wyrażenie stosuje się w odniesieniu do osób obojga płci.) ❏ *Stop reading that book and go out and play! All work and no play makes Jack a dull boy.* ❏ *The doctor told Mr. Jones to stop working on weekends and start playing golf, because all work and no play makes Jack a dull boy.*

An eye for an eye, a tooth for a tooth. powiedzenie biblijne wskazujące, że kara powinna być równa przewinieniu. (Obecnie stosowane jako przysłowie. Nie używane w znaczeniu dosłownym.) ❏ *Little John pulled Jane's hair, so the teacher pulled John's hair as punishment, saying, "An eye for an eye, a tooth for a tooth."* ❏ *He kicked me in the leg, so I kicked him in the leg. After all, an eye for an eye, a tooth for a tooth.*

An ounce of prevention is worth a pound of cure. przysłowie mówiące, że łatwiej i lepiej jest do czegoś nie dopuścić niż mieć do czynienia ze skutkami tego. ❏ *When you ride in a car, buckle your seat belt. An ounce of prevention is worth a pound of cure.* ❏ *Every child should be vaccinated against polio. An ounce of prevention is worth a pound of cure.*

A penny saved is a penny earned. przysłowie mówiące, że pieniądze zaoszczędzone są tym samym, co pieniądze zarobione. (Czasami używane dla usprawiedliwienia chciwości.) ❏ *"I didn't* *want to pay that much for the book," said Mary."After all, a penny saved is a penny earned."* ❏ *Bob put his money in a new bank that pays more interest than his old bank, saying, "A penny saved is a penny earned."*

apple of someone's eye ulubiona osoba lub rzecz; czyjś chłopak lub dziewczyna; rzecz lub osoba, której ktoś pragnie. (Osoba lub rzecz, która wpadła komuś w oko lub zwróciła czyjąś uwagę.) ❏ *Tom is the apple of Mary's eye. She thinks he's great.* ❏ *John's new stereo is the apple of his eye.*

armed to the teeth uzbrojony w wiele rodzajów śmiertelnej broni. (Jakby użyto wszelkiego rodzaju zbroi, po zęby i łącznie z nimi.) ❏ *The bank robber was armed to the teeth when he was caught.* ❏ *There are too many guns around. The entire country is armed to the teeth.*

arm in arm o ludziach trzymających się pod rękę. ❏ *The two lovers walked arm in arm down the street.* ❏ *Arm in arm, the line of dancers kicked high, and the audience roared its approval.*

arms, up in Patrz *up in arms.*

A rolling stone gathers no moss. przysłowie opisujące kogoś, kto stale zmienia pracę lub miejsce zamieszkania i dlatego ani nie gromadzi majątku, ani nie ponosi odpowiedzialności. (Zwykle rozumiane jako krytyka.) ❏ *"John just can't seem to stay in one place," said Sally. "Oh, well, a rolling stone gathers no moss."* ❏ *Bill has no furniture to bother with because he keeps on the move. He keeps saying that a rolling stone gathers no moss.*

as a duck takes to water łatwo i w naturalny sposób. (Odnosi się do kacząt, które potrafią pływać jak tylko wejdą po raz pierwszy do wody.) ❏ *She took to singing, just as a duck takes to water.* ❏ *The baby adapted to bottle-feeding as a duck takes to water.*

as an aside jako uwaga na boku; jako komentarz nie przeznaczony dla wszystkich. ❏ *At the wedding, Tom said as an aside,"The bride doesn't look well."* ❏ *At the ballet, Billy said as an aside to his mother, "I hope the dancers fall off the stage!"*

as bad as all that tak zły, jak się o tym mówi; tak zły, jak się wydaje. (Zwykle w formie przeczącej.) ❏ *Come on! Nothing could be
as bad as all that.* ❏ *Stop crying. It can't be as bad as all that.*

as blind as a bat o słabym wzroku; ślepy. (Pierwsze *as* można
opuścić. Nietoperze nie są jednak ślepe. Wyrażenie przetrwało ze
względu na aliterację.) ❏ *My grandmother is as blind as a bat.*
❏ *I'm getting blind as a bat. I can hardly read this page.*

as busy as a beaver AND **as busy as a bee** bardzo zajęty.
(Pierwsze *as* można opuścić. Wyrażenia przetrwały ze względu na
aliterację.) ❏ *I don't have time to talk to you. I'm as busy as a
beaver.* ❏ *You don't look busy as a beaver to me.* ❏ *Whenever
there is a holiday, we are all as busy as bees.*

as busy as a bee Patrz poprzednie hasło.

as busy as Grand Central Station bardzo ruchliwy; zatłoczony
klientami lub innymi ludźmi. (Pierwsze *as* można opuścić. Wyrażenie odnosi się do Grand Central Station w Nowym Yorku.)
❏ *This house is as busy as Grand Central Station.* ❏ *When the
tourist season starts, this store is busy as Grand Central Station.*

as clear as mud całkowicie niezrozumiały. (Potoczne lub żarto-
bliwe. Pierwsze *as* można opuścić.) ❏ *Your explanation is as
clear as mud.* ❏ *This doesn't make sense. It's clear as mud.*

as comfortable as an old shoe bardzo wygodne; wygodne i
znajome. (Pierwsze *as* można opuścić. Wyrażenie odwołuje się do
noszonych przez jakiś czas i dlatego wygodnych butów.) ❏ *This
old house is fine. It's as comfortable as an old shoe.* ❏ *That's a
great tradition – comfortable as an old shoe.*

as cool as a cucumber spokojny i chłodny; opanowany.
(Pierwsze *as* można opuścić. Jednak ogórki niekoniecznie są
chłodne. Wyrażenie przetrwało ze względu na aliterację.) ❏ *The
captain remained as cool as a cucumber as the passengers
boarded the lifeboats.* ❏ *During the fire the home owner was cool
as a cucumber.*

as crazy as a loon bardzo głupi; kompletnie szalony. (Pierwsze *as* można opuścić. Nur to ptak wodny, którego wołanie brzmi jak głupi śmiech.) ❑ *If you think you can get away with that, you're as crazy as a loon.* ❑ *Poor old John is crazy as a loon.*

as dead as a dodo martwy; już nie istniejący. (Pierwsze *as* można opuścić. Dodo – starożytny ptak z wyspy Mauritius – jest ptakiem wymarłym. Wyrażenie przetrwało ze względu na aliterację.) ❑ *Yes, Adolf Hitler is really dead – as dead as a dodo.* ❑ *That silly old idea is dead as a dodo.*

as dead as a doornail martwy. (Pierwsze *as* można opuścić. O-czywiście, gwoździe w drzwiach nigdy nie były czymś żywym. Wyrażenie przetrwało ze względu na aliterację.) ❑ *This fish is as dead as a doornail.* ❑ *John kept twisting the chicken's neck even though it was dead as a doornail.*

as different as night and day całkowicie różny. (Pierwsze *as* można opuścić.) ❑ *Although Bobby and Billy are twins, they are as different as night and day.* ❑ *Birds and bats appear to be similar, but they are different as night and day.*

as easy as (apple) pie bardzo łatwy. (Pierwsze *as* można opuścić. Zakłada się tutaj, że robienie jabłecznika jest łatwe.) ❑ *Mountain climbing is as easy as pie.* ❑ *Making a simple dress out of cotton cloth is easy as pie.*

as easy as duck soup bardzo łatwe; nie wymagające żadnego wysiłku. (Kaczka podczas gotowania wydziela bardzo dużo tłuszczu i soków, dlatego "zupa" powstaje bez wysiłku. (Pierwsze *as* można opuścić.) ❑ *Finding your way to the shopping center is easy as duck soup.* ❑ *Getting Bob to eat fried chicken is as easy as duck soup.*

as far as it goes na tyle, na ile wystarcza; o tyle, o ile. (Zwykle mówi się tak o czymś niewystarczającym.) ❑ *Your plan is fine as far as it goes. It doesn't seem to take care of everything, though.* ❑ *As far as it goes, this law is a good one. It should require stiffer penalties, however.*

as fit as a fiddle zdrowy i sprawny fizycznie. (Pierwsze *as* można opuścić. Wyrażenie nie ma sensu. Przetrwało ze względu na aliterację.) ❑ *Mary is as fit as a fiddle.* ❑ *Tom used to be fit as a fiddle. Look at him now!*

as flat as a pancake bardzo płaski. (Pierwsze *as* można opuścić.) ❑ *The punctured tire was as flat as a pancake.* ❑ *Bobby squashed the ant flat as a pancake.*

as free as a bird beztroski; całkowicie wolny. (Pierwsze *as* można opuścić.) ❑ *Jane is always happy and free as a bird.* ❑ *The convict escaped from jail and was as free as a bird for two days.* ❑ *In the summer I feel free as a bird.*

as full as a tick AND **as tight as a tick** pełen jedzenia i picia. (Odnosi się do kleszcza, który się opił krwi. Pierwsze *as* można o-puścić.) ❑ *Little Billy ate and ate until he was as full as a tick.* ❑ *Our cat drank the cream until he became full as a tick.*

as funny as a crutch mało zabawny. (Pierwsze *as* można opu-ścić.) ❑ *Your trick is about as funny as a crutch. Nobody thought it was funny.* ❑ *The well-dressed lady slipped and fell in the gutter, which was funny as a crutch.*

as good as done tak samo jakby było zrobione; prawie zrobione. (Wiele różnych imiesłowów może zastąpić *done* w tym wyrażeniu: *cooked, dead, finished, painted, typed,* etc.) ❑ *This job is as good as done. It'll just take another second.* ❑ *Yes, sir, if you hire me to paint your house, it's as good as painted.* ❑ *When I hand my secretary a letter to be typed, I know that it's as good as typed right then and there.*

as good as gold prawdziwy, autentyczny. (Klisza. Pierwsze *as* można opuścić. Wyrażenie przetrwało ze wzgędu na aliterację.) ❑ *Mary's promise is as good as gold.* ❑ *Yes, this diamond is genuine – good as gold.*

as happy as a clam szczęśliwy i zadowolony. (Pierwsze *as* moż-na opuścić. Zauważ zróżnicowanie przykładów. Mięczaki nieko-niecznie są szczęśliwe lub smutne.) ❑ *Tom sat there smiling, as* *happy as a clam.* ❏ *There they all sat, eating corn on the cob and looking happy as clams.*

as happy as a lark widać, że szczęśliwy i radosny. (Pierwsze *as* można opuścić. Zauważ różnice w przykładach.) ❏ *Sally walked along whistling, as happy as a lark.* ❏ *The children danced and sang, happy as larks.*

as hard as nails bardzo twardy; zimny i okrutny. (Odwołuje się do gwoździ przybijanych młotkiem. Pierwsze *as* można opuścić.) ❏ *The old loaf of bread was dried out and became as hard as nails.* ❏ *Ann was unpleasant and hard as nails.*

as high as a kite AND **as high as the sky** (Pierwsze *as* można opuścić.) **1.** bardzo wysoki. ❏ *The tree grew as high as a kite.* ❏ *Our pet bird got outside and flew up high as the sky.* **2.** pijany lub pod wpływem narkotyków. ❏ *Bill drank beer until he got as high as a kite.* ❏ *The thieves were high as the sky on drugs.*

as high as the sky Patrz poprzednie hasło.

as hungry as a bear bardzo głodny. (Pierwsze *as* można opuścić.) ❏ *I'm as hungry as a bear. I could eat anything!* ❏ *Whenever I jog, I get hungry as a bear.*

aside, as an Patrz *as an aside.*

as innocent as a lamb niewinny; naiwny. (Klisza. Pierwsze *as* można opuścić.) ❏ *"Hey! You can't throw me in jail," cried the robber. "I'm innocent as a lamb."* ❏ *Look at the baby, as innocent as a lamb.*

as it were jak można by powiedzieć. (Czasami używane jako zastrzeżenie przy nieprawdopodobnie brzmiących stwierdzeniach.) ❏ *He carefully constructed, as it were, a huge sandwich.* ❏ *The Franklins live in a small, as it were, exquisite house.*

ask for the moon prosić o zbyt wiele; stawiać wielkie wymagania; prosić o coś, co jest trudne lub niemożliwe do uzyskania. (Nie stosowane dosłownie.) ❏ *When you're trying to get a job, it's unwise* *to ask for the moon.* ❑ *Please lend me the money. I'm not asking for the moon!*

ask for trouble zrobić lub powiedzieć coś, co spowoduje kłopot. ❑ *Stop talking to me that way, John. You're just asking for trouble.* ❑ *Anybody who threatens a police officer is just asking for trouble.*

asleep at the switch nie przykładający wagi do pracy; nie wykonujący obowiązków we właściwym czasie. (Wyrażenie niekoniecznie musi mieć związek z prawdziwym kontaktem.) ❑ *The guard was asleep at the switch when the robber broke in.* ❑ *If I hadn't been asleep at the switch, I'd have seen the stolen car.*

as light as a feather niewiele ważący. (Pierwsze *as* można opuścić.) ❑ *Sally dieted until she was as light as a feather.* ❑ *Of course I can lift the box. It's light as a feather.*

as likely as not najprawdopodobniej. (Pierwsze *as* można opuścić. Wyrażenie utarte; nie istnieje w innych formach.) ❑ *He will as likely as not arrive without warning.* ❑ *Likely as not, the game will be cancelled.*

as luck would have it na szczęście lub nieszczęście; jak się okazało; przypadkiem. (Wyrażenie utarte; nie istnieje w innych formach.) ❑ *As luck would have it, we had a flat tire.* ❑ *As luck would have it, the check came in the mail today.*

as mad as a hatter 1. szalony. (Od postaci Szalonego Kapelusznika w "*Alicji w krainie czarów*" Lewisa Carrolla. Pierwsze *as* można opuścić.) ❑ *Poor old John is as mad as a hatter.* ❑ *All these screaming children are driving me mad as a hatter.* **2.** wściekły. (To znaczenie wywodzi się ze złego zrozumienia *mad* w znaczeniu poprzednim. Pierwsze *as* można opuścić.) ❑ *You make me so angry! I'm as mad as a hatter.* ❑ *John can't control his temper. He's always mad as a hatter.*

as mad as a hornet wściekły. (Pierwsze *as* można opuścić. Szerszenie są znane ze złości.) ❑ *You make me so angry. I'm as mad as a hornet.* ❑ *Jane can get mad as a hornet when somebody criticizes her.*

11

as mad as a March hare szalony. (Od imienia postaci w "*Alicji w krainie czarów*" Lewisa Carrolla. Pierwsze *as* można opuścić.) ❑ *Sally is getting as mad as a March hare.* ❑ *My Uncle Bill is mad as a March hare.*

as mad as a wet hen rozgniewany. (Pierwsze *as* można opuścić. Można przypuszczać, że grymaśna kura złości się, kiedy moknie.) ❑ *Bob was screaming and shouting – as mad as a wet hen.* ❑ *What you said made Mary mad as a wet hen.*

as one jakby grupa stanowiła jedność. (Zwłaszcza z *act, move*, lub *speak*.) ❑ *All the dancers moved as one.* ❑ *The chorus spoke as one.*

as plain as day (Pierwsze *as* można opuścić.) **1.** bardzo zwyczajny i prosty. ❑ *Although his face was as plain as day, his smile made him look interesting and friendly.* ❑ *Our house is plain as day, but it's comfortable.* **2.** jasny i zrozumiały. (Tak jasny jak światło dnia.) ❑ *The lecture was as plain as day. No one had to ask questions.* ❑ *His statement was plain as day.*

as plain as the nose on one's face oczywisty; wyraźnie widoczny. (Pierwsze as można opuścić.) ❑ *What do you mean you don't understand? It's as plain as the nose on your face.* ❑ *Your guilt is plain as the nose on your face.*

as poor as a church mouse bardzo biedny. (Klisza. Pierwsze *as* można opuścić. Zakładając, że ci związani z kościołem są biedni, skromna mysz byłaby najbiedniejszym stworzeniem w kościele.) ❑ *My aunt is as poor as a church mouse.* ❑ *The Browns are poor as church mice.*

as pretty as a picture bardzo ładny. (Klisza. Pierwsze *as* można opuścić. Przetrwało ze względu na aliterację.) ❑ *Sweet little Mary is as pretty as a picture.* ❑ *Their new house is pretty as a picture.*

as proud as a peacock bardzo dumny; wyniosły. (Klisza. Pierwsze *as* można opuścić. Odwołuje się do pięknych piór na pawim ogonie. Przetrwało ze względu na aliterację.) ❑ *John is so arrogant. He's as proud as a peacock.* ❑ *The new father was proud as a peacock.*

as quick as a wink bardzo szybko. (Klisza. Pierwsze *as* można opuścić. Odwołuje się do mrugnięcia okiem.) ❏ *As quick as a wink, the thief took the lady's purse.* ❏ *I'll finish this work quick as a wink.*

as quiet as a mouse bardzo spokojny; nieśmiały i milczący. (Często używane w odniesieniu do dzieci. Pierwsze *as* można opuścić.) ❏ *Don't yell; whisper. Be as quiet as a mouse.* ❏ *Mary hardly ever says anything. She's quiet as a mouse.*

as regular as clockwork niezwykle punktualny. (Pierwsze *as* można opuścić.) ❏ *She comes into this store every day, as regular as clockwork.* ❏ *Our tulips come up every year, regular as clockwork.*

as scarce as hens' teeth AND **scarcer than hens' teeth** bardzo rzadki albo nieistniejący. (Klisza. Kury nie mają zębów. Pierwsze *as* można opuścić.) ❏ *I've never seen one of those. They're as scarce as hens' teeth.* ❏ *I was told that the part needed for my car is scarcer than hens' teeth, and it would take a long time to find one.*

as sick as a dog bardzo chory; chory i wymiotujący. (Pierwsze *as* można opuścić. Odwołuje się do bolesnych nudności psa.) ❏ *We've never been so ill. The whole family was sick as dogs.* ❏ *Sally was as sick as a dog and couldn't go to the party.*

as slippery as an eel pokrętny; nie spolegliwy. (Stosowane również dosłownie. Pierwsze *as* można opuścić.) ❏ *Tom can't be trusted. He's as slippery as an eel.* ❏ *It's hard to catch Joe in his office because he's slippery as an eel.*

as smart as a fox sprytny i mądry. (Pierwsze *as* można opuścić.) ❏ *My nephew is as smart as a fox.* ❏ *You have to be smart as a fox to outwit me.*

as snug as a bug in a rug przytulny i wygodny. (Rzeczy tego typu mówi się dzieciom kładąc je spać. Pierwsze *as* można opuścić. Przetrwało ze względu na rym.) ❏ *Let's pull up the covers. There you are, Bobby, as snug as a bug in a rug.* ❏ *What a lovely little house! I know I'll be snug as a bug in a rug.*

13

as sober as a judge (Klisza. Pierwsze *as* można opuścić.) **1.** bardzo oficjalny, trzeźwy lub sztywny. ❑ *You certainly look gloomy, Bill. You're sober as a judge.* ❑ *Tom's as sober as a judge. I think he's angry.* **2.** nie-pijany; czujny i całkowicie trzeźwy. (Wywodzi się z niezrozumienia pierwszego znaczenia.) ❑ *John's drunk? No, he's as sober as a judge.* ❑ *You should be sober as a judge when you drive a car.*

as soft as a baby's bottom bardzo miękki i gładki w dotyku. (Pierwsze *as* można opuścić.) ❑ *This cloth is as soft as a baby's bottom.* ❑ *No, Bob doesn't shave yet. His cheeks are soft as a baby's bottom.*

as soon as possible najszybciej jak można. ❑ *I'm leaving now. I'll be there as soon as possible.* ❑ *Please pay me as soon as possible.*

as strong as an ox bardzo silny. (Pierwsze *as* można opuścić.) ❑ *Tom lifts weights and is as strong as an ox.* ❑ *Now that Ann has recovered from her illness, she's strong as an ox.*

as stubborn as a mule bardzo uparty. (Pierwsze *as* można opuścić.) ❑ *My husband is as stubborn as a mule.* ❑ *Our cat is stubborn as a mule.*

as the crow flies prosto na przełaj, w przeciwieństwie do odległości mierzonych zgodnie z linią drogi, rzeki etc. (Powiedzenie zakłada, że kruki latają prosto.) ❑ *It's twenty miles to town on the highway, but only ten miles as the crow flies.* ❑ *Our house is only a few miles from the lake as the crow flies.*

as thick as pea soup bardzo gęsty. Zwykle używane w odniesieniu do mgły. (Pierwsze *as* można opuścić.) ❑ *This fog is as thick as pea soup.* ❑ *Wow, this coffee is strong! It's thick as pea soup.*

as thick as thieves bardzo blisko związani; zaprzyjaźnieni; złączeni. (Klisza. Pierwsze *as* można opuścić. Przetrwało ze względu na aliterację.) ❑ *Mary, Tom, and Sally are as thick as thieves. They go everywhere together.* ❑ *Those two families are thick as thieves.*

as tight as a tick Patrz pod *as full as a tick.*

as tight as Dick's hatband bardzo ciasny. (Pierwsze *as* można opuścić. Bardzo stare wyrażenie) ❏ *I've got to lose some weight. My belt is as tight as Dick's hatband.* ❏ *This window is stuck tight as Dick's hatband.*

a stone's throw away niewielka odległość; względnie niewielka odległość. (Może odnosić się do odległości w stopach lub milach.) ❏ *John saw Mary across the street, just a stone's throw away.* ❏ *Philadelphia is just a stone's throw away from New York City.*

as weak as a kitten słaby; słaby i chory. (Pierwsze *as* można opuścić. Odwołuje się do nowo narodzonych kociąt.) ❏ *John is as weak as a kitten because he doesn't eat well.* ❏ *Oh! Suddenly I feel weak as a kitten.*

as white as the driven snow bardzo biały. (Klisza. Pierwsze *as* można opuścić.) ❏ *I like my bed sheets to be as white as the driven snow.* ❏ *We have a new kitten whose fur is white as the driven snow.*

as wise as an owl bardzo mądry. (Pierwsze *as* można opuścić.) ❏ *Grandfather is as wise as an owl.* ❏ *My goal is to be wise as an owl.*

at a premium o wysokiej cenie; wysoko wyceniony ze względu na coś specjalnego. ❏ *Sally bought the shoes at a premium because they were of very high quality.* ❏ *This model of car is selling at a premium because so many people want to buy it.*

at a snail's pace bardzo powoli. ❏ *When you watch a clock, time seems to move at a snail's pace.* ❏ *You always eat at a snail's pace. I'm tired of waiting for you.*

at death's door blisko śmierci. (Eufemistyczne i dosłowne.) ❏ *I was so ill that I was at death's door.* ❏ *The family dog was at death's door for three days, and then it finally died.*

at half-mast w połowie drogi, w dół lub w górę. (Pierwotnie odnoszone do flag. Może być użyte jako żart w odniesieniu do rzeczy innych niż flaga.) ❏ *The flag was flying at half-mast because the general had died.* ❏ *Americans fly flags at half-mast on Memorial Day.* ❏ *The little boy ran out of the house with his pants at half-mast.*

at loggerheads w opozycji; w impasie; w niezgodzie. ❏ *Mr. and Mrs. Franklin have been at loggerheads for years.* ❏ *The two political parties were at loggerheads during the entire legislative session.*

at loose ends niespokojny i nieustabilizowany; bezrobotny. ❏ *Just before school starts, all the children are at loose ends.* ❏ *When Tom is home on the weekends, he's always at loose ends.* ❏ *Jane has been at loose ends ever since she lost her job.*

at one fell swoop AND **in one fell swoop** jednorazowo; natychmiast. (W wyrażeniu tym przetrwało stare słowo *fell*, oznaczające "okropny" lub "śmiertelny." Obecnie klisza, czasami o humorystycznym zabarwieniu.) ❏ *The party guests ate up all the snacks at one fell swoop.* ❏ *When the stock market crashed, many large fortunes were wiped out in one fell swoop.*

at one's wit's end na granicy czyichś intelektualnych możliwości. ❏ *I'm at my wit's end with this problem. I cannot figure it out.* ❏ *Tom could do no more. He was at his wit's end.*

at sea (about something) zmieszany; zagubiony i zdezorientowany. (Jakby zagubiony na morzu.) ❏ *Mary is all at sea about getting married.* ❏ *When it comes to higher math, John is totally at sea.*

at sixes and sevens nieuporządkowany; zagubiony i oszołomiony. (Zapożyczone z gry w kości.) ❏ *Mrs. Smith is at sixes and sevens since the death of her husband.* ❏ *Bill is always at sixes and sevens when he's home by himself.*

at someone's doorstep AND **on someone's doorstep** pod czyjąś opieką; jako czyjaś odpowiedzialność. (Nie używane dosłownie.) ❏ *Why do you always have to lay your problems at my doorstep?* ❏ *I shall put this issue on someone else's doorstep.* ❏ *I don't want it on my doorstep.*

at the bottom of the ladder na najniższym szczeblu zapłaty i statusu. ❑ *Most people start work at the bottom of the ladder.* ❑ *When Ann got fired, she had to start all over again at the bottom of the ladder.*

at the drop of a hat natychmiast i bez nalegania. ❑ *John was always ready to go fishing at the drop of a hat.* ❑ *If you need help, just call on me. I can come at the drop of a hat.*

at the eleventh hour w ostatnim możliwym momencie. ❑ *She always turned her term papers in at the eleventh hour.* ❑ *We don't worry about death until the eleventh hour.*

at the end of one's rope AND **at the end of one's tether** na granicy czyjejś wytrzymałości. ❑ *I'm at the end of my rope! I just can't go on this way!* ❑ *These kids are driving me out of my mind. I'm at the end of my tether.*

at the end of one's tether Patrz poprzednie hasło.

at the last minute przy ostatniej możliwej okazji. ❑ *Please don't make reservations at the last minute.* ❑ *Why do you ask all your questions at the last minute?*

at the outside najwyżej, najpóźniej. ❑ *The car repairs will cost $300 at the outside.* ❑ *I'll be there in three weeks at the outside.*

at the top of one's lungs Patrz następne hasło.

at the top of one's voice AND **at the top of one's lungs** bardzo głośno; tak głośno, jak tylko można mówić lub wrzeszczeć. ❑ *Bill called to Mary at the top of his voice.* ❑ *How can I work when you're all talking at the top of your lungs?*

at this stage (of the game) w danym punkcie jakiegoś zdarzenia; obecnie. ❑ *We'll have to wait and see. There isn't much we can do at this stage of the game.* ❑ *At this stage, we are better off not calling the doctor.*

average, on the Patrz *on the average.*

A watched pot never boils. przysłowie mówiące, że skupianie się na problemie nie pomaga w jego rozwiązaniu. (Odwołuje się do długiego - jak czekającemu się wydaje - czasu potrzebnego na zagotowanie wody wtedy, kiedy się ją obserwuje. Mówi się tak o problemie, na którym ktoś się bardzo skupia.) ❏ *John was looking out the window, waiting eagerly for the mail to be delivered. Ann said, "Be patient. A watched pot never boils."* ❏ *Billy weighed himself four times a day while he was trying to lose weight. His mother said, "Relax. A watched pot never boils."*

away from one's desk telefonicznie niedostępny; nie można się z nim widzieć. (Czasami w ten sposób odpowiada osoba odbierająca w biurze telefony. Oznacza, że osoba, do której jest telefon, jest chwilowo nieosiągalna ze względu na jakąś sprawę służbową lub prywatną. Zwykle chodzi o to, że jest w toalecie.) ❏ *I'm sorry, but Ann is away from her desk just now. Can you come back later?* ❏ *Tom is away from his desk, but if you leave your number, he will call you right back.*

ax to grind, have an Patrz *have an ax to grind.*

B

babe in the woods osoba naiwna lub niewinna; niedoświadczona.
❑ *Bill is a babe in the woods when it comes to dealing with plumbers.* ❑ *As a painter, Mary is fine, but she's a babe in the woods as a musician.*

back in circulation **1.** [w stosunku do czegoś, co ma zaistnieć] znów dostępne publicznie. (Używane szczególnie w odniesieniu do rzeczy, które krążą, takich jak pieniądze, książki z biblioteki, magazyny.) ❑ *I've heard that gold coins are back in circulation in Europe.* ❑ *I would like to read* War and Peace. *Is it back in circulation, or is it still checked out?* **2.** [w odniesieniu do osób] znów aktywny towarzysko; znów spotykający się z kimś po rozwodzie lub po rozstaniu z ukochanym/ą. ❑ *Now that Bill is a free man, he's back in circulation.* ❑ *Tom was in the hospital for a month, but now he's back in circulation.*

back-to-back **1.** obok siebie, dotykając się plecami. ❑ *They started the duel by standing back-to-back.* ❑ *Two people who stand back-to-back can manage to see in all directions.* **2.** następujący natychmiast po sobie. (Mówi się tak o rzeczach lub wydarzeniach. W tym przypadku, wydarzenia są określane figuratywnie tyłem-do-przodu.) ❑ *The doctor had appointments set up back-to-back all day long.* ❑ *I have three lecture courses back-to-back every day of the week.*

back to the drawing board czas, by zacząć od nowa; czas, by zacząć coś planować od nowa. (Zauważ różnice w przykładach. Odwołuje się do deski kreślarskiej, na której planuje się budowle lub maszyny.) ❑ *It didn't work. Back to the drawing board.* ❑ *I flunked English this semester. Well, back to the old drawing board.*

back to the salt mines czas, by powrócić do pracy, szkoły, lub czegoś innego, co może być nieprzyjemne. (Wyrażenie implikuje, że mówiący jest niewolnikiem, który pracuje w kopalni soli.) ❑ *It's eight o'clock. Time to go to work! Back to the salt mines.* ❑ *School starts again in the fall, and then it's back to the salt mines again.*

back to the wall, have one's Patrz *have one's back to the wall.*

bad as all that, as Patrz *as bad as all that.*

bad faith, in Patrz *in bad faith.*

bad sorts, in Patrz *in bad sorts.*

bad taste, in Patrz *in bad taste.*

bag and baggage AND **part and parcel** ze swoim bagażem; ze wszystkim, co się posiada. (Wyrażenie utarte.) ❑ *Sally showed up at our door bag and baggage one Sunday morning.* ❑ *All right, if you won't pay the rent, out with you, bag and baggage!* ❑ *Get all your stuff – part and parcel – out of here!*

bag of tricks zbiór specjalnych technik lub metod. ❑ *What have you got in your bag of tricks that could help me with this problem?* ❑ *Here comes Mother with her bag of tricks. I'm sure she can help us.*

bang, go over with a Patrz *go over with a bang.*

bang one's head against a brick wall Patrz pod *beat one's head against the wall.*

bank on something liczyć na coś; polegać na czymś. (Ufać cze- muś tak, jak się ufa bankowi.) ❑ *The weather service said it* *wouldn't rain, but I wouldn't bank on it.* ❏ *My word is to be trusted. You can bank on it.*

bargain, in the Patrz *in the bargain.*

bark up the wrong tree źle wybrać; zapytać niewłaściwą osobę; pójść niewłaściwą drogą. (Odwołuje się do psa myśliwskiego, który zapędził ofiarę na drzewo, ale stoi i szczeka pod innym drzewem.) ❏ *If you think I'm the guilty person, you're barking up the wrong tree.* ❏ *The baseball players blamed their bad record on the pitcher, but they were barking up the wrong tree.*

base, off Patrz *off base.*

bat for someone, go to Patrz *go to bat for someone.*

bat out of hell, like a Patrz *like a bat out of hell.*

bats in one's belfry, have Patrz *have bats in one's belfry.*

batting an eye, without Patrz *without batting an eye.*

be a copycat naśladować kogoś w tym, co on lub ona robi; przedrzeźniać kogoś. (Używane przede wszystkim przez młodzież.) ❏ *Sally wore a pink dress just like Mary's. Mary called Sally a copycat.* ❏ *Bill is such a copycat. He bought a coat just like mine.*

be a fan of someone być czyimś wielbicielem; czynić kogoś swoim idolem. (Słowo *fan* pochodzi od *fanatyczny* [wielbiciel].) ❏ *My mother is still a fan of the Beatles.* ❏ *I'm a great fan of the mayor of the town.*

beard the lion in his den zmierzyć się z przeciwnikiem na jego terenie. (Drażnić się lub straszyć – tak jakby chwytać za brodę czegoś strasznego, na przykład lwa.) ❏ *I went to the tax collector's office to beard the lion in his den.* ❏ *He said he hadn't wanted to come to my home, but it was better to beard the lion in his den.*

bear one's cross AND **carry one's cross** nieść swój ciężar; znosić trudności. (Jest to wyrażenie biblijne. Zawsze używane przenośnie, z wyjątkiem kontekstu biblijnego.) ❑ *It's a very bad disease, but I'll bear my cross.* ❑ *I can't help you with it. You'll just have to carry your cross.*

bear someone or something in mind Patrz pod *keep someone or something in mind.*

bear the brunt (of something) wytrzymać lub znieść najgorszą lub najmocniejszą część czegoś, na przykład ataku. ❑ *I had to bear the brunt of her screaming and yelling.* ❑ *Why don't you talk with her the next time? I'm tired of bearing the brunt.*

bear watching potrzebować obserwacji; wymagać obserwacji lub monitorowania. (Jest to czasownik *to bear.*) ❑ *This problem will bear watching.* ❑ *This is a very serious disease, and it will bear watching for further developments.*

beat about the bush Patrz pod *beat around the bush.*

beat a dead horse kontynuować bitwę, która została wygrana; kontynuować argumentację w odniesieniu do czegoś, co zastało u-stalone. (Wyrażenie oznaczające, że martwy koń nie pobiegnie dalej, nawet gdyby go bardzo mocno bić.) ❑ *Stop arguing! You have won your point. You are just beating a dead horse.* ❑ *Oh, be quiet. Stop beating a dead horse.*

beat a path to someone's door [w odniesieniu do ludzi] tłumnie do kogoś przychodzić. (Wyrażenie oznaczające, że tyle ludzi może chcieć cię odwiedzić, że wydepczą oni ścieżkę do twoich drzwi.) ❑ *I have a product so good that everyone is beating a path to my door.* ❑ *If you really become famous, people will beat a path to your door.*

beat around the bush AND **beat about the bush** unikać odpowiedzi na pytanie; zastygnąć; tracić czas. ❑ *Stop beating around* *the bush and answer my question.* ❑ *Let's stop beating about the bush and discuss this matter.*

be a thorn in someone's side być dla kogoś ciągłym proble- mem; stale kogoś irytować. ❑ *This problem is a thorn in my side. I wish I had a solution to it.* ❑ *John was a thorn in my side for years before I finally got rid of him.*

beat one's head against the wall AND **bang one's head against a brick wall** tracić czas próbując osiągnąć coś, co jest całkowicie nieosiągalne. (Nie używane dosłownie.) ❑ *You're wasting your time trying to fix up this house. You're just beating your head against the wall.* ❑ *You're banging your head against a brick wall trying to get that dog to behave properly.*

beat the gun zdołać coś zrobić przed sygnałem oznaczającym ko- niec. (Pochodzi z języka sportowego i odnosi się do bramki strze- lonej w ostatnich sekundach gry.) ❑ *The ball beat the gun and dropped through the hoop just in time.* ❑ *Tom tried to beat the gun, but he was one second too slow.*

Beauty is only skin deep. przysłowie oznaczające, że wygląd jest sprawą tylko powierzchowną. (Często implikuje, że ktoś bar- dzo piękny może być wewnątrz bardzo okrutny.) ❑ BOB: *Isn't Jane lovely?* TOM: *Yes, but beauty is only skin deep.* ❑ *I know that she looks like a million dollars, but beauty is only skin deep.*

be death on something być dla czegoś bardzo szkodliwe. ❑ *The salt they put on the roads in the winter is death on cars.* ❑ *That teacher is death on slow learners.*

bee in one's bonnet, have a Patrz *have a bee in one's bon- net.*

been through the mill być źle traktowanym; być wyczerpanym. (Niczym ziarno zmielone w młynie.) ❑ *This has been a rough day.*

I've really been through the mill. ❑ *This old car is banged up, and it hardly runs. It's been through the mill.*

before you can say Jack Robinson prawie natychmiast. (Często spotykane w opowiadaniach dla dzieci.) ❑ *And before you could say Jack Robinson, the bird flew away.* ❑ *I'll catch a plane and be there before you can say Jack Robinson.*

be from Missouri wymagać dowodu; domagać się pokazania czegoś. (Od przezwiska stanu Missouri, "Stan-Pokaż-mi".) ❑ *You'll have to prove it to me. I'm from Missouri.* ❑ *She's from Missouri and has to be shown.*

Beggars can't be choosers. przysłowie mówiące, że nie powinno się krytykować czegoś, co się dostało za darmo; jeżeli ktoś prosi lub żebrze o coś, nie ma możliwości wyboru. ❑ *I don't like the old hat that you gave me, but beggars can't be choosers.* ❑ *It doesn't matter whether people like the free food or not. Beggars can't be choosers.*

begin to see daylight zaczynać widzieć koniec długiej pracy. (Tak jakby postrzegać świt pod koniec wypełnionej pracą nocy.) ❑ *I've been working on my thesis for two years, and at last I'm beginning to see daylight.* ❑ *I've been so busy. Only in the last week have I begun to see daylight.*

begin to see the light zaczynać rozumieć (coś). ❑ *My algebra class is hard for me, but I'm beginning to see the light.* ❑ *I was totally confused, but I began to see the light after your explanation.*

be halfhearted (about someone or something) nie być szczególnie zachwyconym czymś lub kimś. ❑ *Ann was halfhearted about the choice of Sally for president.* ❑ *She didn't look halfhearted to me. She looked angry.*

believe it or not możesz wierzyć lub nie. ❑ *Believe it or not, I just got home from work.* ❑ *I'm over fifty years old, believe it or not.*

bench, on the Patrz *on the bench.*

bend, go (a)round the Patrz *go (a)round the bend.*

bend someone's ear mówić do kogoś, być może z irytacją. (Nie
używane dosłownie. Ucha się nie dotyka.) ❏ *Tom is over there,
bending Jane's ear about something.* ❏ *I'm sorry. I didn't mean to
bend your ear for an hour.*

be old hat być staromodnym; być niemodnym. (Odnosi się do
wszystkiego - z wyjątkiem kapelusza - co przypomina staromodny
kapelusz.) ❏ *That's a silly idea. It's old hat.* ❏ *Nobody does that
anymore. That's just old hat.*

be poles apart bardzo się różnić; być bardzo daleko od osiągnięcia
porozumienia. (Odnosi się do północnego i południowego bieguna
Ziemi, o których twierdzi się, że są najbardziej od siebie oddalo-
nymi punktami Ziemi.) ❏ *Mr. and Mrs. Jones don't get along well.
They are poles apart.* ❏ *They'll never sign the contract because
they are poles apart.*

be the spit and image of someone AND **be the spitting
image of someone** być bardzo do kogoś podobnym; bardzo
kogoś przypominać. ❏ *John is the spit and image of his father.*
❏ *I'm not the spit and image of anyone.* ❏ *At first, I thought you
were saying spitting image.*

be the spitting image of someone Patrz poprzednie hasło.

be the teacher's pet być czyimś ulubionym uczniem. (Być trak-
towanym jak ulubione zwierzątko domowe, takie jak pies lub kot.)
❏ *Sally is the teacher's pet. She always gets special treatment.* ❏
The other students don't like the teacher's pet.

between a rock and a hard place AND **between the devil
and the deep blue sea** w bardzo trudnej sytuacji; w obliczu
twardej decyzji. ❏ *I couldn't make up my mind. I was caught*

between a rock and a hard place. ❏ *He had a dilemma on his hands. He was clearly between the devil and the deep blue sea.*

between the devil and the deep blue sea Patrz poprzednie hasło.

beyond one's depth 1. w zbyt głębokiej wodzie. (Dosłowne.) ❏ *Sally swam out until she was beyond her depth.* ❏ *Jane swam out to get her even though it was beyond her depth, too.* **2.** poza możliwością lub zdolnością czyjegoś rozumienia. ❏ *I'm beyond my depth in algebra class.* ❏ *Poor John was involved in a problem that was really beyond his depth.*

beyond one's means więcej niż ktoś może sobie pozwolić. ❏ *I'm sorry, but this house is beyond our means. Please show us a cheaper one.* ❏ *Mr. and Mrs. Brown are living beyond their means.*

beyond the pale nie do zaakceptowania; poza prawem. ❏ *Your behavior is simply beyond the pale.* ❏ *Because of Tom's rudeness, he's considered beyond the pale and is never asked to parties anymore.*

big frog in a small pond ważna osoba pośród mało ważnych ludzi. ❏ *I'd rather be a big frog in a small pond than the opposite.* ❏ *The trouble with Tom is that he's a big frog in a small pond. He needs more competition.*

big mouth, have a Patrz *have a big mouth.*

bird in the hand is worth two in the bush, A. Patrz *A bird in the hand is worth two in the bush.*

birds and the bees ludzka reprodukcja. (Eufemistyczny sposób mówienia o seksie i reprodukcji ludzi.) ❏ *My father tried to teach me about the birds and the bees.* ❏ *He's twenty years old and doesn't understand about the birds and the bees.*

Birds of a feather flock together. przysłowie mówiące, że podobni do siebie ludzie zdają się skupiać razem. ❑ *Bob and Tom are just alike. They like each other's company because birds of a feather flock together.* ❑ *When Mary joined a club for redheaded people, she said, "Birds of a feather flock together."*

birthday suit, in one's Patrz *in one's birthday suit.*

bite off more than one can chew wziąć na siebie więcej niżeli można sobie poradzić; zbytnio sobie ufać. (Wyrażenia używa się dosłownie w odniesieniu do jedzenia i przenośnie w odniesieniu do innych rzeczy, szczególnie trudnych projektów.) ❑ *Billy, stop biting off more than you can chew. You're going to choke on your food someday.* ❑ *Ann is exhausted again. She's always biting off more than she can chew.*

bite one's nails być nerwowym lub obawiać się czegoś; gryźć paznokcie z nerwów lub z obawy. (Używane zarówno dosłownie, jak i przenośnie.) ❑ *I spent all afternoon biting my nails, worrying about you.* ❑ *We've all been biting our nails from worry.*

bite one's tongue walczyć ze sobą, by nie powiedzieć czegoś, co naprawdę chce się powiedzieć. (Używane również dosłownie w odniesieniu do przypadkowego ugryzienia się w język.) ❑ *I had to bite my tongue to keep from telling her what I really thought.* ❑ *I sat through that whole conversation biting my tongue.*

bite the dust upaść pokonanym; umrzeć. (Zwykle słyszy się to wyrażenie w amerykańskich westernach.) ❑ *A bullet hit the sheriff in the chest, and he bit the dust.* ❑ *Poor old Bill bit the dust while mowing the lawn. They buried him yesterday.*

bite the hand that feeds one wyrządzić krzywdę komuś, kto robi ci dobrze. (Nie używane dosłownie. Odwołuje się do niewdzięcznego psa.) ❑ *I'm your mother! How can you bite the hand that feeds you?* ❑ *She can hardly expect much when she bites the hand that feeds her.*

black and white, in Patrz *in black and white.*

27

black, in the Patrz *in the black.*

black sheep of the family najgorszy członek rodziny. (Czarna owca to niechciany potomek w stadzie skądinąd białych owiec.) ❏ *Mary is the black sheep of the family. She's always in trouble with the police.* ❏ *He keeps making a nuisance of himself. What do you expect from the black sheep of the family?*

blind alley, up a Patrz *up a blind alley.*

blind as a bat, as Patrz *as blind as a bat.*

blind leading the blind odnosi się do sytuacji, kiedy ludzie, którzy nie wiedzą, jak co zrobić, próbują wyjaśnić to innym. ❏ *Tom doesn't know anything about cars, but he's trying to teach Sally how to change the oil. It's a case of the blind leading the blind.* ❏ *When I tried to show Mary how to use a computer, it was the blind leading the blind.*

block, on the Patrz *on the block.*

blood, in the Patrz *in the blood.*

blow off steam Patrz pod *let off steam.*

blow one's own horn Patrz pod *toot one's own horn.*

blow someone's cover odkryć czyjąś prawdziwą tożsamość lub cel. ❏ *The spy was very careful not to blow her cover.* ❏ *I tried to disguise myself, but my dog recognized me and blew my cover.*

blow something out of all proportion Patrz pod *out of all proportion.*

blow the whistle (on someone) donieść o czyimś złym postępowaniu komuś (na przykład policji), kto może spowodować zaprzestanie tego postępowania. (Podobnie jak na gwizdek policjanta.) ❏ *The citizens' group blew the whistle on the street gangs by* *calling the police.* ❏ *The gangs were getting very bad. It was definitely time to blow the whistle.*

blue, out of the Patrz *out of the blue.*

boggle someone's mind oszołomić kogoś; zamieszać komuś w głowie; zdumieć kogoś. ❏ *The size of the house boggles my mind.* ❏ *She said that his arrogance boggled her mind.*

bolt out of the blue, like a Patrz *like a bolt out of the blue.*

bone of contention przedmiot lub punkt dysputy: nie ustalony punkt sporu. (Jak kość, z którą walczy pies.) ❏ *We've fought for so long that we've forgotten what the bone of contention is.* ❏ *The question of a fence between the houses has become quite a bone of contention.*

bone to pick (with someone), have a Patrz *have a bone to pick (with someone).*

born with a silver spoon in one's mouth urodzony w bardzo korzystnych okolicznościach; urodzony w bogatej rodzinie; już przy urodzeniu wykazujący oznaki wielkiego bogactwa. ❏ *Sally was born with a silver spoon in her mouth.* ❏ *I'm glad I was not born with a silver spoon in my mouth.*

born yesterday, not Patrz *not born yesterday.*

both hands tied behind one's back, with Patrz *with both hands tied behind one's back.*

bottom of one's heart, from the Patrz *from the bottom of one's heart.*

bottom of the ladder, at the Patrz *at the bottom of the ladder.*

bound hand and foot ze związanymi rękami i nogami. ❑ *The robbers left us bound hand and foot.* ❑ *We remained bound hand and foot until the maid found us and untied us.*

bow and scrape być bardzo pokornym i usłużnym. (Skłonić się nisko i dotknąć ziemi. Zwykle nie używane dosłownie.) ❑ *Please don't bow and scrape. We are all equal here.* ❑ *The salesclerk came in, bowing and scraping, and asked if he could help us.*

bread and butter czyjeś pieniądze na utrzymanie; dochody. (Takie źródło pieniędzy, które sprawia, że chleb i masło, lub jeszcze inna żywność, znajdą się na stole.) ❑ *Selling cars is a lot of hard work, but it's my bread and butter.* ❑ *It was hard to give up my bread and butter, but I felt it was time to retire.*

break camp zamknąć obozowisko; zapakować się i ruszyć dalej. ❑ *Early this morning we broke camp and moved on northward.* ❑ *Okay, everyone. It's time to break camp. Take those tents down and fold them neatly.*

break new ground zacząć robić coś, czego nikt jeszcze nie zrobił; być pionierem jakiegoś przedsięwzięcia. ❑ *Dr. Anderson was breaking new ground in cancer research.* ❑ *They were breaking new ground in consumer electronics.*

break one's back (to do something) Patrz następne hasło.

break one's neck (to do something) AND **break one's back (to do something)** ciężko pracować aby coś zrobić. (Nigdy nie używane dosłownie.) ❑ *I broke my neck to get here on time.* ❑ *That's the last time I'll break my neck to help you.* ❑ *There is no point in breaking your back. Take your time.*

break out in a cold sweat pocić się z gorączki, strachu lub obawy; zacząć się nagle obficie pocić. ❑ *I was so frightened I broke out in a cold sweat.* ❑ *The patient broke out in a cold sweat.*

break (out) into tears AND **break out in tears** zacząć nagle płakać. ❏ *I was so sad that I broke out into tears.* ❏ *I always break into tears at a funeral.* ❏ *It's hard not to break out in tears under those circumstances.*

break someone's fall podeprzeć kogoś, kto się przewraca; zmniejszyć impet upadku. ❏ *When the little boy fell out of the window, the bushes broke his fall.* ❏ *The old lady slipped on the ice, but a snowbank broke her fall.*

break someone's heart sprawić komuś psychiczny ból. (Nie używane dosłownie.) ❏ *It just broke my heart when Tom ran away from home.* ❏ *Sally broke John's heart when she refused to marry him.*

break the ice zainicjować towarzyskie kontakty i rozmowę; rozpocząć coś. (Ten *lód* czasami odnosi się do towarzyskiego chłodu. U-żywane również dosłownie.) ❏ *Tom is so outgoing. He's always the first one to break the ice at parties.* ❏ *It's hard to break the ice at formal events.* ❏ *Sally broke the ice by bidding $20,000 for the painting.*

break the news (to someone) powiedzieć komuś coś bardzo ważnego - zwykle odnosi się do złych wieści. ❏ *The doctor had to break the news to Jane about her husband's cancer.* ❏ *I hope that the doctor broke the news gently.*

breathe down someone's neck 1. uważnie kogoś obserwować; obserwować czyjeś działania. (Odwołuje się do kogoś stojącego blisko za czyimiś plecami. Może być używane dosłownie.) ❏ *I can't work with you breathing down my neck all the time. Go away.* ❏ *I will get through my life without your help. Stop breathing down my neck.* **2.** próbować kogoś poganiać; pospieszać kogoś, by zrobił coś na czas. (Nie musi odnosić się do ludzi. Patrz przykład drugi.) ❏ *I have to finish my taxes today. The tax collector is breathing down my neck.* ❏ *I have a deadline breathing down my neck.*

breathe one's last   umrzeć; wydać ostatnie tchnienie. ❏ *Mrs. Smith breathed her last this morning.* ❏ *I'll keep running every day until I breathe my last.*

bring something to light   wyjawić coś; odkryć coś. (Nawiązuje do wyciągnięcia czegoś ukrytego na światło dzienne.) ❏ *The scientists brought their findings to light.* ❏ *We must bring this new evidence to light.*

bring the house down AND **bring down the house**   rozbawić publiczność w teatrze, albo spowodować oklaski, albo jedno i drugie. (Nie używane dosłownie.) ❏ *This is a great joke. The last time I told it, it brought the house down.* ❏ *It didn't bring down the house; it emptied it.*

bring up the rear   poruszać się z tyłu za wszystkimi; być na końcu kolejki. (Pochodzi od maszerujących żołnierzy.) ❏ *Here comes John, bringing up the rear.* ❏ *Hurry up, Tom! Why are you always bringing up the rear?*

broad daylight, in   Patrz *in broad daylight.*

brush with something, have a   Patrz *have a brush with something.*

build castles in Spain   Patrz następne hasło.

build castles in the air AND **build castles in Spain**   marzyć; planować coś, co nigdy się nie spełni. (Żadne z tych wyrażeń nie jest używane dosłownie.) ❏ *Ann spends most of her time building castles in Spain.* ❏ *I really like to sit on the porch in the evening, just building castles in the air.*

bull in a china shop   ktoś bardzo niezręczny wśród tłukących się rzeczy; osoba bezmyślna lub niezgrabna. (Nawiązuje do delikatnej chińskiej porcelany.) ❏ *Look at Bill, as awkward as a bull in a* *china shop.* ❑ *Get that big dog out of my garden. It's like a bull in a china shop.* ❑ *Bob is so rude, a regular bull in a china shop.*

bullpen, in the Patrz *in the bullpen.*

bump on a log, like a Patrz *like a bump on a log.*

burn one's bridges (behind one) 1. podejmować decyzje, które w przyszłości nie mogą zostać zmienione. ❑ *If you drop out of school now, you'll be burning your bridges behind you.* ❑ *You're too young to burn your bridges that way.* **2.** zachować się nieprzyjemnie w obecnej sytuacji, co uniemożliwi powrót do niej. ❑ *If you get mad and quit your job, you'll be burning your bridges behind you.* ❑ *No sense burning your bridges. Be polite and leave quietly.* **3.** odciąć sobie powrót do sytuacji wyjściowej. ❑ *The army, which had burned its bridges behind it, couldn't go back.* ❑ *By blowing up the road, the spies had burned their bridges behind them.*

burn someone at the stake 1. podpalić kogoś przywiązanego do pala (jako forma egzekucji). ❑ *They used to burn witches at the stake.* ❑ *Look, officer, I only ran a stop sign. What are you going to do, burn me at the stake?* **2.** uspokoić kogoś lub doprowadzić kogoś do porządku, ale bez przemocy. ❑ *Stop yelling. I made a simple mistake, and you're burning me at the stake for it.* ❑ *Sally only spilled her milk. There is no need to shout. Don't burn her at the stake for it.*

burn someone or something to a crisp oparzyć lub spalić kogoś lub coś całkowicie albo w znacznym stopniu. ❑ *The flames burned him to a crisp.* ❑ *The cook burned the meat to a crisp.*

burn the candle at both ends pracować bardzo ciężko do późna w nocy. (Sposób na to, by spalić większą część świecy, albo – przenośnie – siebie.) ❑ *No wonder Mary is ill. She has been burning the candle at both ends for a long time.* ❑ *You can't keep on burning the candle at both ends.*

burn the midnight oil pracować, a szczególnie uczyć się, do późna w nocy. (Nawiązuje do pracy przy lampce oliwnej w przeszłości.) ❑ *I have to go home and burn the midnight oil tonight.* ❑ *If you burn the midnight oil night after night, you'll probably become ill.*

burn with a low blue flame być wściekłym. (Nawiązuje do wyimaginowanego gorąca spowodowanego krańcowym gniewem. Mały niebieski płomień jest bardzo gorący, mimo swego niewielkiego rozmiaru i łagodnego wyglądu.) ❑ *By the time she showed up three hours late, I was burning with a low blue flame.* ❑ *Whenever Ann gets mad, she just presses her lips together and burns with a low blue flame.*

burst at the seams **1.** [w odniesieniu do ludzi] wybuchnąć (przenośnie) śmiechem lub buchać dumą. ❑ *Tom nearly burst at the seams with pride.* ❑ *We laughed so hard we just about burst at the seams.* **2.** pęknąć z nadmiaru. ❑ *The room was so crowded that it almost burst at the seams.* ❑ *I ate so much I almost burst at the seams.*

burst with joy być przepełnionym szczęściem. ❑ *When I got my grades, I could have burst with joy.* ❑ *Joe was not exactly bursting with joy when he got the news.*

bury one's head in the sand AND **hide one's head in the sand** ignorować lub odwracać się od oczywistych oznak niebezpieczeństwa. (Nawiązuje do strusia, którego zwykle rysuje się z głową ukrytą w piasku lub w ziemi.) ❑ *Stop burying your head in the sand. Look at the statistics on smoking and cancer.* ❑ *And stop hiding your head in the sand. All of us will die somehow, whether we smoke or not.*

bury the hatchet zaprzestać walki lub kłótni; zakończyć zadawnione waśnie. (Zakopanie mieczy jest symbolem zakończenia wojny lub bitwy.) ❑ *All right, you two. Calm down and bury the hatchet.* ❑ *I wish Mr. and Mrs. Franklin would bury the hatchet. They argue all the time.*

business, go about one's Patrz *go about one's business.*

busy as a beaver, as Patrz *as busy as a beaver.*

busy as a bee, as Patrz *as busy as a bee.*

busy as Grand Central Station, as Patrz *as busy as Grand Central Station.*

button one's lip zamilknąć i milczeć. (Często używane w odniesieniu do dzieci.) ❏ *All right now, let's button our lips and listen to the story.* ❏ *Button your lip, Tom! I'll tell you when you can talk.*

button, on the Patrz *on the button.*

buy a pig in a poke kupić lub przyjąć coś nie zobaczywszy lub nie zbadawszy tego. (*Poke* oznacza "torbę" lub "worek".) ❏ *Buying a car without test-driving it is like buying a pig in a poke.* ❏ *He bought a pig in a poke when he ordered a diamond ring by mail.*

buy something uwierzyć komuś; przyjąć coś jako fakt. (Używane również dosłownie.) ❏ *It may be true, but I don't buy it.* ❏ *I just don't buy the idea that you can swim that far.*

buy something for a song bardzo tanio coś kupić. ❏ *No one else wanted it, so I bought it for a song.* ❏ *I could buy this house for a song, because it's so ugly.*

buy something sight unseen kupić coś nie zobaczywszy tego najpierw. ❏ *I bought this land sight unseen. I didn't know it was so rocky.* ❏ *It isn't usually safe to buy something sight unseen.*

by a hair's breadth AND **by a whisker** o mało co; bardzo blisko. ❏ *I just missed getting on the plane by a hair's breadth.* ❏ *The arrow missed the deer by a whisker.*

by a whisker Patrz poprzednie hasło.

by leaps and bounds raptownie; poprzez szybki ruch naprzód. (Zdarza się, że używane dosłownie, ale niezbyt często.) ❏ *Our garden is growing by leaps and bounds.* ❏ *The profits of my company are increasing by leaps and bounds.*

35

by return mail kolejną wysyłką (z powrotem do nadawcy). (Wyrażenie oznacza, że odpowiedzi oczekuje się szybko, pocztą.) ❏ *Since this bill is overdue, would you kindly send us your check by return mail?* ❏ *I answered your request by return mail over a year ago. Please check your records.*

by the nape of the neck za kark. (Używane głównie w żartobliwych lub prawdziwych groźbach. Zwykle w ten sposób podnosi się do góry szczenię.) ❏ *He grabbed me by the nape of the neck and told me not to turn around if I valued my life. I stood very still.* ❏ *If you do that again, I'll pick you up by the nape of the neck and throw you out the door.*

by the same token w ten sam sposób; wzajemnie. ❏ *Tom must be good when he comes here, and, by the same token, I expect you to behave properly when you go to his house.* ❏ *The mayor votes for his friend's causes. By the same token, the friend votes for the mayor's causes.*

by the seat of one's pants wyłącznie za pomocą szczęścia, przy bardzo niewielkich umiejętnościach; o mało co. (Najczęściej używane z *to fly*.) ❏ *I got through school by the seat of my pants.* ❏ *The jungle pilot spent most of his days flying by the seat of his pants.*

by the skin of one's teeth o mało co; wielkością równą grubości (wyimaginowanej) skóry na zębach. ❏ *I got through that class by the skin of my teeth.* ❏ *I got to the airport late and missed the plane by the skin of my teeth.*

by the sweat of one's brow by one's efforts; by one's hard work. ❏ *Tom raised these vegetables by the sweat of his brow.* ❏ *Sally polished the car by the sweat of her brow.*

by virtue of something z powodu czegoś; dzięki czemuś. ❏ *She's permitted to vote by virtue of her age.* ❏ *They are members of the club by virtue of their great wealth.*

by word of mouth raczej mówiąc niż pisząc. (Wyrażenie utarte.) ❏ *I learned about it by word of mouth.* ❏ *I need it in writing. I don't trust things I hear about by word of mouth.*

C

cake and eat it too, have one's Patrz *have one's cake and eat it too.*

call a spade a spade nazywać coś po imieniu; mówić o czymś szczerze, nawet jeżeli jest to nieprzyjemne. ❏ *Well, I believe it's time to call a spade a spade. We are just avoiding the issue.* ❏ *Let's call a spade a spade. The man is a liar.*

call it a day zostawić pracę i pójść do domu; powiedzieć, że praca na dany dzień została wykonana. ❏ *I'm tired. Let's call it a day.* ❏ *The boss was mad because Tom called it a day at noon and went home.*

call it quits porzucić; zrezygnować z czegoś; oznajmić, że ktoś rezygnuje. ❏ *Okay! I've had enough! I'm calling it quits.* ❏ *Time to go home, John. Let's call it quits.*

call someone on the carpet dać komuś repremendę. (Wyrażenie nawiązuje do obrazu kogoś wezwanego do wyścielanego dywanem gabinetu szefa na reprymendę.) ❏ *One more error like that and the boss will call you on the carpet.* ❏ *I'm sorry it went wrong. I really hope he doesn't call me on the carpet again.*

call the dogs off AND **call off the dogs** zaprzestać grożenia, ścigania lub prześladowania kogoś; (dosłownie) kazać psom zaprzestać polowania. (Zwróć uwagę na zróżnicowanie w przykładach.) ❏ *All right, I surrender. You can call your dogs off.* ❏ *Tell the sheriff to call off the dogs. We caught the robber.* ❏ *Please call off your dogs!*

can't carry a tune niezdolny do zaśpiewania nawet prostej melodii; nie posiadający zdolności muzycznych. (Prawie zawsze w znaczeniu negatywnym. Również z *cannot*.) ❑ *I wish that Tom wouldn't try to sing. He can't carry a tune.* ❑ *Listen to poor old John. He really cannot carry a tune.*

can't hold a candle to someone nierówny komuś; niegodny towarzyszenia komuś; nie dający się porównać z kimś. (Również z *cannot*. Odwołuje się do tego, że ktoś jest niegodny nawet nieść świecę, by oświetlić komuś innemu drogę.) ❑ *Mary can't hold a candle to Ann when it comes to auto racing.* ❑ *As for singing, John can't hold a candle to Jane.*

can't make heads or tails (out) of someone or something niezdolny, by zrozumieć kogoś lub coś; niezdolny, by odróżnić koniec czegoś od końca czego innego. (Ponieważ dana osoba lub rzecz jest niejasna lub myląca. Również z *cannot*.) ❑ *John is so strange. I can't make heads or tails of him.* ❑ *Do this report again. I can't make heads or tails out of it.*

can't see beyond the end of one's nose nieświadom rzeczy, które mogą zaistnieć w przyszłości; niezdolny do widzenia rzeczy w perspektywie; skupiony na sobie. (Również z *cannot*.) ❑ *John is a very poor planner. He can't see beyond the end of his nose.* ❑ *Ann can't see beyond the end of her nose. She is very self-centered.*

can't see one's hand in front of one's face nie móc widzieć daleko, zwykle z powodu ciemności lub mgły. (Również z *cannot*.) ❑ *It was so dark that I couldn't see my hand in front of my face.* ❑ *Bob said that the fog was so thick he couldn't see his hand in front of his face.*

cards, in the Patrz *in the cards.*

carry a torch (for someone) AND **carry the torch** kochać się w kimś, kto cię nie kocha; przemyśliwać o beznadziejnej miłości. ❑ *John is carrying a torch for Jane.* ❑ *Is John still carrying a torch?* ❑ *Yes, he'll carry the torch for months.*

carry coals to Newcastle robić coś, co nie jest konieczne; robić coś w nadmiarze lub powtarzać czyjąś robotę. (Stare angielskie przysłowie. Newcastle to miasto, skąd wysyłano węgiel do innych części Anglii. Byłoby bez sensu przywozić węgiel do Newcastle. ❑ *Taking food to a farmer is like carrying coals to Newcastle.* ❑ *Mr. Smith is so rich he doesn't need any more money. To give him money is like carrying coals to Newcastle.*

carry one's cross Patrz pod *bear one's cross.*

carry the ball **1.** być tym graczem, który trzyma piłkę, zwłaszcza w piłce nożnej po celnym strzale. ❑ *It was the fullback carrying the ball.* ❑ *Yes, Tom always carries the ball.* **2.** być odpowiedzialnym za wykonanie czegoś; zapewnić, że praca zostanie wykonana. ❑ *We need someone who knows how to get the job done. Hey, Sally! Why don't you carry the ball for us?* ❑ *John can't carry the ball. He isn't organized enough.*

carry the torch podtrzymywać dążenie do celów; prowadzić lub uczestniczyć w (przenośnej) wyprawie krzyżowej. ❑ *The battle was over, but John continued to carry the torch.* ❑ *If Jane hadn't carried the torch, no one would have followed, and the whole thing would have failed.*

carry the weight of the world on one's shoulders wydawać się obciążonym wszystkimi problemami na świecie. ❑ *Look at Tom. He appears to be carrying the weight of the world on his shoulders.* ❑ *Cheer up, Tom! You don't need to carry the weight of the world on your shoulders.*

carry weight (with someone) [w odniesieniu do kogoś] ma wpływ; [w odniesieniu do rzeczy] mieć dla kogoś znaczenie. (Często w formie przeczącej.) ❑ *Everything Mary says carries weight with me.* ❑ *Don't pay any attention to John. What he says carries no weight around here.* ❑ *Your proposal is quite good, but since you're not a member of the club, it carries no weight.*

case in point przykład czegoś, o czym ktoś mówi. ❑ *Now, as a case in point, let's look at nineteenth-century England.* ❑ *Fireworks can be dangerous. For a case in point, look what happened to Bob Smith last week.*

39

cash-and-carry odnoszący się do takiego sposobu sprzedaży towarów, który wymaga zapłacenia w momencie sprzedaży i zabrania towaru. ❑ *I'm sorry. We don't deliver. It's strictly cash-and-carry.* ❑ *You cannot get credit at that drugstore. They only sell cash-and-carry.*

cash in (on something) zarobić na czymś mnóstwo pieniędzy; mieć z czegoś zysk. ❑ *This is a good year for farming, and you can cash in on it if you're smart.* ❑ *It's too late to cash in on that particular clothing fad.*

cast (one's) pearls before swine stracić coś wartościowego dla kogoś, kogo to nic nie obchodzi. (Cytat z Biblii. Nawiązuje do rzucania czegoś wielkiej wartości pod nogi świń. Uważa się za obrazę, jeśli o człowieku powie się, że jest świnią.) ❑ *To sing for them is to cast pearls before swine.* ❑ *To serve them French cuisine is like casting one's pearls before swine.*

cast the first stone zrobić pierwszą uwagę krytyczną; być tym, kto zaatakuje pierwszy. (Cytat z Biblii.) ❑ *Well, I don't want to be the one to cast the first stone, but she sang horribly.* ❑ *John always casts the first stone. Does he think he's perfect?*

catch cold AND **take cold** zaziębić się. ❑ *Please close the window, or we'll all catch cold.* ❑ *I take cold every year at this time.*

catch one's death (of cold) AND **take one's death of cold** zaziębić się; zaziębić się poważnie. ❑ *If I go out in this weather, I'll catch my death of cold.* ❑ *Dress up warm or you'll take your death of cold.* ❑ *Put on your raincoat or you'll catch your death.*

catch someone off-balance złapać kogoś, że jest nieprzygotowany; zaskoczyć kogoś. (Używane również dosłownie.) ❑ *Sorry I acted so flustered. You caught me off-balance.* ❑ *The robbers caught Ann off-balance and stole her purse.*

catch someone's eye AND **get someone's eye** nawiązać z kimś kontakt wzrokowy; przyciągnąć czyjąś uwagę. (Również z *have*, jak w przykładach.) ❑ *The shiny red car caught Mary's eye.*

❏ *Tom got Mary's eye and waved to her.* ❏ *When Tom had her eye, he smiled at her.*

caught in the cross fire złapany pomiędzy dwoje walczących lub kłócących się ludzi lub grupy. (Tak jakby ktoś zabłądził pomiędzy ogień karabinowy dwóch wrogich armii.) ❏ *In western movies, innocent people are always getting caught in the cross fire.* ❏ *In the war, Corporal Smith was killed when he got caught in the cross fire.*

caught short zostać bez czegoś, czego potrzebujesz, zwłaszcza bez pieniędzy. ❏ *I needed eggs for my cake, but I was caught short.* ❏ *Bob had to borrow money from John to pay for the meal. Bob is caught short quite often.*

cause (some) eyebrows to raise zaszokować kogoś; nieprzyjemnie kogoś zaskoczyć. ❏ *John caused eyebrows to raise when he married a poor girl from Toledo.* ❏ *If you want to cause some eyebrows to raise, just start singing as you walk down the street.*

cause (some) tongues to wag stać się przyczyną plotek; dać ludziom temat do plotek. ❏ *The way John was looking at Mary will surely cause some tongues to wag.* ❏ *The way Mary was dressed will also cause tongues to wag.*

champ at the bit być gotowym i palić się do zrobienia czegoś. (Pochodzi od koni.) ❏ *The kids were champing at the bit to get into the swimming pool.* ❏ *The dogs were champing at the bit to begin the hunt.*

change horses in midstream podejmować zasadnicze zmiany w czymś, co się już zaczęło; wybrać kogoś lub coś innego wtedy, kiedy jest już za późno. (Zwykle odnosi się do złych pomysłów.) ❏ *I'm already baking a cherry pie. I can't bake an apple pie. It's too late to change horses in midstream.* ❏ *The house is half-built. It's too late to hire a different architect. You can't change horses in midstream.*

channels, go through Patrz *go through channels.*

Charity begins at home. przysłowie mówiące, że należy być uprzejmym dla swojej rodziny, przyjaciół lub współobywateli, zanim zacznie się podejmować próby pomagania innym. ❑ *"Mother, may I please have some pie?" asked Mary. "Remember, charity begins at home."* ❑ *At church, the minister reminded us that charity begins at home, but we must remember others also.*

chip off the old block, a Patrz *a chip off the old block.*

chip on one's shoulder, have a Patrz *have a chip on one's shoulder.*

circulation, back in Patrz *back in circulation.*

circulation, out of Patrz *out of circulation.*

clean hands, have Patrz *have clean hands.*

clear as mud, as Patrz *as clear as mud.*

clear blue sky, out of a Patrz *out of a clear blue sky.*

clear the table sprzątnąć talerze i inne naczynia ze stołu po posiłku. ❑ *Will you please help clear the table?* ❑ *After you clear the table, we'll play cards.*

climb on the bandwagon dołączyć się do poparcia dla czegoś lub kogoś. ❑ *Come join us! Climb on the bandwagon and support Senator Smith!* ❑ *Look at all those people climbing on the bandwagon! They don't know what they are getting into!*

clip someone's wings ograniczyć kogoś; zmniejszyć lub położyć koniec przywilejom nastolatków. (Ptakom lub ptactwu domowemu przycina się skrzydła, aby je zatrzymać.) ❑ *You had better learn to get home on time, or I will clip your wings.* ❑ *My mother clipped my wings. I can't go out tonight.*

clock, against the Patrz *against the clock.*

clockwork, go like Patrz *go like clockwork.*

close at hand   w zasięgu ręki; podręczny. ❏ *I'm sorry, but your letter isn't close at hand. Please remind me what you said in it.* ❏ *When you're cooking, you should keep all the ingredients close at hand.*

close call, have a   Patrz *have a close call.*

close ranks   **1**. poruszać się blisko siebie w wojskowym ordynku. ❏ *The soldiers closed ranks and marched on the enemy.* ❏ *All right! Stop that talking and close ranks.* **2**. dołączyć do kogoś. ❏ *We can fight this menace only if we close ranks.* ❏ *Let's all close ranks behind Ann and get her elected.*

close shave, have a   Patrz *have a close shave.*

cloud nine, on   Patrz *on cloud nine.*

cloud (of suspicion), under a   Patrz *under a cloud (of suspicion).*

coast is clear, The.   Patrz *The coast is clear.*

coast-to-coast   od Atlantyku po Ocean Spokojny (w U.S.A.); cały kraj pomiędzy Atlantykiem i Pacyfikiem. ❏ *My voice was once heard on a coast-to-coast radio broadcast.* ❏ *Our car made the coast-to-coast trip in eighty hours.*

cock-and-bull story   głupia, wymyślona historyjka; historyjka będąca kłamstwem. ❏ *Don't give me that cock-and-bull story.* ❏ *I asked for an explanation, and all I got was your ridiculous cock-and-bull story!*

cold, out   Patrz *out cold.*

color, off   Patrz *off-color.*

come a cropper   mieć jakieś niepowodzenie; nie udać się. (Dosłownie, spaść z konia.) ❏ *Bob invested all his money in the stock market just before it fell. Boy, did he come a cropper.* ❏ *Jane*

43

was out all night before she took her tests. She really came a cropper.

come apart at the seams   nagle stracić panowanie nad sobą. (Dosłownie pochodzi od rozpadającej się w szwach odzieży.) ❑ *Bill was so upset that he almost came apart at the seams.* ❑ *I couldn't take anymore. I just came apart at the seams.*

come away empty-handed   wrócić bez niczego. ❑ *All right, go gambling. Don't come away empty-handed, though.* ❑ *Go to the bank and ask for the loan again. This time don't come away empty-handed.*

come by something   **1.** podróżować jakimś określonym środkiem lokomocji, na przykład samolotem, statkiem lub samochodem. (Znaczenie dosłowne.) ❑ *We came by train. It's more relaxing.* ❑ *Next time, we'll come by plane. It's faster.* **2.** znaleźć lub otrzymać coś. ❑ *How did you come by that haircut?* ❑ *Where did you come by that new shirt?*

come down in the world   stracić pozycję towarzyską lub podstawy finansowe. ❑ *Mr. Jones has really come down in the world since he lost his job.* ❑ *If I were unemployed, I'm sure I'd come down in the world, too.*

come home (to roost)   powrócić po to, by spowodować komuś kłopot. (Tak jak kurczęta lub inne ptaki wracają na grzędę.) ❑ *As I feared, all my problems came home to roost.* ❑ *Yes, problems all come home eventually.*

come in out of the rain   stać się czujnym i świadomym. (Używane również dosłownie.) ❑ *Pay attention, Sally! Come in out of the rain!* ❑ *Bill will fail if he doesn't come in out of the rain and study.*

come into one's or its own   **1.** [w odniesieniu do kogoś] zostać docenionym. ❑ *Sally finally came into her own.* ❑ *After years of trying, she finally came into her own.* **2.** [w odniesieniu do czegoś] docenić coś. ❑ *The idea of an electric car finally came into its own.* ❑ *Film as an art medium finally came into its own.*

come of age osiągnąć taki wiek, kiedy można posiąść jakąś własność, ożenić się lub wyjść za mąż, i podpisywać prawne dokumenty. ❑ *When Jane comes of age, she will buy her own car.* ❑ *Sally, who came of age last month, entered into an agreement to purchase a house.*

come off second-best zdobyć drugie lub jeszcze dalsze miejsce; przegrać z kimś. ❑ *John came off second-best in the race.* ❑ *Why do I always come off second-best in an argument with you?*

come out ahead osiągnąć jakiś zysk; poprawić swoją sytuację. ❑ *I hope you come out ahead with your investments.* ❑ *It took a lot of money to buy the house, but I think I'll come out ahead.*

come out in the wash dobrze coś rozwiązać. (Oznacza to, że problemy lub kłopoty znikną tak jak brud znika w praniu.) ❑ *Don't worry about that problem. It'll all come out in the wash.* ❑ *This trouble will go away. It'll come out in the wash.*

come out of the closet **1.** wyjawić czyjeś poufne zainteresowania. ❑ *Tom Brown came out of the closet and admitted that he likes to knit.* ❑ *It's time that all of you lovers of chamber music came out of the closet and attended our concerts.* **2.** wyjawić, że ktoś jest homoseksualistą. ❑ *Tom surprised his parents when he came out of the closet.* ❑ *It was difficult for him to come out of the closet.*

come to a bad end mieć jakieś nieszczęście, być może zasłużone lub oczekiwane; nieszczęśliwie zginąć. ❑ *My old car came to a bad end. Its engine burned up.* ❑ *The evil merchant came to a bad end.*

come to a dead end dojść do punktu, z którego niemożliwa jest kontynuacja. ❑ *The building project came to a dead end.* ❑ *The street came to a dead end.* ❑ *We were driving along and came to a dead end.*

come to a head dojść do punktu kluczowego; dojść do punktu, w którym problem musi zostać rozwiązany. ❑ *Remember my problem with my neighbors? Well, last night the whole thing came to a* *head.* ❑ *The battle between the two factions of the city council came to a head yesterday.*

come to an end zatrzymać; skończyć. ❑ *The party came to an end at midnight.* ❑ *Her life came to an end late yesterday.*

come to an untimely end wcześnie umrzeć. ❑ *Poor Mr. Jones came to an untimely end in a car accident.* ❑ *Cancer caused Mrs. Smith to come to an untimely end.*

come to a standstill zatrzymać, tymczasowo lub na stałe. ❑ *The building project came to a standstill because the workers went on strike.* ❑ *The party came to a standstill until the lights were turned on again.*

come to grief nie udać się; mieć problem lub zmartwienie. ❑ *The artist wept when her canvas came to grief.* ❑ *The wedding party came to grief when the bride passed out.*

come to grips with something zmierzyć się z czymś; zrozumieć coś. ❑ *He found it difficult to come to grips with his grandmother's death.* ❑ *Many students have a hard time coming to grips with algebra.*

come to light stać się znanym. ❑ *Some interesting facts about your past have just come to light.* ❑ *If too many bad things come to light, you may lose your job.*

come to one's senses obudzić się; oprzytomnieć; zacząć jasno myśleć. ❑ *John, come to your senses. You're being quite stupid.* ❑ *In the morning I don't come to my senses until I have had two cups of coffee.*

come to pass wydarzyć się. (Literackie.) ❑ *When did all of this come to pass?* ❑ *When will this event come to pass?*

come to the point AND **get to the point** dotrzeć do ważnej części (czegoś). ❑ *He has been talking a long time. I wish he would come to the point.* ❑ *Quit wasting time! Get to the point!* ❑ *We are talking about money, Bob! Come on, get to the point.*

come to think of it właśnie sobie przypomniałem...; teraz kiedy o tym pomyślę... ❏ *Come to think of it, I know someone who can help.* ❏ *I have a screwdriver in the trunk of my car, come to think of it.*

come true urzeczywistnić się [sen albo życzenie], rzeczywiście zaistnieć. ❏ *When I got married, all my dreams came true.* ❏ *Coming to the big city was like having my wish come true.*

come up in the world polepszyć status lub życiową sytuację. ❏ *Since Mary got her new job, she has really come up in the world.* ❏ *A good education helped my brother come up in the world.*

come what may niezależnie, co się stanie. ❏ *I'll be home for the holidays, come what may.* ❏ *Come what may, the mail will get delivered.*

comfortable as an old shoe, as Patrz *as comfortable as an old shoe.*

commission, out of Patrz *out of commission.*

conspicuous by one's absence zauważyć czyjąś nieobecność (na imprezie). ❏ *We missed you last night. You were conspicuous by your absence.* ❏ *How could the bride's father miss the wedding party? He was certainly conspicuous by his absence.*

construction, under Patrz *under construction.*

contrary, on the Patrz *on the contrary.*

control the purse strings odpowiadać za pieniądze w interesie albo w domu. ❏ *I control the purse strings at our house.* ❏ *Mr. Williams is the treasurer. He controls the purse strings.*

cook someone's goose zniszczyć lub zrujnować kogoś. (Zrobić coś, czego nie można zmienić.) ❏ *I cooked my own goose by not showing up on time.* ❏ *Sally cooked Bob's goose for treating her the way he did.*

cook the accounts oszukiwać w księgowości; pokazywać, że rachunki się bilansują, podczs gdy w rzeczywistości jest inaczej. ❑ *Jane was sent to jail for cooking the accounts of her mother's store.* ❑ *It's hard to tell whether she really cooked the accounts or just didn't know how to add.*

cool as a cucumber, as Patrz *as cool as a cucumber.*

cool one's heels czekać (na kogoś). ❑ *I spent all afternoon cooling my heels in the waiting room while the doctor talked on the telephone.* ❑ *All right. If you can't behave properly, just sit down here and cool your heels until I call you.*

copycat, be a Patrz *be a copycat.*

corner of one's eye, out of the Patrz *out of the corner of one's eye.*

cost an arm and a leg Patrz pod *pay an arm and a leg (for something).*

cost a pretty penny kosztować mnóstwo pieniędzy. ❑ *I'll bet that diamond cost a pretty penny.* ❑ *You can be sure that house cost a pretty penny. It has seven bathrooms.*

counter, under the Patrz *under the counter.*

count noses AND **count heads** policzyć ludzi. (Każdy człowiek ma tylko jedną głowę lub nos.) ❑ *I'll tell you how many people are here after I count noses.* ❑ *Everyone is here. Let's count noses so we can order hamburgers.*

count one's chickens before they hatch planować, jak wykorzystać dobre wyniki czegoś zanim wyniki te zostały osiągnięte. (Często używane w formie przeczącej.) ❑ *You're way ahead of yourself. Don't count your chickens before they hatch.* ❑ *You may be disappointed if you count your chickens before they hatch.*

cover a lot of ground **1.** daleko podróżować; zbadać szeroki płat ziemi. ❑ *The prospectors covered a lot of ground, looking for gold.* ❑ *My car can cover a lot of ground in one day.* **2.** mieć do czynienia z ogromną ilością informacji i faktów. ❑ *The history lecture covered a lot of ground today.* ❑ *Mr. and Mrs. Franklin always cover a lot of ground when they argue.*

cover for someone **1.** znajdować dla kogoś usprawiedliwienia; ukrywać czyjeś błędy. ❑ *If I miss class, please cover for me.* ❑ *If you're late, I'll cover for you.* **2.** wykonywać pracę kogoś innego. ❑ *Dr. Johnson's partner agreed to cover for him during his vacation.* ❑ *I'm on duty this afternoon. Will you please cover for me? I have a doctor's appointment.*

crack a joke powiedzieć żart. ❑ *She's never serious. She's always cracking jokes.* ❑ *As long as she's cracking jokes, she's okay.*

crack a smile trochę się uśmiechnąć, być może z oporami. ❑ *She cracked a smile, so I knew she was kidding.* ❑ *The soldier cracked a smile at the wrong time and had to march for an hour as punishment.*

cramp someone's style w jakiś sposób kogoś ograniczać. ❑ *I hope this doesn't cramp your style, but could you please not hum while you work?* ❑ *To ask him to keep regular hours would really be cramping his style.*

crazy as a loon, as Patrz *as crazy as a loon.*

cream of the crop najlepszy ze wszystkich. (Klisza.) ❑ *This particular car is the cream of the crop.* ❑ *The kids are very bright. They are the cream of the crop.*

creation, in Patrz *in creation.*

Crime doesn't pay. przysłowie mówiące, że zbrodnia korzyści nie przynosi. ❑ *At the end of the radio program, a voice said, "Remember, crime doesn't pay."* ❑ *No matter how tempting it may appear, crime doesn't pay.*

cross a bridge before one comes to it bardzo się czymś martwić zanim to się stanie. (Zwróć uwagę na zróżnicowanie w przykładach.) ❑ *There is no sense in crossing that bridge before you* *come to it.* ❏ *She's always crossing bridges before coming to them. She needs to learn to relax.*

cross a bridge when one comes to it zająć się problemem dopiero wtedy, kiedy zaistnieje. (Zwróć uwagę na zróżnicowanie w przykładach.) ❏ *Please wait and cross that bridge when you come to it.* ❏ *He shouldn't worry about it now. He can cross that bridge when he comes to it.*

cross-examine someone zadawać komuś bardzo szczegółowe pytania; zadawać wiele dokładnych pytań świadkowi lub podejrzanemu. ❏ *The police cross-examined the suspect for three hours.* ❏ *The lawyer plans to cross-examine the witness tomorrow morning.*

cross one's heart (and hope to die) zaświadczać lub przysięgać, że mówi się prawdę. ❏ *It's true, cross my heart and hope to die.* ❏ *It's really true – cross my heart.*

cross swords (with someone) zacząć się z kimś sprzeczać. (Nie używane dosłownie.) ❏ *I don't want to cross swords with Tom.* ❏ *The last time we crossed swords, we had a terrible time.*

crow flies, as the Patrz *as the crow flies.*

crux of the matter najważniejszy punkt sprawy. (*Crux* to stare słowo oznaczające "krzyż.") ❏ *All right, this is the crux of the matter.* ❏ *It's about time that we looked at the crux of the matter.*

cry before one is hurt płakać lub skarżyć się zanim stanie się krzywda. ❏ *Bill always cries before he's hurt.* ❏ *There is no point in crying before one is hurt.*

cry bloody murder AND **scream bloody murder** krzyczeć tak jakby wydarzyło się coś strasznego. (Krzyczeć tak, jakby ktoś odkrył krwawe morderstwo.) ❏ *Now that Bill is really hurt, he's screaming bloody murder.* ❏ *There is no point in crying bloody murder about the bill if you aren't going to pay it.*

cry one's eyes out mocno płakać. (Nie używane dosłownie.) ❏ *When we heard the news, we cried our eyes out with joy.* ❏ *She cried her eyes out after his death.*

cry over spilled milk rozpaczać nad czymś, co zostało zrobione i czego nie można zmienić. (Zwykle traktowane jako dziecinada. *Spilled* można także pisać *spilt.*) ❏ *I'm sorry that you broke your bicycle, Tom. But there is nothing that can be done now. Don't cry over spilled milk.* ❏ *Ann is always crying over spilt milk.*

cry wolf płakać lub uskarżać się wtedy, kiedy w rzeczywistości nic złego się nie stało. ❏ *Pay no attention. She's just crying wolf again.* ❏ *Don't cry wolf too often. No one will come.*

cup of tea, not someone's Patrz *not someone's cup of tea.*

Curiosity killed the cat. przysłowie mówiące, że ciekawość jest niebezpieczna. ❏ *Don't ask so many questions, Billy. Curiosity killed the cat.* ❏ *Curiosity killed the cat. Mind your own business.*

curl someone's hair bardzo kogoś przestraszyć; zaszokować kogoś wyglądem, dźwiękiem lub smakiem. (Używane również dosłownie.) ❏ *Don't ever sneak up on me like that again. You really curled my hair.* ❏ *The horror film curled my hair.*

curl up and die wycofać się i umrzeć. ❏ *When I heard you say that, I could have curled up and died.* ❏ *No, it wasn't an illness. She just curled up and died.*

cut class opuścić zajęcia. (Odnosi się do szkoły średniej lub kolegiów.) ❏ *If Mary keeps cutting classes, she'll fail the course.* ❏ *I can't cut that class. I've missed too many already.*

cut off one's nose to spite one's face wyrażenie mówiące, że szkodzi się sobie próbując ukarać kogoś innego. (Wyrażenie jest zróżnicowane w formie, co pokazują przykłady.) ❏ *Billy loves the zoo, but he refused to go with his mother because he was mad at her. He cut off his nose to spite his face.* ❏ *Find a better way to be angry. It is silly to cut your nose off to spite your face.*

cut one's (own) throat [w odniesieniu do ludzi] doświadczyć jakiejś porażki; wyrządzić komuś szkodę. (Również używane dosłownie.) ❏ *If I were to run for office, I'd just be cutting my throat.* ❏ *Judges who take bribes are cutting their own throats.*

cut someone or something (off) short uciąć coś zanim jest to ukończone; przeciąć czyjąś wypowiedź przed jej skończeniem. ❏ *We cut the picnic short because of the storm.* ❏ *I'm sorry to cut you off short, but I must go now.*

cut someone or something to the bone 1. przeciąć do kości. (Znaczenie dosłowne.) ❏ *The knife cut John to the bone. He had to be sewed up.* ❏ *Cut each slice of ham to the bone. Then each slice will be as big as possible.* 2. [z *something*] dokonać ostrego cięcia. (Nie używane dosłownie.) ❏ *We cut our expenses to the bone and are still losing money.* ❏ *Congress had to cut the budget to the bone in order to balance it.*

cut someone's losses zredukować straty pieniędzy, towarów lub innych wartościowych rzeczy. ❏ *I sold the stock as it went down, thus cutting my losses.* ❏ *He cut his losses by putting better locks on the doors. There were fewer robberies.* ❏ *The mayor's reputation suffered because of the scandal. He finally resigned to cut his losses.*

cut someone to the quick głęboko zranić czyjeś uczucia. (Wyrażenia można użyć dosłownie, jeżeli *quick* odnosi się do wrażliwych części ciała pod paznokciami.) ❏ *Your criticism cut me to the quick.* ❏ *Tom's sharp words to Mary cut her to the quick.*

cut the ground out from under someone AND **cut out the ground from under someone** zburzyć podstawy czyichś planów lub czyichś argumentów. ❏ *The politician cut the ground out from under his opponent.* ❏ *Congress cut out the ground from under the president.*

D

dance to another tune   szybko zmienić zachowanie; zmienić czyjeś zachowanie lub stanowisko. ❑ *After being yelled at, Ann danced to another tune.* ❑ *A stern talking-to will make her dance to another tune.*

dash cold water on something   Patrz pod *pour cold water on something.*

date back (to sometime)   rozszerzyć wstecz do określonej daty; żyć w określonym czasie w przeszłości. ❑ *My late grandmother dated back to the Civil War.* ❑ *This record dates back to the sixties.* ❑ *How far do you date back?*

Davy Jones's locker, go to   Patrz *go to Davy Jones's locker.*

dead and buried   odszedł na zawsze. (W znaczeniu dosłownym odnosi się do ludzi, a przenośnie - do idei i innych rzeczy. ❑ *Now that Uncle Bill is dead and buried, we can read his will.* ❑ *That kind of thinking is dead and buried.*

dead as a dodo, as   Patrz *as dead as a dodo.*

dead as a doornail, as   Patrz *as dead as a doornail.*

dead heat, in a   Patrz *in a dead heat.*

dead to rights, have someone   Patrz *have someone dead to rights.*

dead to the world zmęczony, wyczerpany; pogrążony w zdrowym śnie. (Śpiący i niepomny tego, co się dzieje w świecie wokół niego.) ❏ *I've had such a hard day. I'm really dead to the world.* ❏ *Look at her sleep. She's dead to the world.*

death on someone or something **1.** bardzo skuteczny w działaniu przeciwko komuś lub czemuś. ❏ *This road is terribly bumpy. It's death on tires.* ❏ *The sergeant is death on lazy soldiers.* **2.** [z *something*] dokładny lub do ostateczności skuteczny w robieniu czegoś wymagającego umiejętności lub wielkiego wysiłku. ❏ *John is death on curve balls. He's our best pitcher.* ❏ *The boxing champ is really death on those fast punches.*

death on something, be Patrz *be death on something.*

death's door, at Patrz *at death's door.*

deep end, go off the Patrz *go off the deep end.*

deep water, in Patrz *in deep water.*

depth, beyond one's Patrz *beyond one's depth.*

desert a sinking ship AND **leave a sinking ship** opuścić miejsce, człowieka lub sytuację wtedy, kiedy bieg rzeczy staje się trudny lub nieprzyjemny. (Mówi się, że to szczury pierwsze opuszczają okręt, który tonie.) ❏ *I hate to be the one to desert a sinking ship, but I can't stand it around here anymore.* ❏ *There goes Tom. Wouldn't you know he'd leave a sinking ship rather than stay around and try to help?*

devil and the deep blue sea, between the Patrz *between the devil and the deep blue sea.*

devil of it, for the Patrz *for the devil of it.*

diamond in the rough cenny lub potencjalnie znakomity człowiek lub rzecz, ukryta pod szorstką lub niewygładzoną powłoką. ❏ *Ann looks like a stupid woman, but she's a fine person – a real diamond in the rough.* ❏ *That piece of property is a diamond in the rough. Someday it will be valuable.*

dibs on something, have Patrz *have dibs on something.*

die of a broken heart **1.** umrzeć z powodu jakiegoś uczuciowego nieszczęścia. ❑ *I was not surprised to hear of her death. They say she died of a broken heart.* ❑ *In the movie, the heroine appeared to die of a broken heart, but the audience knew she was poisoned.* **2.** cierpieć z powodu jakiegoś uczuciowego nieszczęścia, szczególnie zaś nieudanego romansu. ❑ *Tom and Mary broke off their romance and both died of broken hearts.* ❑ *Please don't leave me. I know I'll die of a broken heart.*

die of boredom cierpieć nudę, być bardzo znudzonym. ❑ *No one has ever really died of boredom.* ❑ *We sat there and listened politely, even though we almost died of boredom.*

die on the vine Patrz pod *wither on the vine.*

different as night and day, as Patrz *as different as night and day.*

dig some dirt up on someone AND **dig up some dirt on someone** wyjawić coś złego o kimś. (Ten brud to plotka.) ❑ *If you don't stop trying to dig some dirt up on me, I'll get a lawyer and sue you.* ❑ *The citizens' group dug up some dirt on the mayor and used it against her at election time.*

dirty one's hands Patrz pod *get one's hands dirty.*

dishes, do the Patrz *do the dishes.*

distance, go the Patrz *go the distance.*

do a land-office business zrobić wiele interesów w krótkim czasie. (Niczym w sytuacji szybkiego sprzedania ziemi.) ❑ *The ice-cream shop always does a land-office business on a hot day.* ❑ *The tax collector's office did a land-office business on the day that taxes were due.*

doghouse, in the Patrz *in the doghouse.*

dogs, go to the Patrz *go to the dogs.*

doldrums, in the Patrz *in the doldrums.*

dollar for dollar biorąc pod uwagę kwotę, która wchodzi w grę; biorąc pod uwagę koszty. (Często używane w reklamie.) ❏ *Dollar for dollar, you cannot buy a better car.* ❏ *Dollar for dollar, this laundry detergent washes cleaner and brighter than any other product on the market.*

Don't hold your breath. Nie wstrzymuj oddechu (czekając, aż coś się stanie). ❏ *You think he'll get a job? Ha! Don't hold your breath.* ❏ *I'll finish building the fence as soon as I have time, but don't hold your breath.*

Don't let someone or something get you down. Nie pozwalaj, by ktoś lub coś zbiło cię z tropu. ❏ *Don't let their constant teasing get you down.* ❏ *Don't let Tom get you down. He's not always unpleasant.*

Don't look a gift horse in the mouth. przysłowie mówiące, że nie należy oczekiwać idealnych prezentów. (Zwykle używane w formie przeczącej. Zauważ zróżnicowanie w przykładach. Wiek konia, a co za tym idzie, jego przydatność, można ocenić patrząc na jego zęby. Byłoby chciwością oglądanie otrzymanemu w prezencie koniowi zębów po to, by sprawdzić, czy jest on najwyższej jakości.) ❏ *Don't complain. You shouldn't look a gift horse in the mouth.* ❏ *John complained that the television set he got for his birthday was black and white rather than color. He was told, "Don't look a gift horse in the mouth."*

doorstep, at someone's Patrz *at someone's doorstep.*

doorstep, on someone's Patrz *on someone's doorstep.*

dose of one's own medicine takie samo traktowanie, które ktoś oferuje innym. (Często z *get* lub *have.*) ❏ *Sally never is very friendly. Someone is going to give her a dose of her own medicine someday.* ❏ *He didn't like getting a dose of his own medicine.*

do someone's heart good sprawić, by się ktoś dobrze czuł psychicznie. (Używane również dosłownie.) ❏ *It does my heart good to hear you talk that way.* ❏ *When she sent me a get-well card, it really did my heart good.*

do something by hand zrobić coś raczej ręcznie niż maszynowo. ❏ *The computer was broken so I had to do the calculations by hand.* ❏ *All this tiny stitching was done by hand. Machines cannot do this kind of work.*

do something hands down zrobić coś łatwo i bez protestów. (Nikt nie podnosi ręki, by zgłosić protest.) ❏ *The mayor won the election hands down.* ❏ *She was the choice of the people hands down.*

do the dishes umyć naczynia; umyć i wysuszyć naczynia. ❏ *Bill, you cannot go out and play until you've done the dishes.* ❏ *Why am I always the one who has to do the dishes?*

do the honors występować w roli gospodarza lub gospodyni i usługiwać gościom nalewając drinki, krojąc mięso, wznosząc (pijąc) toasty etc. ❏ *All the guests were seated, and a huge juicy turkey sat on the table. Jane Thomas turned to her husband and said, "Bob, will you do the honors?" Mr. Jones smiled and began slicing thick slices of meat from the turkey.* ❏ *The mayor stood up and addressed the people who were still eating their salads. "I'm delighted to do the honors this evening and propose a toast to your friend and mine, Bill Jones. Bill, good luck and best wishes in your new job in Washington." And everyone sipped a bit of wine.*

dot, on the Patrz *on the dot.*

down in the dumps smutny lub przygnębiony. ❏ *I've been down in the dumps for the past few days.* ❏ *Try to cheer Jane up. She's down in the dumps for some reason.*

down in the mouth o smutnej twarzy; przygnębiony i bez uśmiechu. (Odwołuje się do ust zmarszczonych lub ściągniętych w dół.) ❏ *Since her dog died, Barbara has been down in the mouth.* ❏ *Bob has been down in the mouth since the car wreck.*

down the drain stracony na zawsze; zmarnowany. (Używane również dosłownie.) ❏ *I just hate to see all that money go down the drain.* ❏ *Well, there goes the whole project, right down the drain.*

down to the wire w ostatniej minucie; do ostatniej chwili. (Odwołuje się do drutu, który oznacza koniec trasy wyścigów konnych.) ❏ *I have to turn this in tomorrow, and I'll be working down to the wire.* ❏ *When we get down to the wire, we'll know better what to do.*

drain, down the Patrz *down the drain.*

draw a blank **1.** nie otrzymać żadnej odpowiedzi; nic nie znaleźć. ❏ *I asked him about Tom's financial problems, and I just drew a blank.* ❏ *We looked in the files for an hour, but we drew a blank.* **2.** nie zapamiętać (czegoś). ❏ *I tried to remember her telephone number, but I could only draw a blank.* ❏ *It was a very hard test with just one question to answer, and I drew a blank.*

draw a line between something and something else oddzielić dwie rzeczy; rozróżnić między dwoma rzeczami. (*A* może być zastąpione *the.* Również używane dosłownie.) ❏ *It's necessary to draw a line between bumping into people and striking them.* ❏ *It's very hard to draw the line between slamming a door and just closing it loudly.*

draw blood **1.** uderzyć lub ugryźć (człowieka lub zwierzę), tak że powstała rana krwawi. ❏ *The dog chased me and bit me hard, but it didn't draw blood.* ❏ *The boxer landed just one punch and drew blood immediately.* **2.** rozgniewać lub obrazić kogoś. ❏ *Sally screamed out a terrible insult at Tom. Judging by the look on his face, she really drew blood.* ❏ *Tom started yelling and cursing, trying to insult Sally. He wouldn't be satisfied until he had drawn blood, too.*

dream come true życzenie lub marzenie, które się spełniło. ❏ *Going to Hawaii is like having a dream come true.* ❏ *Having you for a friend is a dream come true.*

drink to excess pić zbyt wiele alkoholu; pić stale alkohol. ❑ *Mr. Franklin drinks to excess.* ❑ *Some people drink to excess only at parties.*

drive a hard bargain pracować ciężko, by wynegocjować warunki lub umowę na swoją korzyść. ❑ *I saved $200 by driving a hard bargain when I bought my new car.* ❑ *All right, sir, you drive a hard bargain. I'll sell you this car for $12,450.* ❑ *You drive a hard bargain, Jane, but I'll sign the contract.*

drive someone to the wall Patrz pod *force someone to the wall.*

drop in one's tracks stanąć lub zemdleć z wyczerpania; nagle umrzeć. ❑ *If I keep working this way, I'll drop in my tracks.* ❑ *Uncle Bob was working in the garden and dropped in his tracks. We are all sorry that he's dead.*

drop of a hat, at the Patrz *at the drop of a hat.*

drop someone a few lines Patrz następne hasło.

drop someone a line AND **drop someone a few lines** napisać do kogoś list lub notatkę. (*Line* odnosi się do linijek pisma.) ❑ *I dropped Aunt Jane a line last Thanksgiving.* ❑ *She usually drops me a few lines around the first of the year.*

drop the ball popełnić błąd; ponieść jakąś porażkę. (Używane też dosłownie, w sporcie: pomyłkowo rzucić piłkę.) ❑ *Everything was going fine in the election until my campaign manager dropped the ball.* ❑ *You can't trust John to do the job right. He's always dropping the ball.*

drop the other shoe wykonać coś, co kończy jakieś działanie; wykonać spodziewaną pozostałą część czegoś. (Nawiązuje do zdjęcia butów przed pójściem do łóżka. Ściąga się jednego buta, a dzieło kończy się ściągnięciem drugiego.) ❑ *Mr. Franklin has left his wife. Soon he'll drop the other shoe and divorce her.* ❑ *Tommy has just failed three classes in school. We expect him to drop the other shoe and quit altogether any day now.*

drown one's sorrows Patrz następne hasło.

drown one's troubles AND **drown one's sorrows** próbować zapomnieć o problemach pijąc mnóstwo alkoholu. ❑ *Bill is in the bar, drowning his troubles.* ❑ *Jane is at home, drowning her sorrows.*

drug on the market w ogromnej ilości na rynku; cała masa na rynku. ❑ *Right now, small computers are a drug on the market.* ❑ *Ten years ago, small transistor radios were a drug on the market.*

drum some business up AND **drum up some business** stymulować ludzi do kupienia tego, co sprzedajesz. (Nawiązuje do bicia w bębny w celu przyciągnięcia uwagi klientów.) ❑ *I need to do something to drum some business up.* ❑ *A little bit of advertising would drum up some business.*

dry behind the ears bardzo młody i niedojrzały. (Używane zwykle w formie przeczącej.) ❑ *Tom is going into business by himself? Why, he's hardly dry behind the ears.* ❑ *That kid isn't dry behind the ears. He'll go broke in a month.*

duck takes to water, as a Patrz *as a duck takes to water.*

dumps, down in the Patrz *down in the dumps.*

Dutch, go Patrz *go Dutch.*

duty, off Patrz *off duty.*

duty, on Patrz *on duty.*

E

early bird gets the worm, The. Patrz *The early bird gets the worm.*

Early to bed, early to rise, (makes a man healthy, wealthy, and wise). przysłowie mówiące, że wczesne kładzenie się spać i wczesne wstawanie jest dla ciebie czymś dobrym. (Czasami używane dla wyjaśnienia, dlaczego ktoś wcześnie kładzie się spać. Ostatnia część przysłowia bywa nie dopowiadana.) ❑ *Tom left the party at ten o'clock, saying "Early to bed, early to rise, makes a man healthy, wealthy, and wise."* ❑ *I always get up at six o'clock. After all, early to bed, early to rise.*

earn one's keep pomagać w domu w zamian za jedzenie i mieszkanie; zarabiać poprzez robienie tego, czego ktoś oczekuje. ❑ *I earn my keep at college by shoveling snow in the winter.* ❑ *Tom hardly earns his keep around here. He should be fired.*

ears (in something), up to one's Patrz *up to one's ears (in something).*

earth, on Patrz *on earth.*

ear to the ground, have one's Patrz *have one's ear to the ground.*

easy as (apple) pie, as Patrz *as easy as (apple) pie.*

easy as duck soup, as Patrz *as easy as duck soup.*

easy come, easy go używane dla wyjaśnienia straty czegoś, o-
trzymanie czego kosztowało niewiele wysiłku. ❏ *Ann found twenty
dollars in the morning and spent it foolishly at noon. "Easy come,
easy go," she said.* ❏ *John spends his money as fast as he can earn
it. With John it's easy come, easy go.*

Easy does it. Postępuj ostrożnie. ❏ *Be careful with that glass
vase. Easy does it!* ❏ *Now, now, Tom. Don't get angry. Easy does
it.*

eat humble pie **1.** zachowywać się bardzo pokornie po pokazaniu,
że ktoś postąpił źle. ❏ *I think I'm right, but if I'm wrong, I'll eat
humble pie.* ❏ *You think you're so smart. I hope you have to eat
humble pie.* **2.** zaakceptować obrazę i upokorzenie. ❏ *John, stand
up for your rights. You don't have to eat humble pie all the time.*
❏ *Beth seems quite happy to eat humble pie. She should stand up
for her rights.*

eat like a bird jeść bardzo niewiele; "dziobać" posiłek. ❏ *Jane is
very slim because she eats like a bird.* ❏ *Bill is trying to lose
weight by eating like a bird.*

eat like a horse bardzo dużo jeść. ❏ *No wonder he's so fat. He
eats like a horse.* ❏ *John works like a horse and eats like a horse,
so he never gets fat.*

eat one's cake and have it too Patrz pod *have one's cake
and eat it too.*

eat one's hat wyrażenie mówiące, że jeśli coś się stanie, to jest to
na tyle nieprawdopodobne, że ktoś jest gotów zjeść kapelusz.
(Zawsze używane z *if.* Nigdy nie używane dosłownie.) ❏ *If we get
there on time, I'll eat my hat.* ❏ *I'll eat my hat if you get a raise.*
❏ *He said he'd eat his hat if she got elected.*

eat one's heart out **1.** być bardzo smutnym (z powodu kogoś lub
czegoś). ❏ *Bill spent a lot of time eating his heart out after his
divorce.* ❏ *Sally ate her heart out when she had to sell her house.*
2. być zazdrosnym (o kogoś lub coś). ❏ *Do you like my new
watch? Well, eat your heart out. It was the last one in the store.*

62

❏ *Don't eat your heart out about my new car. Go get one of your own.*

eat one's words musieć wycofać się ze swoich twierdzeń; przyznać, że przewidywania nie były słuszne. ❏ *You shouldn't say that to me. I'll make you eat your words.* ❏ *John was wrong about the election and had to eat his words.*

eat out of someone's hands robić to, czego chce ktoś inny; chętnie być komuś posłusznym. (Często używane z *have*; patrz przykłady.) ❏ *Just wait! I'll have everyone eating out of my hands. They'll do whatever I ask.* ❏ *The president has Congress eating out of his hands.* ❏ *A lot of people are eating out of his hands.*

eat someone out of house and home zjeść ogromne ilości jedzenia (w czyimś domu); zjeść wszystko, co było w domu. ❏ *Billy has a huge appetite. He almost eats us out of house and home.* ❏ *When the kids come home from college, they always eat us out of house and home.*

egg on one's face, have Patrz *have egg on one's face.*

element, out of one's Patrz *out of one's element.*

eleventh hour, at the Patrz *at the eleventh hour.*

empty-handed, come away Patrz *come away empty-handed.*

empty-handed, go away Patrz *go away empty-handed.*

end in itself dla czegoś samego w sobie; dla celu jako takiego; tylko dla tego celu. ❏ *For Bob, art is an end in itself. He doesn't hope to make any money from it.* ❏ *Learning is an end in itself. Knowledge does not have to have a practical application.*

end of one's rope, at the Patrz *at the end of one's rope.*

end of one's tether, at the Patrz *at the end of one's tether.*

end of the line Patrz następne hasło.

end of the road AND **end of the line** koniec; koniec całego procesu; śmierć. (*Line* początkowo odnosiła się do torów kolejowych.) ❏ *Our house is at the end of the road.* ❏ *We rode the train to the end of the line.* ❏ *When we reach the end of the road on this project, we'll get paid.* ❏ *You've come to the end of the line. I'll not lend you another penny.* ❏ *When I reach the end of the road, I wish to be buried in a quiet place, near some trees.*

ends of the earth, to the Patrz *to the ends of the earth.*

end up with the short end of the stick Patrz *get the short end of the stick.*

Enough is enough. To wystarczy, i nie powinno być więcej. ❏ *Stop asking for money! Enough is enough!* ❏ *I've heard all the complaining from you that I can take. Stop! Enough is enough!*

enter one's mind przyjść do głowy; uświadomić sobie [pomysł lub wspomnienie]; myśleć o. ❏ *Leave you behind? The thought never even entered my mind.* ❏ *A very interesting idea just entered my mind. What if I ran for Congress?*

Every cloud has a silver lining. przysłowie mówiące, że każde zło zawiera w sobie coś dobrego. ❏ *Jane was upset when she saw that all her flowers had died from the frost. But when she saw that the weeds had died too, she said, "Every cloud has a silver lining."* ❏ *Sally had a sore throat and had to stay home from school. When she learned she missed a math test, she said, "Every cloud has a silver lining."*

Every dog has its day. AND **Every dog has his day.** przysłowie mówiące, że każdy, nawet najniżej stojący w społecznej hierarchii, ma swoją szansę. ❏ *Don't worry, you'll get chosen for the team. Every dog has its day.* ❏ *You may become famous someday. Every dog has his day.*

every living soul każdy. ❏ *I expect every living soul to be there and be there on time.* ❏ *This is the kind of problem that affects every living soul.*

every minute counts AND **every moment counts** czas jest bardzo ważny. ❏ *Doctor, please try to get here quickly. Every minute counts.* ❏ *When you take a test, you must work rapidly because every minute counts.* ❏ *When you're trying to meet a deadline, every moment counts.*

every (other) breath, with Patrz *with every (other) breath.*

everything but the kitchen sink wszystko, co było możliwe. ❏ *When Sally went off to college, she took everything but the kitchen sink.* ❏ *John orders everything but the kitchen sink when he goes out to dinner, especially if someone else is paying for it.*

everything from A to Z Patrz następne hasło.

everything from soup to nuts AND **everything from A to Z** prawie wszystko, o czym tylko można pomyśleć. (Pierwszego wyrażenia używa się głównie wtedy, kiedy mówimy o wielu daniach podawanych podczas posiłku.) ❏ *For dinner we had everything from soup to nuts.* ❏ *In college I studied everything from soup to nuts.* ❏ *She mentioned everything from A to Z.*

expecting (a child) w ciąży. (Eufemizm.) ❏ *Tommy's mother is expecting a child.* ❏ *Oh, I didn't know she was expecting.*

eye for an eye, a tooth for a tooth, An. Patrz *An eye for an eye, a tooth for a tooth.*

eye out (for someone or something), have an Patrz *have an eye out (for someone or something).*

eyes bigger than one's stomach, have Patrz *have eyes bigger than one's stomach.*

eyes in the back of one's head, have Patrz *have eyes in the back of one's head.*

F

face the music zostać ukaranym; zaakceptować nieprzyjemne rezultaty swoich działań. ❑ *Mary broke a dining-room window and had to face the music when her father got home.* ❑ *After failing a math test, Tom had to go home and face the music.*

fair-weather friend ktoś, kto jest twoim przyjacielem tylko wtedy, kiedy wszystko idzie ci dobrze. (Ten ktoś opuści cię wtedy, kiedy ci się nie powiedzie.) ❑ *Bill wouldn't help me with my homework. He's just a fair-weather friend.* ❑ *A fair-weather friend isn't much help in an emergency.*

fall down on the job nie zrobić czegoś dobrze; nie zrobić czegoś właściwie. (Również używane dosłownie.) ❑ *The team kept losing because the coach was falling down on the job.* ❑ *Tom was fired because he fell down on the job.*

fall flat (on one's face) AND **fall flat (on its face)** ponieść całkowitą porażkę. ❑ *I fell flat on my face when I tried to give my speech.* ❑ *The play fell flat on its face.* ❑ *My jokes fall flat most of the time.*

fall in(to) place pasować do siebie; organizować się. ❑ *After we heard the whole story, things began to fall in place.* ❑ *When you get older, the different parts of your life begin to fall into place.*

fall short (of something) **1.** brakować czegoś; brakować wystarczającej ilości czegoś. ❑ *We fell short of money at the end of the month.* ❑ *When baking a cake, the cook fell short of eggs and had to go to the store for more.* **2.** nie osiągnąć celu. ❑ *We fell short of our goal of collecting a thousand dollars.* ❑ *Ann ran a fast race, but fell short of the record.*

Familiarity breeds contempt. przysłowie mówiące, że bliska znajomość przez długi czas rodzi złe uczucia. ❑ *Bill and his brothers are always fighting. As they say: "Familiarity breeds contempt."* ❑ *Mary and John were good friends for many years. Finally they got into a big argument and became enemies. That just shows that familiarity breeds contempt.*

familiar ring, have a Patrz *have a familiar ring.*

fan of someone, be a Patrz *be a fan of someone.*

far as it goes, as Patrz *as far as it goes.*

farm someone or something out AND **farm out someone or something** **1.** [z *someone*] wysłać kogoś gdzieś dla roztoczenia nad nim opieki i umożliwienia rozwoju. ❑ *When my mother died, they farmed me out to my aunt and uncle.* ❑ *The team manager farmed out the baseball player to the minor leagues until he improved.* **2.** [z *something*] przekazać coś gdzieś po to, by się tym zająć. ❑ *I farmed out various parts of the work to different people.* ❑ *Bill farmed his chores out to his brothers and sisters and went to a movie.*

fat is in the fire, The. Patrz *The fat is in the fire.*

fear of something, for Patrz *for fear of something.*

feast one's eyes (on someone or something) spoglądać na kogoś lub na coś z przyjemnością, zazdrością i podziwem. (Tak jakby taki widok stanowił ucztę wizualnej rozkoszy dla czyichś oczu.) ❑ *Just feast your eyes on that beautiful juicy steak!* ❑ *Yes, feast your eyes. You won't see one like that again for a long time.*

feather in one's cap honor; nagroda za coś. ❑ *Getting a new client was really a feather in my cap.* ❑ *John earned a feather in his cap by getting an A in physics.*

feather one's (own) nest **1.** umeblować i ozdobić swój dom stylowo i wygodnie. (Ptaki obramowują swoje gniazda piórami po to, by uczynić je ciepłymi i wygodnymi.) ❑ *Mr. and Mrs. Simpson have feathered their nest quite comfortably.* ❑ *It costs a great deal* *of money to feather one's nest these days.* **2.** wykorzystywać władzę i prestiż po to, by odnieść osobiste korzści. (Mówi się tak głównie o politykach, którzy wykorzystują swój urząd po to, by zrobić pieniądze.) ❏ *The mayor seemed to be helping people, but she was really feathering her own nest.* ❏ *The building contractor used a lot of public money to feather his nest.*

feed the kitty dać pieniądze na jakiś cel. (*Kitty* to nazwa pojemnika, do którego wkładane są pieniądze.) ❏ *Please feed the kitty. Make a contribution to help sick children.* ❏ *Come on, Bill. Feed the kitty. You can afford a dollar for a good cause.*

feel like a million (dollars) czuć się dobrze i zdrowo, zarówno psychicznie, jak i fizycznie. (Czuć się jak coś niewiarygodnie dobrego.) ❏ *A quick swim in the morning makes me feel like a million dollars.* ❏ *What a beautiful day! It makes you feel like a million.*

feel like a new person czuć się odświeżonym i odnowionym, zwłaszcza po wyzdrowieniu lub po wystrojeniu się. ❏ *I bought a new suit, and now I feel like a new person.* ❏ *Bob felt like a new person when he got out of the hospital.*

feel out of place czuć się obco w danym miejscu. ❏ *I feel out of place at formal dances.* ❏ *Bob and Ann felt out of place at the picnic, so they went home.*

feel something in one's bones AND **know something in one's bones** przeczuwać coś; mieć intuicyjne odczucia w stosunku do czegoś. ❏ *The train will be late. I feel it in my bones.* ❏ *I failed the test. I know it in my bones.*

feet of clay, have Patrz *have feet of clay.*

feet, on one's Patrz *on one's feet.*

fell swoop, at one Patrz *at one fell swoop.*

fell swoop, in one Patrz *in one fell swoop.*

fight someone or something hammer and tongs AND **fight someone or something tooth and nail; go at it hammer and tongs; go at it tooth and nail** walczyć przeciwko komuś lub czemuś energicznie i z wielką determinacją. (Te wyrażenia są stare i odnoszą się do walki z bronią i bez broni.) ❏ *They fought against the robber tooth and nail.* ❏ *The dogs were fighting each other hammer and tongs.* ❏ *The mayor fought the new law hammer and tongs.* ❏ *We'll fight this zoning ordinance tooth and nail.*

fight someone or something tooth and nail Patrz poprzednie hasło.

fill someone's shoes zająć czyjeś miejsce i dobrze wykonywać pracę tej osoby. (To tak, jakby nosić czyjeś buty, wypełniając je swoją stopą.) ❏ *I don't know how we'll be able to do without you. No one can fill your shoes.* ❏ *It'll be difficult to fill Jane's shoes. She did her job very well.*

fill the bill być dokładnie tą rzeczą, która jest potrzebna. ❏ *Ah, this steak is great. It really fills the bill.* ❏ *This new pair of shoes fills the bill nicely.*

Finders keepers,(losers weepers). wyrażenie używane wtedy, kiedy się coś znalazło. (Przysłowie oznacza, że ten, kto coś znajduje, zatrzymuje to. Ten, kto gubi, może tylko płakać.) ❏ *John lost a quarter in the dining room yesterday. Ann found the quarter there today. Ann claimed that since she found it, it was hers. She said, "Finders keepers, losers weepers."* ❏ *John said, "I'll say finders keepers when I find something of yours!"*

find it in one's heart (to do something) mieć odwagę lub pasję, aby coś zrobić. ❏ *She couldn't find it in her heart to refuse to come home to him.* ❏ *I can't do it! I can't find it in my heart.*

find one's or something's way somewhere **1.** [z *one's*] odkryć drogę do danego miejsca. ❏ *Mr. Smith found his way to the museum.* ❏ *Can you find your way home?* **2.** [z *something's*] wylądować gdzieś. (Używając tego wyrażenia, unikamy oskarżania kogoś o przeniesienie czegoś.) ❏ *The money found its way into the mayor's pocket.* ❏ *The secret plans found their way into the enemy's hands.*

fine feather, in Patrz *in fine feather.*

fine kettle of fish prawdziwy chaos; niezadowalająca sytuacja. (Dosłownie nic nie znaczy.) ❑ *The dog has eaten the steak we were going to have for dinner. This is a fine kettle of fish!* ❑ *This is a fine kettle of fish. It's below freezing outside, and the furnace won't work.*

fine-tooth comb, go over something with a Patrz *go over something with a fine-tooth comb.*

finger in the pie, have one's Patrz *have one's finger in the pie.*

fingertips, have something at one's Patrz *have something at one's fingertips.*

fire, under Patrz *under fire.*

first and foremost przede wszystkim. (Klisza.) ❑ *First and foremost, I think you should work harder on your biology.* ❑ *Have this in mind first and foremost: Keep smiling!*

First come, first served. Ci, którzy przybędą pierwsi, będą pierwsi obsłużeni. (Klisza.) ❑ *They ran out of tickets before we got there. It was first come, first served, but we didn't know that.* ❑ *Please line up and take your turn. It's first come, first served.*

first of all przede wszystkim; zanim zrobimy cokolwiek innego. (Wyrażenia podobne: "second of all" lub "third of all," są używane, ale nie mają większego sensu.) ❑ *First of all, put your name on this piece of paper.* ❑ *First of all, we'll try to find a place to live.*

first thing (in the morning) przed czymkolwiek innym rano. ❑ *Please call me first thing in the morning. I can't help you now.* ❑ *I'll do that first thing.*

first things first rzeczy najważniejsze muszą być wzięte pod uwagę w pierwszej kolejności. ❑ *It's more important to get a job than to buy new clothes. First things first!* ❑ *Do your homework now. Go out and play later. First things first.*

first water, of the Patrz *of the first water.*

fish for a compliment próbować kogoś sprowokować do powiedzenia sobie komplementu. (Tak jakby kusić kogoś do powiedzenia komplementu.) ❏ *When she showed me her new dress, I could tell that she was fishing for a compliment.* ❏ *Tom was certainly fishing for a compliment when he modeled his fancy haircut for his friends.*

fishing expedition, go on a Patrz *go on a fishing expedition.*

fish or cut bait albo wykonać pracę w taki sposób, w jaki się tego oczekuje, albo zostawić ją i pozwolić ją wykonać komu innemu. (Albo zwracaj uwagę na swoją wędkę, abo odsuń się i przygotuj przynętę dla innych, bardziej aktywnych w łowieniu.) ❏ *Mary is doing much better on the job since her manager told her to fish or cut bait.* ❏ *The boss told Tom, "Quit wasting time! Fish or cut bait!"*

fish out of water, like a Patrz *like a fish out of water.*

fish to fry, have other Patrz *have other fish to fry.*

fit as a fiddle, as Patrz *as fit as a fiddle.*

fit for a king całkowicie odpowiadające; odpowiednie dla króla. (Klisza.) ❏ *What a delicious meal. It was fit for a king.* ❏ *Our room at the hotel was fit for a king.*

fit like a glove bardzo dobrze pasujące; ciasno lub idealnie dopasowane. ❏ *My new shoes fit like a glove.* ❏ *My new coat is a little tight. It fits like a glove.*

fit someone to a T Patrz pod *suit someone to a T.*

fix someone's wagon ukarać kogoś; wyrównać z kimś rachunki; spiskować przeciwko komuś. ❏ *If you ever do that again, I'll fix your wagon!* ❏ *Tommy! You clean up your room this instant, or I'll fix your wagon!* ❏ *He reported me to the boss, but I fixed his wagon. I knocked his lunch on the floor.*

flames, go up in Patrz *go up in flames.*

flash, in a Patrz *in a flash.*

flash in the pan ktoś lub coś przyciągające wiele uwagi, ale bardzo krótko. ❏ *I'm afraid that my success as a painter was just a flash in the pan.* ❏ *Tom had hoped to be a singer, but his career was only a flash in the pan.*

flat as a pancake, as Patrz *as flat as a pancake.*

flat broke całkowity bankrut; zupełnie bez żadnych pieniędzy. ❏ *I spent my last dollar, and I'm flat broke.* ❏ *The bank closed its doors to the public. It was flat broke!*

flesh and blood **1.** żywe ludzkie ciało, zwłaszcza w odniesieniu do jego naturalnych ograniczeń; istota ludzka. ❏ *This cold weather is more than flesh and blood can stand.* ❏ *Carrying 300 pounds is beyond mere flesh and blood.* **2.** Żyjący, żywy, z życiem. ❏ *The paintings of this artist are lifeless. They lack flesh and blood.* ❏ *These ideas have no flesh and blood.* **3.** krewni; swoja krew. ❏ *That's no way to treat one's own flesh and blood.* ❏ *I want to leave my money to my own flesh and blood.* ❏ *Grandmother was happier living with her flesh and blood.*

flesh, in the Patrz *in the flesh.*

float a loan otrzymać pożyczkę; wystąpić o pożyczkę. ❏ *I couldn't afford to pay cash for the car, so I floated a loan.* ❏ *They needed money, so they had to float a loan.*

flying colors, with Patrz *with flying colors.*

fly in the face of someone or something AND **fly in the teeth of someone or something** zlekceważyć, zanegować lub okazać brak szacunku dla kogoś lub czegoś. ❏ *John loves to fly in the face of tradition.* ❏ *Ann made it a practice to fly in the face of standard procedures.* ❏ *John finds great pleasure in flying in the teeth of his father.*

fly in the ointment   mała, nieprzyjemna sprawa, która coś psuje; wada. ❑ *We enjoyed the play, but the fly in the ointment was not being able to find our car afterward.* ❑ *It sounds like a good idea, but there must be a fly in the ointment somewhere.*

fly in the teeth of someone or something   Patrz pod   *fly in the face of someone or something.*

fly off the handle   stracić panowanie nad sobą. ❑ *Every time anyone mentions taxes, Mrs. Brown flies off the handle.* ❑ *If she keeps flying off the handle like that, she'll have a·heart attack.*

foam at the mouth   być bardzo rozgniewanym. (Wyrażenie odwołuje się do psa chorego na wściekliznę, który ma pianę na pysku.) ❑ *Bob was raving—foaming at the mouth. I've never seen anyone so angry.* ❑ *Bill foamed at the mouth in anger.*

follow one's heart   działać zgodnie ze swoimi uczuciami: być pusłusznym uczuciu sympatii lub współczucia. ❑ *I couldn't decide what to do, so I just followed my heart.* ❑ *I trust that you will follow your heart in this matter.*

food for thought   temat do myślenia. ❑ *I don't like your idea very much, but it's food for thought.* ❑ *Your lecture was very good. It contained much food for thought.*

fool and his money are soon parted, A.   Patrz *A fool and his money are soon parted.*

Foot-in-mouth disease, have   Patrz pod   *have foot-in-mouth disease.*

foot the bill   zapłacić rachunek; zapłacić (za coś). ❑ *Let's go out and eat. I'll foot the bill.* ❑ *If the bank goes broke, don't worry. The government will foot the bill.*

force someone's hand   zmusić kogoś, aby odkrył swoje plany, strategie, lub tajemnice. (Odnosi się do kart trzymanych w ręku podczas gry.) ❑ *We didn't know what she was doing until Tom forced her hand.* ❑ *We couldn't plan our game until we forced the other team's hand in the last play.*

force someone to the wall AND **drive someone to the wall** zepchnąć kogoś na ekstremalne pozycje, postawić kogoś w dziwnej sytuacji. ❑ *He wouldn't tell the truth until we forced him to the wall.* ❑ *They don't pay their bills until you drive them to the wall.*

for fear of something ze strachu przed czymś; z powodu obawy przed czymś. ❑ *He doesn't drive for fear of an accident.* ❑ *They lock their doors for fear of being robbed.*

forgive and forget przebaczyć komuś coś i zapomnieć, że się to zdarzyło. (Klisza.) ❑ *I'm sorry, John. Let's forgive and forget. What do you say?* ❑ *It was nothing. We'll just have to forgive and forget.*

fork money out (for something) AND **fork out money (for something)** zapłacić (prawdopodobnie niechętnie) za coś. (Wyrażeniu temu często towarzyszy wzmianka o kwocie pieniędzy. Patrz przykłady.) ❑ *I like that stereo, but I don't want to fork out a lot of money.* ❑ *Do you think I'm going to fork twenty dollars out for that book?* ❑ *I hate having to fork out money day after day.* ❑ *Forking money out to everyone is part of life in a busy economy.*

form an opinion przemyśleć lub zdecydować się na opinię. (Zwróć uwagę na różnice w przykładach.) ❑ *I don't know enough about the issue to form an opinion.* ❑ *Don't tell me how to think! I can form my own opinion.* ❑ *I don't form opinions without careful consideration.*

for the devil of it AND **for the heck of it; for the hell of it** po prostu dla zabawy; ponieważ jest w tym coś w niewielkim stopniu złego; dla żadnego uzasadnionego powodu. (Niektórzy mogą mieć obiekcje do słowa *hell.*) ❑ *We filled their garage with leaves just for the devil of it.* ❑ *Tom tripped Bill for the heck of it.* ❑ *John picked a fight with Tom just for the hell of it.*

for the heck of it Patrz poprzednie hasło.

for the odds to be against one ponieważ stan rzeczy ogólnie jest przeciwko komuś. ❑ *You can give it a try, but the odds are against you.* ❑ *I know the odds are against me, but I wish to run in the race anyway.*

for the record po to, żeby (w czyjejś własnej wersji) fakty stały się znane; po to, żeby pozostało świadectwo określonego faktu. (Często się tak mówi, kiedy obecni są reporterzy.) ❑ *I'd like to say – for the record – that at no time have I ever accepted a bribe from anyone.* ❑ *For the record, I've never been able to get anything done around city hall without bribing someone.*

foul play nielegalna działalność; złe praktyki. ❑ *The police investigating the death suspect foul play.* ❑ *Each student got an A on the test, and the teacher imagined it was the result of foul play.*

free and easy nieformalnie. ❑ *John is so free and easy. How can anyone be so relaxed?* ❑ *Now, take it easy. Just act free and easy. No one will know you're nervous.*

free as a bird, as Patrz *as free as a bird.*

free-for-all zdezorganizowana kłótnia lub zawody angażujące wszystkich; burda. ❑ *The picnic turned into a free-for-all after midnight.* ❑ *The race started out in an organized manner, but ended up being a free-for-all.*

friend in need is a friend indeed, A. Patrz *A friend in need is a friend indeed.*

from hand to hand od jednej osoby do grupy innych osób; przekazywane z ręki do ręki. ❑ *The book traveled from hand to hand until it got back to its owner.* ❑ *By the time the baby had been passed from hand to hand, it was crying.*

from pillar to post z jednego miejsca do wielu innych miejsc; (przenośnie) od człowieka do człowieka, podobnie jak plotka. (Klisza.) ❑ *My father was in the army, and we moved from pillar* *to post year after year.* ❏ *After I told one person my secret, it went quickly from pillar to post.*

from rags to riches z biedy do bogactwa; od skromności do elegancji. ❏ *The princess used to be quite poor. She certainly moved from rags to riches.* ❏ *After I inherited the money, I went from rags to riches.*

from start to finish od początku do końca; poprzez. ❏ *I disliked the whole business from start to finish.* ❏ *Mary caused problems from start to finish.*

from stem to stern z jednego końca na drugi. (Odnosi się do części przedniej i tylniej statku. Również używane dosłownie w odniesieniu do statków.) ❏ *Now, I have to clean the house from stem to stern.* ❏ *I polished my car carefully from stem to stern.*

from the bottom of one's heart szczerze. ❏ *When I returned the lost kitten to Mrs. Brown, she thanked me from the bottom of her heart.* ❏ *Oh, thank you! I'm grateful from the bottom of my heart.*

from the ground up od początku; od początku do końca. (Używane dosłownie w odniesieniu do domów lub innych budynków.) ❏ *We must plan our sales campaign carefully from the ground up.* ❏ *Sorry, but you'll have to start all over again from the ground up.*

from the word go od początku; od samego momentu powstania czegoś. (Od momentu wypowiedzenia słowa *go*.) ❏ *I knew about the problem from the word go.* ❏ *She was failing the class from the word go.*

from top to bottom od punktu najwyższego do najniższego; poprzez. ❏ *I have to clean the house from top to bottom today.* ❏ *We need to replace our elected officials from top to bottom.*

frying pan into the fire, out of the Patrz *out of the frying pan into the fire.*

full as a tick, as Patrz *as full as a tick.*

full swing, in Patrz *in full swing.*

fun and games zabawiając się; robiąc rzeczy bezużyteczne; działania, które są stratą czasu. ❑ *All right, Bill, the fun and games are over. It's time to get down to work.* ❑ *This isn't a serious course. It's nothing but fun and games.*

funny as a crutch, as Patrz *as funny as a crutch.*

further ado, without Patrz *without further ado.*

G

gas, out of Patrz *out of gas.*

get a black eye (Używane również z *have.* Uwaga: *Get* można zastąpić *have.* Zwróć uwagę na różnice w przykładach. *Get* zwykle znaczy stać się, dostać, lub spowodować. *Have* zwykle znaczy posiadać, być, lub spowodować.) **1.** mieć sińca koło oczu od uderzenia. ❏ *I got a black eye from walking into a door.* ❏ *I have a black eye where John hit me.* **2.** mieć albo zły charakter, albo złą opinię. ❏ *Mary got a black eye because of her complaining.* ❏ *The whole group now has a black eye.* ALSO: **give someone a black eye 1.** uderzyć kogoś w oczy, tak że pokazuje się siniec. ❏ *John became angry and gave me a black eye.* **2.** nadwerężyć komuś charakter lub opinię. ❏ *The constant complaining gave the whole group a black eye.*

get a clean bill of health [w odniesieniu do ludzi] otrzymać świadectwo dobrego zdrowia od lekarza. (Używane również z *have.* Patrz uwaga dotycząca *get a black eye.*) ❏ *Sally got a clean bill of health from the doctor.* ❏ *Now that Sally has a clean bill of health, she can go back to work.* ALSO: **give someone a clean bill of health** [w odniesieniu do lekarza] dać komuś świadectwo dobrego zdrowia. ❏ *The doctor gave Sally a clean bill of health.*

get (all) dolled up wystroić się. (Zwykle w odniesieniu do kobiet, ale niekoniecznie.) ❏ *I have to get all dolled up for the dance tonight.* ❏ *I just love to get dolled up in my best clothes.*

get a load off one's feet AND **take a load off one's feet** usiąść; cieszyć się z faktu, że można usiąść. ❏ *Come in, John. Sit* *down and take a load off your feet.* ❏ *Yes, I need to get a load off my feet. I'm really tired.*

get a load off one's mind powiedzieć to, co się myśli. ❏ *He sure talked a long time. I guess he had to get a load off his mind.* ❏ *You aren't going to like what I'm going to say, but I have to get a load off my mind.*

get along (on a shoestring) umieć wyżyć z bardzo niewielkich pieniędzy. ❏ *For the last two years, we have had to get along on a shoestring.* ❏ *With so little money, it's hard to get along.*

get a lump in one's throat mieć uczucie ucisku w gardle – jak gdyby zamierzało się rozpłakać. (Również z *have.* Patrz uwaga przy *get a black eye.*) ❏ *Whenever they play the national anthem, I get a lump in my throat.* ❏ *I have a lump in my throat because I'm frightened.*

get a word in edgewise AND **get a word in edgeways** zdołać coś powiedzieć wtedy, kiedy inni rozmawiają i nie zauważają cię. (Często używane w formie przeczącej. To tak, jakby ktoś próbował wcisnąć coś do rozmowy.) ❏ *It was such an exciting conversation that I could hardly get a word in edgewise.* ❏ *Mary talks so fast that nobody can get a word in edgeways.*

get cold feet być onieśmielonym lub przestraszonym; mieć jak gdyby marznące ze strachu stopy. (Również z *have.* Patrz uwaga przy *get a black eye.*) ❏ *I usually get cold feet when I have to speak in public.* ❏ *John got cold feet and wouldn't run in the race.* ❏ *I can't give my speech now. I have cold feet.*

get down to brass tacks zacząć rozmawiać o ważnych rzeczach. ❏ *Let's get down to brass tacks. We've wasted too much time chatting.* ❏ *Don't you think that it's about time to get down to brass tacks?*

get down to business AND **get down to work** zacząć rozmawiać poważnie; zacząć negocjować lub prowadzić interesy. ❏ *All right, everyone. Let's get down to business. There has been enough playing around.* ❏ *When the president and vice president arrive,* *we can get down to business.* ❏ *They're here. Let's get down to work.*

get down to work Patrz poprzednie hasło.

get fresh (with someone) być zbyt śmiałym lub impertynenckim. ❏ *When I tried to kiss Mary, she slapped me and shouted, "Don't get fresh with me!"* ❏ *I can't stand people who get fresh.*

get goose bumps AND **get goose pimples** [w odniesieniu do skóry] dostać gęsiej skórki ze strachu lub podekscytowania. (Również z *have*. Patrz uwaga przy *get a black eye*. To tak, jakby czyjeś ciało przypominało oskubaną gęś. Bardzo niewielu Amerykanów kiedykolwiek widziało oskubaną gęś.) ❏ *When he sings, I get goose bumps.* ❏ *I never get goose pimples.* ❏ *That really scared her. Now she's got goose pimples.*

get goose pimples Patrz poprzednie hasło.

get in someone's hair sprawiać komuś kłopot lub irytować go. (Zwykle nie używane dosłownie.) ❏ *Billy is always getting in his mother's hair.* ❏ *I wish you'd stop getting in my hair.*

get into the swing of things dołączyć się do rutyny lub do zaczętych już działań. (Nawiązuje do rytmu zrutynizowanych działań.) ❏ *Come on, Bill. Try to get into the swing of things.* ❏ *John just couldn't seem to get into the swing of things.*

get off scot-free Patrz *go scot-free*.

get one's ducks in a row poukładać swoje sprawy; przygotować się. (Nieformalne lub slang. Tak jakby ktoś układał w rzędzie drewniane kaczki, jedna po drugiej, by je zestrzelić, tak jak w zabawie karnawałowej.) ❏ *You can't hope to go into a company and sell something until you get your ducks in a row.* ❏ *As soon as you people get your ducks in a row, we'll leave.*

get one's feet on the ground być mocno ustabilizowanym lub ustabilizować się ponownie. (Również z *have*. Patrz uwaga przy *get a black eye*.) ❏ *He's new at the job, but soon he'll get his feet on the ground.* ❏ *Her productivity will improve after she gets her* *feet on the ground again.* ❏ *Don't worry about Sally. She has her feet on the ground.* ALSO: **keep one's feet on the ground** pozostawać mocno ustabilizowanym. ❏ *Sally will have no trouble keeping her feet on the ground.*

get one's feet wet zacząć coś; zdobywać pierwsze doświadczenia w czymś. (Tak jakby ktoś brodził w wodzie.) ❏ *Of course he can't do the job right. He's hardly got his feet wet yet.* ❏ *I'm looking forward to learning to drive. I can't wait to get behind the steering wheel and get my feet wet.*

get one's fill of someone or something mieć dosyć kogoś lub czegoś. (Używane również z *have*. Patrz uwaga przy *get a black eye*.) ❏ *You'll soon get your fill of Tom. He can be quite a pest.* ❏ *I can never get my fill of shrimp. I love it.* ❏ *Three weeks of visiting grandchildren is enough. I've had my fill of them.*

get one's fingers burned mieć złe doświadczenie. (Również używane dosłownie.) ❏ *I tried that once before and got my fingers burned. I won't try it again.* ❏ *If you go swimming and get your fingers burned, you won't want to swim again.*

get one's foot in the door uzyskać korzystną pozycję (dla dalszych działań); podjąć pierwsze kroki. (Sprzedawcy krążący od domu do domu zwykle blokują drzwi stopą, by ich nie zamknąć. Również z *have*. Patrz uwaga przy *get a black eye*.) ❏ *I think I could get the job if I could only get my foot in the door.* ❏ *It pays to get your foot in the door. Try to get an appointment with the boss.* ❏ *I have a better chance now that I have my foot in the door.*

get one's hands dirty AND **dirty one's hands; soil one's hands** wplątać się w coś nielegalnego; zrobić coś wstydliwego; zrobić coś poniżej swojego poziomu. ❏ *The mayor would never get his hands dirty by giving away political favors.* ❏ *I will not dirty my hands by breaking the law.* ❏ *Sally felt that to talk to the hobo was to soil her hands.*

get one's head above water poradzić sobie z problemami; dawać sobie radę z pracą lub odpowiedzialnością. (Używane również dosłownie. Także z *have*. Patrz uwaga przy *get a black eye*.) ❏ *I can't seem to get my head above water. Work just keeps piling up.* ❏ *I'll be glad when I have my head above water.* ALSO: **keep**

one's head above water bez trudu radzić sobie z odpowiedzialnością. ❏ *Now that I have more space to work in, I can easily keep my head above water.*

get one's just deserts dostać to, na co się zasługuje. ❏ *I feel better now that Jane got her just deserts. She really insulted me.* ❏ *Bill got back exactly the treatment that he gave out. He got his just deserts.*

get one's second wind (Używane również z *have*. Patrz uwaga przy *get a black eye.*) **1.** [w odniesieniu do ludzi] odzyskać oddech po krótkim wysiłku. ❏ *John was having a hard time running until he got his second wind.* ❏ *Bill had to quit the race because he never got his second wind.* ❏ *"At last," thought Ann, "I have my second wind. Now I can really swim fast."* **2.** stać się bardziej aktywnym lub produktywnym (po powolnym starcie). ❏ *I usually get my second wind early in the afternoon.* ❏ *Mary is a better worker now that she has her second wind.*

get one's teeth into something poważnie coś rozpocząć, zwłaszcza jakieś trudne zadanie. (Używane również dosłownie w odniesieniu do jedzenia.) ❏ *Come on, Bill. You have to get your teeth into your biology.* ❏ *I can't wait to get my teeth into this problem.*

get on someone's nerves zirytować kogoś. ❏ *Please stop whistling. It's getting on my nerves.* ❏ *All this arguing is getting on their nerves.*

get on the bandwagon AND **jump on the bandwagon** dołączyć do czegoś cieszącego się popularnością; zająć popularne stanowisko. ❏ *You really should get on the bandwagon. Everyone else is.* ❏ *Jane has always had her own ideas about things. She's not the kind of person to jump on the bandwagon.*

get out of the wrong side of the bed Patrz pod *get up on the wrong side of the bed.*

get second thoughts about someone or something mieć wątpliwości w stosunku do czegoś lub kogoś. (Używane również z *have*. Patrz uwaga przy *get a black eye.*) ❏ *I'm beginning to get* *second thoughts about Tom.* ❑ *Tom is getting second thoughts about it, too.* ❑ *We now have second thoughts about going to Canada.*

get (someone) off the hook uwolnić kogoś od zobowiązań; pomóc komuś w kłopotliwej sytuacji. ❑ *Thanks for getting me off the hook. I didn't want to attend that meeting.* ❑ *I couldn't get off the hook by myself.*

get someone over a barrel AND **get someone under one's thumb** skazać kogoś na czyjąś łaskę; mieć nad kimś kontrolę. (Używane również z *have.* Patrz uwaga przy *get a black eye.*) ❑ *He got me over a barrel, and I had to do what he said.* ❑ *Ann will do exactly what I say. I've got her over a barrel.* ❑ *All right, John. You've got me under your thumb. What do you want me to do?*

get someone's back up Patrz następne hasło.

get someone's dander up AND **get someone's back up; get someone's hackles up; get someone's Irish up** rozzłościć kogoś. (Używane również z *have.* Patrz uwaga przy *get a black eye.*) ❑ *Now, don't get your dander up. Calm down.* ❑ *Bob had his Irish up all day yesterday. I don't know what was wrong.* ❑ *She really got her back up when I asked her for money.* ❑ *Now, now, don't get your hackles up. I didn't mean any harm.*

get someone's ear sprawić, by ktoś cię posłuchał; przyciągnąć czyjąś uwagę. (Używane również z *have.* Patrz uwaga przy *get a black eye.* Nie używane dosłownie.) ❑ *He got my ear and talked for an hour.* ❑ *While I have your ear, I'd like to tell you about something I'm selling.*

get someone's eye Patrz pod *catch someone's eye.*

get someone's hackles up Patrz pod *get someone's dander up.*

get someone's Irish up Patrz pod *get someone's dander up.*

83

get someone under one's thumb Patrz pod *get someone over a barrel*.

get something into someone's thick head Patrz pod *get something through someone's thick skull*.

get something off one's chest powiedzieć o jakimś swoim zmartwieniu czy kłopocie. (Używane również z *have*. Patrz uwaga przy *get a black eye*.) ❑ *I have to get this off my chest. I broke your window with a stone.* ❑ *I knew I'd feel better when I had that off my chest.*

get something off (the ground) rozpocząć coś. ❑ *I can relax after I get this project off the ground.* ❑ *You'll have a lot of free time when you get the project off.*

get something sewed up (Używane również z *have*. Patrz uwaga przy *get a black eye*.) **1.** sprawić, by coś zostało zeszyte (przez kogoś). (Używane dosłownie.) ❑ *I want to get this tear sewed up now.* ❑ *I'll have this hole sewed up tomorrow.* **2.** AND **get something wrapped up** sprawić, by coś zostało ustalone lub zakończone. (Używane również z *have*.) ❑ *I'll take the contract to the mayor tomorrow morning. I'll get the whole deal sewed up by noon.* ❑ *Don't worry about the car loan. I'll have it sewed up in time to make the purchase.* ❑ *I'll get the loan wrapped up, and you'll have the car this week.*

get something straight jasno coś zrozumieć. (Używane również z *have*. Patrz uwaga przy *get a black eye*.) ❑ *Now get this straight. You're going to fail history.* ❑ *Let me get this straight. I'm supposed to go there in the morning?* ❑ *Let me make sure I have this straight.*

get something through someone's thick skull AND **get something into someone's thick head** sprawić, by ktoś coś zrozumiał; wcisnąć komuś do głowy jakąś informację. ❑ *He can't seem to get it through his thick skull.* ❑ *If I could get this into my thick head once, I'd remember it.*

get something under one's belt (Używane również z *have*. Patrz uwaga przy *get a black eye*.) **1.** zjeść lub wypić coś.

(Oznacza, że jedzenie idzie do żołądka, który jest pod paskiem.) ❏ *I'd feel a lot better if I had a cool drink under my belt.* ❏ *Come in out of the cold and get a nice warm meal under your belt.* **2.** dobrze się czegoś nauczyć; zasymilować jakąś informację. (Nie używane dosłownie. Wiedza znajduje się w umyśle, a nie pod paskiem.) ❏ *I have to study tonight. I have to get a lot of algebra under my belt.* ❏ *Now that I have my lessons under my belt, I can rest easy.*

get something under way zacząć coś. (Używane również z *have*. Patrz uwaga przy *get a black eye*. Pochodzenie żeglarskie.) ❏ *The time has come to get this meeting under way.* ❏ *Now that the president has the meeting under way, I can relax.*

get something wrapped up Patrz pod *get something sewed up*.

get stars in one's eyes mieć obsesję na punkcie show businessu; mieć obsesję na punkcie sceny. (Również z *have*. Patrz uwaga przy *get a black eye*. Odnosi się do gwiazd Hollywood czy New Yorku.) ❏ *Many young people get stars in their eyes at this age.* ❏ *Ann has stars in her eyes. She wants to go to Hollywood.*

get the benefit of the doubt otrzymać korzystny dla siebie wyrok wtedy, kiedy dowody ani nie są za tobą, ani przeciwko tobie. (Również z *have*. Patrz uwaga przy *get a black eye*.) ❏ *I was right between a B and an A. I got the benefit of the doubt – an A.* ❏ *I thought I should have had the benefit of the doubt, but the judge made me pay a fine.* ALSO: **give someone the benefit of the doubt** ❏ *I'm glad the teacher gave me the benefit of the doubt.* ❏ *Please, judge. Give me the benefit of the doubt.*

get the blues pogrążyć się w smutku lub w depresji; pogrążyć się w melancholii. (Również z *have*. Patrz uwaga przy *get a black eye*.) ❏ *You'll have to excuse Bill. He has the blues tonight.* ❏ *I get the blues every time I hear that song.*

get the final word Patrz pod *get the last word*.

get the hang of something nauczyć się, jak coś zrobić; nauczyć się, jak coś działa. (Również z *have*. Patrz uwaga przy *get a black* *eye.*) ❑ *As soon as I get the hang of this computer, I'll be able to work faster.* ❑ *Now that I have the hang of starting the car in cold weather, I won't have to get up so early.*

get the inside track uzyskać przewagę (nad kimś) dzięki specjalnym powiązaniom, wiedzy lub względom. (Również z *have.* Patrz uwaga przy *get a black eye.*) ❑ *If I could get the inside track, I could win the contract.* ❑ *The boss likes me. Since I have the inside track, I'll probably be the new office manager.*

get the jump on someone zrobić coś przed kimś; wyprzedzić kogoś. (Również z *have.* Patrz uwaga przy *get a black eye.*) ❑ *I got the jump on Tom and got a place in line ahead of him.* ❑ *We'll have to work hard to get the contract, because they have the jump on us.*

get the last laugh wyśmiać lub ośmieszyć kogoś, kto przedtem wyśmiał lub ośmieszył ciebie; postawić kogoś w takiej samej niedobrej sytuacji, w jakiej ty byłeś poprzednio. (Również z *have.* Patrz uwaga przy *get a black eye.*) ❑ *John laughed when I got a D on the final exam. I got the last laugh, though. He failed the course.* ❑ *Mr. Smith said I was foolish when I bought an old building. I had the last laugh when I sold it a month later for twice what I paid for it.*

get the last word AND **get the final word** mieć ostatnie słowo (w dyskusji, w kłótni); podjąć ostateczną decyzję (w jakiejś sprawie). (Również z *have.* Patrz uwaga przy *get a black eye.*) ❑ *The boss gets the last word in hiring.* ❑ *Why do you always have to have the final word in an argument?*

get the message Patrz pod *get the word.*

get the nod zostać wybranym. (Również z *have.* Patrz uwaga przy *get a black eye.*) ❑ *The boss is going to pick the new sales manager. I think Ann will get the nod.* ❑ *I had the nod for captain of the team, but I decided not to do it.*

get the red-carpet treatment być specjalnie traktowanym; być traktowanym po królewsku. (Wyrażenie nawiązuje – czasami w sensie dosłownym – do rozkładania czerwonego dywanu dla kogoś do przejścia po nim.) ❏ *I love to go to fancy stores where I get the red-carpet treatment.* ❏ *The queen expects to get the red-carpet treatment wherever she goes.* ALSO: **give someone the red-carpet treatment** specjalnie kogoś traktować; traktować kogoś po królewsku. ❏ *We always give the queen the red-carpet treatment when she comes to visit.* ALSO: **roll out the red carpet for someone** zapewnić komuś specjalne traktowanie. ❏ *There's no need to roll out the red carpet for me.* ❏ *We rolled out the red carpet for the king and queen.*

get the runaround otrzymać serię wymówek, odwlekań i odesłań do kogoś innego. ❏ *You'll get the runaround if you ask to see the manager.* ❏ *I hate it when I get the runaround.* ALSO: **give someone the runaround** kilka razy kogoś odsyłać; odwlekać coś lub wymyślać wymówki. ❏ *If you ask to see the manager, they'll give you the runaround.*

get the shock of one's life doznać poważnego emocjonalnego szoku. (Również z *have.* Patrz uwaga przy *get a black eye.*) ❏ *I opened the telegram and got the shock of my life.* ❏ *I had the shock of my life when I won $5,000.*

get the short end of the stick AND **end up with the short end of the stick** w końcu uzyskać mniej niż ktoś inny; zostać o-szukanym. (Również z *have.* Patrz uwaga przy *get a black eye.*) ❏ *Why do I always get the short end of the stick? I want my fair share!* ❏ *She's unhappy because she has the short end of the stick again.* ❏ *I hate to end up with the short end of the stick.*

get the upper hand (on someone) uzyskać pozycję wyższą w stosunku do kogoś innego; mieć nad kimś przewagę. (Również z *have.* Patrz uwaga przy *get a black eye.*) ❏ *John is always trying to get the upper hand on someone.* ❏ *He never ends up having the upper hand, though.*

get the word AND **get the message** otrzymać wyjaśnienie; otrzymać ostateczne i autorytatywne wyjaśnienie. (Również z *have.* Patrz uwaga przy *get a black eye.*) ❏ *I'm sorry, I didn't get the word. I didn't know the matter had been settled.* ❏ *Now that I have the message, I can be more effective in answering questions.*

get time to catch one's breath znaleźć wystarczająco dużo czasu, by odpocząć lub zachowywać się normalnie. (Również z *have*.
Patrz uwaga przy *get a black eye*.) ❑ *When things slow down
around here, I'll get time to catch my breath.* ❑ *Sally was so busy
she didn't even have time to catch her breath.*

get to first base (with someone or something) AND **reach
first base (with someone or something)** poczynić zasadni-
czy pierwszy krok w stosunku do kogoś lub czegoś. (*First base* odnosi się do baseballu.) ❑ *I wish I could get to first base with this
business deal.* ❑ *John adores Sally, but he can't even reach first
base with her. She won't even speak to him.* ❑ *He smiles and acts
friendly, but he can't get to first base.*

get to one's feet wstać. ❑ *On a signal from the director, the
singers got to their feet.* ❑ *I was so weak, I could hardly get to my
feet.*

get to the bottom of something zrozumieć przyczyny czegoś.
❑ *We must get to the bottom of this problem immediately.* ❑ *There
is clearly something wrong here, and I want to get to the bottom of
it.*

get to the heart of the matter dotrzeć do sedna sprawy. ❑ *We
have to stop wasting time and get to the heart of the matter.*
❑ *You've been very helpful. You really seem to be able to get to the
heart of the matter.*

get to the point Patrz pod *come to the point.*

get two strikes against one mieć kilka rzeczy przeciwko sobie;
znajdować się w pozycji, w której sukces jest niemożliwy.
(pochodzi od baseballu, gdzie gracz wychodzi po trzech uderze-
niach. Również z *have*. Patrz uwaga przy *get a black eye*.)
❑ *Poor Bob got two strikes against him when he tried to explain
where he was last night.* ❑ *I can't win. I've got two strikes against
me before I start.*

get under someone's skin sprawiać komuś kłopot lub złościć
kogoś. (Nawiązuje do substancji drażniącej od ugryzienia owada
lub chemikaliów dostających się pod skórę.) ❑ *John is so*

annoying. He really gets under my skin. ❏ *I know he's bothersome, but don't let him get under your skin.* ❏ *This kind of problem gets under my skin.*

get up enough nerve (to do something) być dość odważnym, by coś zrobić. ❏ *I could never get up enough nerve to sing in public.* ❏ *I'd do it if I could get up enough nerve, but I'm shy.*

get up on the wrong side of the bed AND **get out of the wrong side of the bed** wstać rano w złym nastroju. (Jakby wybór strony łóżka miał wpływ na nastrój.) ❏ *What's wrong with you? Did you get up on the wrong side of the bed today?* ❏ *Excuse me for being grouchy. I got out of the wrong side of the bed.*

get wind of something usłyszeć o czymś; otrzymać informację o czymś. (*Wind* może to być czyjś oddech lub słowa, ale prawdopodobnie wyrażenie odwołuje się do zapachu przyniesionego przez wiatr na długo przed pojawieniem się tego czegoś.) ❏ *I just got wind of your marriage. Congratulations.* ❏ *Wait until the boss gets wind of this. Somebody is going to get in trouble.*

get worked up about something Patrz następne hasło.

get worked up (over something) AND **get worked up about something** denerwować się lub martwić czymś. ❏ *Please don't get worked up over this matter.* ❏ *They get worked up about these things very easily.* ❏ *I try not to get worked up.*

gild the lily dodać jakąś ozdobę do czegoś, co z natury swojej jest ładne; starać się poprawić coś, co już jest dobre. (Często odnosi się do pochlebstwa lub do przesady. Lilia uważana jest za wystarczająco ładną sama w sobie. Pozłocenie jej jest przesadą.) ❏ *Your house has lovely brickwork. Don't paint it. That would be gilding the lily.* ❏ *Oh, Sally. You're beautiful the way you are. You don't need makeup. You would be gilding the lily.*

gird (up) one's loins przygotować się (do czegoś). (Klisza. Zasadniczo oznacza wystrojenie się w przygotowaniu do czegoś. Pochodzi z Biblii.) ❏ *Well, I guess I had better gird up my loins and go to work.* ❏ *Somebody has to do something about the problem. Why don't you gird your loins and do something?*

give a good account of oneself robić coś dobrze lub całościowo; wystawić sobie dobre świadectwo. ❏ *John gave a good account of himself when he gave his speech last night.* ❏ *Mary was not hungry, and she didn't give a good account of herself at dinner.*

give as good as one gets dać tyle, ile się otrzymało; odpłacić komuś tym samym. (Zwykle w czasie teraźniejszym.) ❏ *John can take care of himself in a fight. He can give as good as he gets.* ❏ *Sally usually wins a formal debate. She gives as good as she gets.*

give credit where credit is due obdarzyć zaufaniem kogoś, kto na to zasługuje; podziękować komuś, kto na to zasługuje. (Klisza.) ❏ *We must give credit where credit is due. Thank you very much, Sally.* ❏ *Let's give credit where credit is due. Mary is the one who wrote the report, not Jane.*

Give one an inch, and one will take a mile. AND **If you give one an inch, one will take a mile.** przysłowie oznaczające, że ktoś, komu się dało trochę czegoś (np. wyrozumiałości lub odroczyło się coś) będzie chciał więcej. ❏ *I told John he could turn in his paper one day late, but he turned it in three days late. Give him an inch, and he'll take a mile.* ❏ *First we let John borrow our car for a day. Now he wants to go on a two-week vacation. If you give him an inch, he'll take a mile.*

give one an inch, one will take a mile, If you. Patrz poprzednie hasło.

give one one's freedom uwolnić kogoś; dać komuś rozwód. (Zwykle eufemizm oznaczający rozwód.) ❏ *Mrs. Brown wanted to give her husband his freedom.* ❏ *Well, Tom, I hate to break it to you this way, but I have decided to give you your freedom.*

give oneself airs zachowywać się zarozumiale lub z wyższością. ❏ *Sally is always giving herself airs. You'd think she had royal blood.* ❏ *Come on, John. Don't act so haughty. Stop giving yourself airs.*

give one's right arm (for someone or something) chcieć ofiarować coś bardzo wartościowego dla kogoś lub czegoś. (Nigdy nie używane dosłownie.) ❑ *I'd give my right arm for a nice cool drink.* ❑ *I'd give my right arm to be there.* ❑ *Tom really admired John. Tom would give his right arm for John.*

give someone a black eye Patrz pod *get a black eye.*

give someone a buzz Patrz pod *give someone a ring.*

give someone a clean bill of health Patrz pod *get a clean bill of health.*

give someone a piece of one's mind zwymyślać kogoś; nakrzyczeć na kogoś. (Jakby dać komuś część swoich myśli o nim.) ❑ *I've had enough from John. I'm going to give him a piece of my mind.* ❑ *Sally, stop it, or I'll give you a piece of my mind.*

give someone a ring AND **give someone a buzz** zadzwonić do kogoś. (*Ring* i *buzz* odnosi się do dzwonka telefonu.) ❑ *Nice talking to you. Give me a ring sometime.* ❑ *Give me a buzz when you're in town.*

give someone or something a wide berth trzymać się od kogoś lub czegoś w rozsądnej odległości; unikać kogoś lub czegoś. (Pochodzi od żaglowców.) ❑ *The dog we are approaching is very mean. Better give it a wide berth.* ❑ *Give Mary a wide berth. She's in a very bad mood.*

give someone the benefit of the doubt Patrz pod *get the benefit of the doubt.*

give someone the eye patrzeć na kogoś w sposób komunikujący romantyczne zainteresowanie. (Nie używane dosłownie.) ❑ *Ann gave John the eye. It really surprised him.* ❑ *Tom kept giving Sally the eye. She finally left.*

give someone the red-carpet treatment Patrz pod *get the red-carpet treatment.*

give someone the runaround Patrz pod *get the runaround.*

give someone the shirt off one's back być w stosunku do kogoś bardzo szlachetnym lub hojnym. ❑ *Tom really likes Bill. He'd give Bill the shirt off his back.* ❑ *John is so friendly that he'd give anyone the shirt off his back.*

give someone tit for tat dać komuś coś równoważnego w stosunku do tego, co było dane tobie; wymienić serię rzeczy, jedną po drugiej, z kimś. ❑ *They gave me the same kind of difficulty that I gave them. They gave me tit for tat.* ❑ *He punched me, so I punched him. Every time he hit me, I hit him. I just gave him tit for tat.*

give something a lick and a promise zrobić coś źle – szybko i niestarannie. ❑ *John! You didn't clean your room! You just gave it a lick and a promise.* ❑ *This time, Tom, comb your hair. It looks as if you just gave it a lick and a promise.*

give the bride away [w odniesieniu do ojca panny młodej] towarzyszyć państwu młodym w ceremonii ślubnej. ❑ *Mr. Brown is ill. Who'll give the bride away?* ❑ *In the traditional wedding ceremony, the bride's father gives the bride away.*

give the devil his due AND **give the devil her due** przyznać, że twój wróg robi jakąś rzecz dobrze. (Klisza. Zwykle odnosi się do osoby, która postępuje źle - niczym diabeł.) ❑ *She's generally impossible, but I have to give the devil her due. She cooks a terrific cherry pie.* ❑ *John may cheat on his taxes and yell at his wife, but he keeps his car polished. I'll give the devil his due.*

give up the ghost umrzeć; wyzionąć ducha. (Klisza. Wyrażenie literackie lub humorystyczne.) ❑ *The old man sighed, rolled over, and gave up the ghost.* ❑ *I'm too young to give up the ghost.*

go about one's business pilnować swojego interesu; odejść i pilnować swojego interesu. ❑ *Leave me alone! Just go about your business!* ❑ *I have no more to say. I would be pleased if you would go about your business.*

go against the grain postępować odwrotnie w stosunku do naturalnego porządku rzeczy lub inklinacji. (Nawiązuje do ułożenia słoi w drzewie. Odwrotnie do kierunku słoi oznacza ułożenie pionowe.) ❑ *Don't expect me to help you cheat. That goes against the grain.* ❑ *Would it go against the grain for you to call in sick for me?*

go along for the ride towarzyszyć komuś dla samej przyjemności przejażdżki; towarzyszyć komuś bez żadnej specjalnej przyczyny. ❑ *Join us. You can go along for the ride.* ❑ *I don't really need to go to the grocery store, but I'll go along for the ride.* ❑ *We're having a little party next weekend. Nothing fancy. Why don't you come along for the ride?*

go and never darken my door again odejść i nie powrócić więcej. (Klisza.) ❑ *The heroine of the drama told the villain never to darken her door again.* ❑ *She touched the back of her hand to her forehead and said, "Go and never darken my door again!"*

go (a)round the bend **1.** przejść za zakręt lub skrzyżowanie; skręcić. ❑ *You'll see the house you're looking for as you go round the bend.* ❑ *John waved to his father until the car went round the bend.* **2.** oszaleć; postradać zmysły. ❑ *If I don't get some rest, I'll go round the bend.* ❑ *Poor Bob. He has been having trouble for a long time. He finally went around the bend.*

go away empty-handed odejść z niczym. ❑ *I hate for you to go away empty-handed, but I cannot afford to contribute any money.* ❑ *They came hoping for some food, but they had to go away empty-handed.*

go back on one's word nie dotrzymać poczynionej obietnicy. ❑ *I hate to go back on my word, but I won't pay you $100 after all.* ❑ *Going back on your word makes you a liar.*

go down in history pozostać w pamięci jako coś historycznie ważnego. (Klisza.) ❑ *Bill is so great. I'm sure that he'll go down in history.* ❑ *This is the greatest party of the century. I bet it'll go down in history.*

go Dutch dzielić koszt posiłku lub jakiejś innej imprezy. ❑ JANE: *Let's go out and eat.* MARY: *Okay, but let's go Dutch.* ❑ *It's getting expensive to have Sally for a friend. She never wants to go Dutch.*

go in one ear and out the other usłyszeć coś i zapomnieć o tym. (Nie używane dosłownie.) ❑ *Everything I say to you seems to go in one ear and out the other. Why don't you pay attention?* ❑ *I can't concentrate. Things people say to me just go in one ear and out the other.*

go into a nosedive AND **take a nosedive 1.** [w odniesieniu do samolotu] nurkować gwałtownie w kierunku ziemi, dziobem naprzód. ❑ *It was a bad day for flying, and I was afraid we'd go into a nosedive.* ❑ *The small plane took a nosedive. The pilot was able to bring it out at the last minute, so the plane didn't crash.* **2.** przechodzić gwałtowne finansowe lub uczuciowe pogorszenie, lub też pogorszenie stanu zdrowia. ❑ *Our profits took a nosedive last year.* ❑ *After he broke his hip, Mr. Brown's health went into a nosedive, and he never recovered.*

go into a tailspin 1. [w odniesieniu do samolotu] stracić kontrolę i spadać na ziemię ruchem wirowym, dziobem naprzód. ❑ *The plane shook and then suddenly went into a tailspin.* ❑ *The pilot was not able to bring the plane out of the tailspin, and it crashed into the sea.* **2.** [w odniesieniu do kogoś] być zdezorientowanym lub wpaść w panikę; [w odniesieniu do czyjegoś życia] rozlecieć się w kawałki. ❑ *Although John was a great success, his life went into a tailspin. It took him a year to get straightened out.* ❑ *After her father died, Mary's world fell apart, and she went into a tailspin.*

go into one's song and dance about something zacząć podawać swoje typowe wyjaśnienia lub wymówki dotyczące czegoś. (Klisza. *One's* można zastąpić *the same old.* Nie dotyczy śpiewu lub tańca.) ❑ *Please don't go into your song and dance about how you always tried to do what was right.* ❑ *John went into his song and dance about how he won the war all by himself.* ❑ *He always goes into the same old song and dance every time he makes a mistake.*

go like clockwork dokonywać postępu regularnie i w sposób godny zaufania. (Bardziej odnosi się do ogólnych prac mechanicznych niż do zegarów.) ❑ *The building project is progressing nicely. Everything is going like clockwork.* ❑ *The elaborate pageant was a great success. It went like clockwork from start to finish.*

good as done, as Patrz *as good as done.*

good as gold, as Patrz *as good as gold.*

good condition, in Patrz *in good condition.*

good head on one's shoulders, have a Patrz *have a good head on one's shoulders.*

good shape, in Patrz *in good shape.*

go off the deep end AND **jump off the deep end** bardzo się zaangażować - w coś albo uczuciowo, zanim jest się do tego przygotowanym; iść za głosem uczuć w konkretnej sytuacji. (Nawiązuje do wejścia do basenu pływackiego od strony głębokiej wody i znalezienia się w niej. Odnosi się zwłaszcza do zakochania się.) ❏ *Look at the way Bill is looking at Sally. I think he's about to go off the deep end.* ❏ *Now, John, I know you really want to go to Australia, but don't go jumping off the deep end. It isn't all perfect there.*

go on a fishing expedition próbować znaleźć jakąś informację. (Używane również dosłownie. Jak gdyby ktoś zapuszczał przynętę w niewidoczne głębiny wody próbując złowić coś, ale nic szczególnie określonego.) ❏ *We are going to have to go on a fishing expedition to try to find the facts.* ❏ *One lawyer went on a fishing expedition in court, and the other lawyer objected.*

go, on the Patrz *on the go.*

go (out) on strike [w odniesieniu do grupy ludzi] przestać pracować na swoich stanowiskach dopóki jakieś żądania nie zostaną uwzględnione. ❏ *If we don't have a contract by noon tomorrow, we'll go out on strike.* ❏ *The entire work force went on strike at noon today.*

go overboard **1.** wypaść z łodzi lub statku. ❏ *My fishing pole just went overboard. I'm afraid it's lost.* ❏ *That man just went overboard. I think he jumped.* **2.** zrobić czegoś za wiele; być ekstrawaganckim. ❏ *Look, Sally, let's have a nice party, but don't go* *overboard. It doesn't need to be fancy.* ❑ *Okay, you can buy a big comfortable car, but don't go overboard.*

go over someone's head [w odniesieniu do intelektualnej zawartości czegoś] być zbyt trudne dla kogoś do zrozumienia. (Tak jakby coś przelatywało nad czyjąś głową zamiast do niej wejść.) ❑ *All that talk about computers went over my head.* ❑ *I hope my lecture didn't go over the students' heads.*

go over something with a fine-tooth comb AND **search something with a fine-tooth comb** bardzo starannie coś przeszukiwać. (Tak jakby ktoś poszukiwał czegoś bardzo drobnego zagubionego wewnątrz jakiegoś włókna.) ❑ *I can't find my calculus book. I went over the whole place with a fine-tooth comb.* ❑ *I searched this place with a fine-tooth comb and didn't find my ring.*

go over with a bang [w odniesieniu do czegoś] śmieszne i zabawne. (Odnosi dię głównie do żartów i przedstawień na scenie.) ❑ *The play was a success. It really went over with a bang.* ❑ *That's a great joke. It went over with a bang.*

go scot-free AND **get off scot-free** nie zostać ukaranym; być oczyszczonym z przestępstwa. (Słowo *scot* jest słowem starym, oznaczającym "podatek" lub "obciążenie podatkowe.") ❑ *The thief went scot-free.* ❑ *Jane cheated on the test and got caught, but she got off scot-free.*

go stag pójść na imprezę (która w założeniu była przeznaczona dla par) bez partnera płci przeciwnej. (Początkowo wyrażenie odnosiło się tylko do mężczyzn.) ❑ *Is Tom going to take you, or are you going stag?* ❑ *Bob didn't want to go stag, so he took his sister to the party.*

go the distance wykonać całą część; zagrać całą grę; przebiec cały wyścig. (Początkowo wyrażenie odnosiło się tylko do sportu.) ❑ *That horse runs fast. I hope it can go the distance.* ❑ *This is going to be a long, hard project. I hope I can go the distance.*

go the limit zrobić tyle, ile było możliwe. ❏ *What do I want on my hamburger? Go the limit!* ❏ *Don't hold anything back. Go the limit.*

go through channels postępować odwołując się do konsultacji właściwych osób lub biur. (*Channels* nawiązuje do drogi, jaką sprawa musi przejść poprzez stopnie hierarchii lub biurokracji.) ❏ *If you want an answer to your questions, you'll have to go through channels.* ❏ *If you know the answers, why do I have to go through channels?*

go through the motions zrobić niewielki wysiłek, by coś wykonać; robić coś nieszczerze. ❏ *Jane isn't doing her best. She's just going through the motions.* ❏ *Bill was supposed to be raking the yard, but he was just going through the motions.*

go through the roof dojść bardzo wysoko; osiągnąć bardzo wysoki stopień (czegoś). (W tym znaczeniu nie używane dosłownie.) ❏ *It's so hot! The temperature is going through the roof.* ❏ *Mr. Brown got so angry he almost went through the roof.*

go to bat for someone poprzeć kogoś lub pomóc komuś. (Wyrażenie wzięte z gry w baseball.) ❏ *I tried to go to bat for Bill, but he said he didn't want any help.* ❏ *I heard them gossiping about Sally, so I went to bat for her.*

go to Davy Jones's locker pójść na dno morza. (Uważane za wyrażenie żeglarskie.) ❏ *My camera fell overboard and went to Davy Jones's locker.* ❏ *My uncle was a sailor. He went to Davy Jones's locker during a terrible storm.*

go to pot AND **go to the dogs** pójść w ruinę; pogarszać, niszczyć się. ❏ *My whole life seems to be going to pot.* ❏ *My lawn is going to pot. I had better weed it.* ❏ *The government is going to the dogs.*

go to rack and ruin AND **go to wrack and ruin** iść w ruinę. (Słowa *rack* i *wrack* oznaczają "wrak" i są używane tylko w tym wyrażeniu.) ❏ *That lovely old house on the corner is going to go to rack and ruin.* ❏ *My lawn is going to wrack and ruin.*

97

go to seed Patrz pod *run to seed.*

go to someone's head stać się zarozumiałym; wpaść w nadmierną dumę. ❑ *You did a fine job, but don't let it go to your head.* ❑ *He let his success go to his head, and soon he became a complete failure.*

go to the dogs Patrz pod *go to pot.*

go to the wall ponieść klęskę lub nie udać się po znalezieniu się w sytuacji ekstremalnej. ❑ *We really went to the wall on that deal.* ❑ *The company went to the wall because of that contract. Now it's broke.*

go to town pracować ciężko lub szybko. (Używane również w sensie dosłownym.) ❑ *Look at all those ants working. They are really going to town.* ❑ *Come on, you guys! Let's go to town. We have to finish this job before noon.*

go to wrack and ruin Patrz pod *go to rack and ruin.*

go up in flames AND **go up in smoke** spłonąć; być zniszczonym w płomieniach. ❑ *The whole museum went up in flames.* ❑ *My paintings – my whole life's work – went up in flames.* ❑ *What a shame for all that to go up in smoke.*

go up in smoke Patrz poprzednie hasło.

grain, go against the Patrz *go against the grain.*

green thumb, have a Patrz *have a green thumb.*

green with envy zazdrosny. (Klisza. Nie używane dosłownie.) ❑ *When Sally saw me with Tom, she turned green with envy. She likes him a lot.* ❑ *I feel green with envy whenever I see you in your new car.*

grin and bear it wytrzymać coś nieprzyjemnego w dobrym humorze. ❑ *There is nothing you can do but grin and bear it.* ❑ *I hate having to work for rude people. I guess I have to grin and bear it.*

grind to a halt zwalniać przed zatrzymaniem się; zwalniać. ❏ *By the end of the day, the factory had ground to a halt.* ❏ *The car ground to a halt, and we got out to stretch our legs.*

grit one's teeth zgrzytać zębami z gniewu lub determinacji. ❏ *I was so mad, all I could do was stand there and grit my teeth.* ❏ *All through the race, Sally was gritting her teeth. She was really determined.*

ground up, from the Patrz *from the ground up.*

gun for someone szukać kogoś, przypuszczalnie po to, by go zastrzelić. (Pochodzi z westernów i filmów gangsterskich.) ❏ *The coach is gunning for you. I think he's going to bawl you out.* ❏ *I've heard that the sheriff is gunning for me, so I'm getting out of town.*

gutter, in the Patrz *in the gutter.*

H

hail-fellow-well-met   przyjazny w stosunku do wszystkich; fałszywie miły w stosunku do wszystkich. (Zwykle używane w odniesieniu do mężczyzn.) ❏ *Yes, he's friendly, sort of hail-fellow-well-met.* ❏ *He's not a very sincere person. Hail-fellow-well-met – you know the type.* ❏ *What a pain he is! Good old Mr. Hail-fellow-well-met. What a phony!*

hair of the dog that bit one   łyk alkoholu kiedy ma się kaca; łyk alkoholu podczas dochodzenia do siebie po przepiciu. (Nie ma nic wspólnego ani z psem, ani z włosami.) ❏ *Oh, I'm miserable. I need some of the hair of the dog that bit me.* ❏ *That's some hangover you've got there, Bob. Here, drink this. It's some of the hair of the dog that bit you.*

hair's breadth, by a   Patrz *by a hair's breadth.*

hale and hearty   w dobrym humorze i zdrowy. ❏ *Doesn't Ann look hale and hearty?* ❏ *I don't feel hale and hearty. I'm really tired.*

Half a loaf is better than none.   przysłowie mówiące, że część czegoś jest lepsza niż nic. ❏ *When my raise was smaller than I wanted, Sally said, "Half a loaf is better than none."* ❏ *People who keep saying "Half a loaf is better than none" usually have as much as they need.*

halfhearted (about someone or something), be   Patrz *be halfhearted (about someone or something).*

half-mast, at Patrz *at half-mast.*

hand, do something by Patrz *do something by hand.*

hand, have something at Patrz *have something at hand.*

hand in glove (with someone) bardzo blisko kogoś. ❏ *John is really hand in glove with Sally.* ❏ *The teacher and the principal work hand in glove.*

hand in the till, have one's Patrz *have one's hand in the till.*

handle someone with kid gloves być bardzo ostrożnym w stosunkach z kimś wrażliwym; mieć do czynienia z kimś bardzo trudnym. ❏ *Bill has become so sensitive. You really have to handle him with kid gloves.* ❏ *You don't have to handle me with kid gloves. I can take it.*

hand, out of Patrz *out of hand.*

hand over fist [w odniesieniu do pieniędzy i towaru na wymianę] bardzo szybko. ❏ *What a busy day. We took in money hand over fist.* ❏ *They were buying things hand over fist.*

hand over hand [przesuwając] jedną ręką za drugą (stale powtarzając). ❏ *Sally pulled in the rope hand over hand.* ❏ *The man climbed the rope hand over hand.*

hands down, do something Patrz *do something hands down.*

hands full (with someone or something), have one's Patrz *have one's hands full (with someone or something).*

hands, have someone or something in one's Patrz *have someone or something in one's hands.*

hands tied, have one's Patrz *have one's hands tied.*

hand tied behind one's back, with one Patrz *with one hand tied behind one's back.*

hand to hand, from Patrz *from hand to hand.*

hang by a hair AND **hang by a thread** mieć niepewną pozycję; zależeć od czegoś bardzo niewystarczającego jako poparcie. (Również z *on*, tak jak w drugim przykładzie.) ❑ *Your whole argument is hanging by a thread.* ❑ *John isn't failing geometry, but he's just hanging on by a hair.*

hang by a thread Patrz poprzednie hasło.

hanging over one's head, have something Patrz *have something hanging over one's head.*

hang in the balance być niezdecydowanym; być między dwoma równymi możliwościami. ❑ *The prisoner stood before the judge with his life hanging in the balance.* ❑ *This whole issue will have to hang in the balance until Jane gets back from her vacation.*

Hang on! być przygotowanym na szybki lub ostry ruch. ❑ *Hang on! Here we go!* ❑ *The airplane passengers suddenly seemed weightless. Someone shouted, "Hang on!"*

hang on someone's every word uważnie słuchać czegoś, co ktoś mówi. ❑ *He gave a great lecture. We hung on his every word.* ❑ *Look at the way John hangs on Mary's every word. He must be in love with her.*

Hang on to your hat! AND **Hold on to your hat!** "Łap swój kapelusz"; "Przygotuj się na nagłą niespodziankę lub szok." ❑ *What a windy day. Hang on to your hat!* ❑ *Here we go! Hold on to your hat!* ❑ *Are you ready to hear the final score? Hang on to your hat! We won ten to nothing!*

hang someone in effigy powiesić kukłę lub jakąś inną postać znienawidzonej osoby. ❑ *They hanged the dictator in effigy.* ❑ *The angry mob hanged the president in effigy.*

happy as a clam, as Patrz *as happy as a clam.*

happy as a lark, as Patrz *as happy as a lark.*

hard-and-fast rule surowy przepis. ❏ *It's a hard-and-fast rule that you must be home by midnight.* ❏ *You should have your project completed by the end of the month, but it's not a hard-and-fast rule.*

hard as nails, as Patrz *as hard as nails.*

hardly have time to breathe być bardzo zajętym. ❏ *This was such a busy day. I hardly had time to breathe.* ❏ *They made him work so hard that he hardly had time to breathe.*

hard on someone's heels poruszać się bardzo blisko za kimś; poruszać się bardzo blisko za czyimiś piętami. ❏ *I ran as fast as I could, but the dog was still hard on my heels.* ❏ *Here comes Sally, and John is hard on her heels.*

Haste makes waste. przysłowie mówiące, że czas zyskany na zrobieniu czegoś szybko i niestarannie będzie stracony, kiedy tę rzecz trzeba będzie zrobić od nowa. ❏ *Now, take your time. Haste makes waste.* ❏ *Haste makes waste, so be careful as you work.*

hat, be old Patrz *be old hat.*

hate someone's guts bardzo kogoś nienawidzieć. (Potoczne i wulgarne.) ❏ *Oh, Bob is terrible. I hate his guts!* ❏ *You may hate my guts for saying so, but I think you're getting gray hair.*

haul someone over the coals Patrz pod *rake someone over the coals.*

have a bee in one's bonnet mieć pomysł lub ideę, która ciągle tkwi w głowie; mieć jakąś obsesję. (Pszczoła - to idea w głowie, która to głowa jest wewnątrz beretu.) ❏ *I have a bee in my bonnet that you'd be a good manager.* ❏ *I had a bee in my bonnet about swimming. I couldn't stop wanting to go swimming.* ALSO: **put a bee in someone's bonnet** podsunąć komuś pomysł (czegoś). ❏ *Somebody put a bee in my bonnet that we should go to a movie.* ❏ *Who put a bee in your bonnet?*

have a big mouth być plotkarzem; być osobą, która zdradza sekrety. (Takie duże usta są zbyt głośne lub zbyt dobrze słyszane przez wiele ludzi.) ❑ *Mary has a big mouth. She told Bob what I was getting him for his birthday.* ❑ *You shouldn't say things like that about people all the time. Everyone will say you have a big mouth.*

have a bone to pick (with someone) mieć sprawę do omówienia z kimś; mieć jakiś sporny temat do przedyskutowania z kimś. ❑ *Hey, Bill. I've got a bone to pick with you. Where is the money you owe me?* ❑ *I had a bone to pick with her, but she was so sweet that I forgot about it.* ❑ *You always have a bone to pick.*

have a brush with something mieć z kimś krótki kontakt; mieć jakieś doświadczenie z czymś. (Szczególnie dotyczy prawa. Czasami w formie *close brush*.) ❑ *Ann had a close brush with the law. She was nearly arrested for speeding.* ❑ *When I was younger, I had a brush with scarlet fever, but I got over it.*

have a chip on one's shoulder prowokować kogoś do kłótni lub walki. (Zaproszenie do walki można wyrazić jako zaproszenie do strącenia drzazgi z czyjegoś ramienia, co jest już wystarczającą prowokacją. Ktoś, kto wydaje się mieć taką drzazgę na ramieniu zawsze prowokuje do walki lub kłótni.) ❑ *Who are you mad at? You always seem to have a chip on your shoulder.* ❑ *John's had a chip on his shoulder ever since he got his speeding ticket.*

have a close call Patrz następne hasło.

have a close shave AND **have a close call** ledwie uniknąć czegoś niebezpiecznego. ❑ *What a close shave I had! I nearly fell off the roof when I was working there.* ❑ *I almost got struck by a speeding car. It was a close shave.*

have a familiar ring [w odniesieniu do opowiadania lub wyjaśnienia] wydawać się znajome. ❑ *Your excuse has a familiar ring. Have you done this before?* ❑ *This term paper has a familiar ring. I think it has been copied.*

have a good head on one's shoulders mieć zdrowy rozsądek; być rozsądnym i inteligentnym. ❑ *Mary doesn't do well in school, but she's got a good head on her shoulders.* ❑ *John has a good* *head on his shoulders and can be depended on to give good advice.*

have a green thumb mieć zdolności do hodowania roślin. (Nie używane dosłownie.) ❏ *Just look at Mr. Simpson's garden. He has a green thumb.* ❏ *My mother has a green thumb when it comes to house plants.*

have a heart umieć współczuć; być szlachetnym i przebaczającym; mieć serce pełne współczucia. ❏ *Oh, have a heart! Give me some help!* ❏ *If Ann had a heart, she'd have made us feel more welcome.*

have a heart of gold być hojnym, szczerym i przyjaznym. (Nie używane dosłownie. Mieć wspaniały charakter i osobowość.) ❏ *Mary is such a lovely person. She has a heart of gold.* ❏ *You think Tom stole your watch? Impossible! He has a heart of gold.*

have a heart of stone być zimnym, nieczułym i nieprzyjaznym. (Nie używane dosłownie.) ❏ *Sally has a heart of stone. She never even smiles.* ❏ *The villain in the play had a heart of stone. He was an ideal villain.*

have a lot going (for one) mieć wiele rzeczy pracujących na swoją korzyść. ❏ *Jane is so lucky. She has a lot going for her.* ❏ *She has a good job and a nice family. She has a lot going.*

have a low boiling point łatwo wpadać w złość. ❏ *Be nice to John. He's upset and has a low boiling point.* ❏ *Mr. Jones sure has a low boiling point. I hardly said anything, and he got angry.*

have an ax to grind mieć się na co poskarżyć. ❏ *Tom, I need to talk to you. I have an ax to grind.* ❏ *Bill and Bob went into the other room to argue. They had an ax to grind.*

have an eye out (for someone or something) AND **keep an eye out (for someone or something)** oczekiwać przybycia lub ukazania się kogoś lub czegoś. (*An* można zastąpić *one's*.) ❏ *Please try to have an eye out for the bus.* ❏ *Keep an eye out for rain.* ❏ *Have your eye out for a raincoat on sale.* ❏ *Okay. I'll keep my eye out.*

105

have an in (with someone) mieć sposób na uzyskanie specjalnych przywilejów od kogoś; mieć na kogoś wpływ. (*In* jest rzeczownikiem.) ❑ *Do you have an in with the mayor? I have to ask him a favor.* ❑ *Sorry, I don't have an in, but I know someone who does.*

have an itchy palm AND **have an itching palm** potrzebować napiwku; zamierzać poprosić o napiwek; potrzebować pieniędzy. (Jak gdyby umieszczenie pieniędzy na dłoni uciszyłoby swędzenie.) ❑ *All the waiters at that restaurant have itchy palms.* ❑ *The cab driver was troubled by an itching palm. Since he refused to carry my bags, I gave him nothing.*

have a price on one's head być poszukiwanym przez władze, które zaoferowały nagrodę za schwytanie. (Nie używane dosłownie. Zwykle ograniczone do westernów i filmów gangsterskich. Jak gdyby dostarczenie czyjejś głowy spowodowało nagrodę lub zapłatę.) ❑ *We captured a thief who had a price on his head, and the sheriff gave us the reward.* ❑ *The crook was so mean, he turned in his own brother, who had a price on his head.*

have a scrape (with someone or something) wejść w kontakt z kimś lub czymś; mieć małą bitwę z kimś lub czymś. ❑ *I had a scrape with the county sheriff.* ❑ *John and Bill had a scrape, but they are friends again now.*

have a soft spot in one's heart for someone or something lubić kogoś lub coś. ❑ *John has a soft spot in his heart for Mary.* ❑ *I have soft spot in my heart for chocolate cake.*

have a sweet tooth lubić słodycze – szczególnie ciastka i cukierki. (Tak jakby któryś ząb prosił o słodycze.) ❑ *I have a sweet tooth, and if I don't watch it, I'll really get fat.* ❑ *John eats candy all the time. He must have a sweet tooth.*

have a weakness for someone or something nie móc się oprzeć komuś lub czemuś; lubić kogoś lub coś; być (w przenośni) bezbronnym wobec kogoś lub czegoś. ❑ *I have a weakness for chocolate.* ❑ *John has a weakness for Mary. I think he's in love.*

have bats in one's belfry być odrobinę szalonym. (*The belfry* – dzwonnica – symbolizuje głowę lub umysł. Nietoperze symbolizują urojenia.) ❏ *Poor old Tom has bats in his belfry.* ❏ *Don't act so silly, John. People will think you have bats in your belfry.*

have clean hands być niewinnym. (Jak gdyby człowiek winny miał pokrwawione ręce.) ❏ *Don't look at me. I have clean hands.* ❏ *The police took him in, but let him go again because he had clean hands.*

have dibs on something AND **put one's dibs on something** zarezerwować coś dla siebie; zgłaszać pretensje do czegoś dla siebie. ❏ *I have dibs on the last piece of cake.* ❏ *John put his dibs on the last piece again. It isn't fair.*

have egg on one's face być zakłopotanym z powodu błędu oczywistego dla wszystkich. (Rzadko używane dosłownie.) ❏ *Bob has egg on his face because he wore jeans to the party and everyone else wore formal clothing.* ❏ *John was completely wrong about the weather for the picnic. It snowed! Now he has egg on his face.*

have eyes bigger than one's stomach Patrz pod *one's eyes are bigger than one's stomach.*

have eyes in the back of one's head wyczuwać coś, co jest poza zasięgiem wzroku. (Nie używane dosłownie.) ❏ *My teacher seems to have eyes in the back of her head.* ❏ *My teacher doesn't need to have eyes in the back of his head. He watches us very carefully.*

have feet of clay [w odniesieniu do kogoś silnego] mieć jakąś wadę charakteru. ❏ *All human beings have feet of clay. No one is perfect.* ❏ *Sally was popular and successful. She was nearly fifty before she learned that she, too, had feet of clay.*

have foot-in-mouth disease czuć się zakłopotanym z powodu głupiej wpadki. (Jest to parodia *foot-and-mouth disease* lub *hoof-and-mouth disease*, która atakuje bydło i zwierzynę łowną.) ❏ *I'm sorry I keep saying stupid things. I guess I have foot-in-*

mouth disease. ❏ *Yes, you really have foot-in-mouth disease tonight.*

have mixed feelings (about someone or something) być niepewnym kogoś lub czegoś. ❏ *I have mixed feelings about Bob. Sometimes I think he likes me; other times I don't.* ❏ *I have mixed feelings about my trip to England. I love the people, but the climate upsets me.* ❏ *Yes, I also have mixed feelings.*

have money to burn mieć dużo pieniędzy; mieć więcej pieniędzy niżeli się potrzebuje; mieć na tyle pieniędzy, że część można zmarnować. ❏ *Look at the way Tom buys things. You'd think he had money to burn.* ❏ *If I had money to burn, I'd just put it in the bank.*

have one's back to the wall znajdować się w pozycji defensywnej. ❏ *He'll have to give in. He has his back to the wall.* ❏ *How can I bargain when I've got my back to the wall?*

have one's cake and eat it too AND **eat one's cake and have it too** chcieć jednocześnie coś i posiadać, i zużywać. (Zwykle w formie przeczącej.) ❏ *Tom wants to have his cake and eat it too. It can't be done.* ❏ *Don't buy a car if you want to walk and stay healthy. You can't eat your cake and have it too.*

have one's ear to the ground AND **keep one's ear to the ground** słuchać uważnie, z nadzieją usłyszenia jakiegoś ostrzeżenia. (Nie używane dosłownie. Jak gdyby ktoś nasłuchiwał odgłosu kopyt pędzących daleko koni.) ❏ *John had his ear to the ground, hoping to find out about new ideas in computers.* ❏ *His boss told him to keep his ear to the ground so that he'd be the first to know of a new idea.*

have one's finger in the pie być w coś wciągniętym. (Nie używane dosłownie.) ❏ *I like to have my finger in the pie so I can make sure things go my way.* ❏ *As long as John has his finger in the pie, things will happen slowly.*

have one's hand in the till kraść pieniądze firmie lub organizacji. (*The till* to kaseta lub szuflada z pieniędzmi.) ❏ *Mr. Jones had his hand in the till for years before he was caught.* ❏ *I think that* *the new clerk has her hand in the till. There is cash missing every morning.*

have one's hands full (with someone or something) być zajętym lub całkowicie zaabsorbowanym kimś lub czymś. ❑ *I have my hands full with my three children.* ❑ *You have your hands full with the store.* ❑ *We both have our hands full.*

have one's hands tied nie móc czegoś zrobić. ❑ *I can't help you. I was told not to, so I have my hands tied.* ❑ *John can help. He doesn't have his hands tied.*

have one's head in the clouds być nieświadomym tego, co się dzieje wokół. ❑ *"Bob, do you have your head in the clouds?" said the teacher.* ❑ *She walks around all day with her head in the clouds. She must be in love.*

have one's heart in one's mouth mieć silne uczucia w stosunku do kogoś lub czegoś. ❑ *"Gosh, Mary," said John, "I have my heart in my mouth whenever I see you."* ❑ *My heart is in my mouth whenever I hear the national anthem.* ALSO: **one's heart is in one's mouth** [w odniesieniu do kogoś] odczuwać coś bardzo mocno. ❑ *It was a touching scene. My heart was in my mouth the whole time.*

have one's heart set on something pragnąć i oczekiwać czegoś. ❑ *Jane has her heart set on going to London.* ❑ *Bob will be disappointed. He had his heart set on going to college this year.* ❑ *His heart is set on it.* ALSO: **set one's heart on something** być zdeterminowanym w odniesieniu do czegoś. ❑ *Jane set her heart on going to London.* ALSO: **one's heart is set on something** pragnąć i oczekiwać czegoś. ❑ *Jane's heart is set on going to London.*

have one's nose in a book czytać książkę; cały czas czytać książki. ❑ *Bob has his nose in a book every time I see him.* ❑ *His nose is always in a book. He never gets any exercise.*

have one's tail between one's legs być przestraszonym lub zastraszonym. (Nawiązuje do przestraszonego psa. Używane również dosłownie w odniesieniu do psów.) ❑ *John seems to lack* *courage. Whenever there is an argument, he has his tail between his legs.* ❏ *You can tell that the dog is frightened because it has its tail between its legs.* ALSO: **one's tail is between one's legs** ktoś zachowuje się jak osoba przestraszona lub zastraszona. ❏ *He should have stood up and argued, but – as usual – his tail was between his legs.*

have one's words stick in one's throat być tak przytłoczonym emocjami, że nie można wydobyć głosu. ❏ *I sometimes have my words stick in my throat.* ❏ *John said that he never had his words stick in his throat.* ALSO: **one's words stick in one's throat** nie móc mówić z powodu emocji. ❏ *My words stick in my throat whenever I try to say something kind or tender.*

have other fish to fry mieć co innego do roboty; mieć coś ważniejszego do zrobienia. (*Other* można zastąpić *bigger, better, more important*, etc. Nie używane w sensie dosłownym.) ❏ *I can't take time for your problem. I have other fish to fry.* ❏ *I won't waste time on your question. I have bigger fish to fry.*

have someone dead to rights udowodnić komś winę ponad wszelką wątpliwość. ❏ *The police burst in on the robbers while they were at work. They had the robbers dead to rights.* ❏ *All right, Tom! I've got you dead to rights! Get your hands out of the cookie jar.*

have someone in one's pocket kontrolować kogoś. ❏ *Don't worry about the mayor. She'll cooperate. I've got her in my pocket.* ❏ *John will do just what I tell him. I've got him and his brother in my pocket.*

have someone or something in one's hands mieć nad kimś lub nad czymś kontrolę lub być odpowiedzialnym za kogoś lub za coś. (*Have* można zastąpić *leave* lub *put*.) ❏ *You have the whole project in your hands.* ❏ *The boss put the whole project in your hands.* ❏ *I have to leave the baby in your hands while I go to the doctor.*

have something at hand Patrz następne hasło.

have something at one's fingertips AND **have something at hand** mieć coś w zasięgu ręki. (*Have* można zastąpić *keep.*) ❏ *I have a dictionary at my fingertips.* ❏ *I try to have everything I need at hand.* ❏ *I keep my medicine at my fingertips.*

have something hanging over one's head mieć jakieś zmartwienie lub kłopot; mieć nad głową jakiś termin. (Używane również dosłownie.) ❏ *I keep worrying about getting drafted. I hate to have something like that hanging over my head.* ❏ *I have a history paper that is hanging over my head.*

have something in stock mieć towar dostępny i gotowy do sprzedaży. ❏ *Do you have extra large sizes in stock?* ❏ *Of course, we have all sizes and colors in stock.*

have something to spare mieć czegoś więcej niż dość. ❏ *Ask John for some firewood. He has firewood to spare.* ❏ *Do you have any candy to spare?*

have the right-of-way mieć legalne prawo do zajmowania określonej przestrzeni na drodze publicznej. ❏ *I had a traffic accident yesterday, but it wasn't my fault. I had the right-of-way.* ❏ *Don't pull out onto a highway if you don't have the right-of-way.*

have the shoe on the other foot przeżyć coś odwrotnego w stosunku do sytuacji poprzedniej. (Również z *be* zamiast *have*. Patrz przykłady.) ❏ *I used to be a student, and now I'm the teacher. Now I have the shoe on the other foot.* ❏ *You were mean to me when you thought I was cheating. Now that I have caught you cheating, the shoe is on the other foot.*

have the time of one's life cudownie się bawić; mieć najwspanialszy okres w życiu. ❏ *What a great party! I had the time of my life.* ❏ *We went to Florida last winter and had the time of our lives.*

have too many irons in the fire robić zbyt wiele rzeczy na raz. (Klisza. Tak jakby kowal miał zbyt wiele rzeczy jednocześnie w ogniu, by móc sobie z nimi poradzić.) ❏ *Tom had too many irons in the fire and missed some important deadlines.* ❏ *It's better if you don't have too many irons in the fire.*

head and shoulders above someone or something wyraźnie nad czymś górować. (Często z *stand,* tak jak w przykładach.) ❏ *This wine is head and shoulders above that one.* ❏ *John stands head and shoulders above Bob.*

head, go over someone's Patrz *go over someone's head.*

head, go to someone's Patrz *go to someone's head.*

head, in over one's Patrz *in over one's head.*

head in the clouds, have one's Patrz *have one's head in the clouds.*

head, on someone's Patrz *on someone's head.*

head, out of one's Patrz *out of one's head.*

heart and soul, with all one's Patrz *with all one's heart and soul.*

heart good, do someone's Patrz *do someone's heart good.*

heart, have a Patrz *have a heart.*

heart in one's mouth, have one's Patrz *have one's heart in one's mouth.*

heart of gold, have a Patrz *have a heart of gold.*

heart of stone, have a Patrz *have a heart of stone.*

heart set on something, have one's Patrz *have one's heart set on something.*

heat, in Patrz *in heat.*

heck of it, for the Patrz *for the heck of it.*

heels of something, on the Patrz *on the heels of something.*

He laughs best who laughs last. Patrz następne hasło.

He who laughs last, laughs longest. AND **He laughs best who laughs last.** przysłowie mówiące, że ten, komu udaje się zrobić ostatni ruch lub wykonać ostatni trik, ma najwięcej uciechy. ❑ *Bill had pulled many silly tricks on Tom. Finally Tom pulled a very funny trick on Bill and said, "He who laughs last, laughs longest."* ❑ *Bill pulled another, even bigger trick on Tom, and said, laughing, "He laughs best who laughs last."*

hide one's head in the sand Patrz pod *bury one's head in the sand.*

hide one's light under a bushel ukrywać swoje dobre pomysły lub talenty. (Temat biblijny.) ❑ *Jane has some good ideas, but she doesn't speak very often. She hides her light under a bushel.* ❑ *Don't hide your light under a bushel. Share your gifts with other people.*

high as a kite, as Patrz *as high as a kite.*

high as the sky, as Patrz *as high as the sky.*

high man on the totem pole osoba na szczycie hierarchii; osoba odpowiedzialna za organizację. (Patrz również *low man on the totem pole.*) ❑ *I don't want to talk to a secretary. I demand to talk to the high man on the totem pole.* ❑ *Who's in charge around here? Who's high man on the totem pole?*

hill, over the Patrz *over the hill.*

history, go down in Patrz *go down in history.*

hit a happy medium Patrz pod *strike a happy medium.*

hit a snag napotkać problem. ❑ *We've hit a snag with the building project.* ❑ *I stopped working on the roof when I hit a snag.*

113

hit a sour note Patrz pod *strike a sour note.*

hit bottom osiągnąć najniższy lub najgorszy punkt. ❏ *Our profits have hit bottom. This is our worst year ever.* ❏ *When my life hit bottom, I began to feel much better. I knew that if there was going to be any change, it would be for the better.*

hitch a ride Patrz pod *thumb a ride.*

hit someone between the eyes stać się zupełnie jasnym; zaskoczyć kogoś lub zrobić na kimś wrażenie. (Również z *right,* jak w przykładach. Używane również w znaczeniu dosłownym.) ❏ *Suddenly, it hit me right between the eyes. John and Mary were in love.* ❏ *Then – as he was talking – the exact nature of the evil plan hit me between the eyes.*

hit (someone) like a ton of bricks zaskoczyć, przestraszyć lub zaszokować kogoś. ❏ *Suddenly, the truth hit me like a ton of bricks.* ❏ *The sudden tax increase hit like a ton of bricks. Everyone became angry.*

hit the bull's-eye **1.** trafić w środek okrągłego celu. (Dosłowne.) ❏ *The archer hit the bull's-eye three times in a row.* ❏ *I didn't hit the bull's-eye even once.* **2.** idealnie osiągnąć cel. ❏ *Your idea really hit the bull's-eye. Thank you!* ❏ *Jill has a lot of insight. She knows how to hit the bull's-eye.*

hit the nail (right) on the head zrobić dokładnie to, co trzeba; zrobić coś w sposób najbardziej wydajny i skuteczny. (Klisza.) ❏ *You've spotted the flaw, Sally. You hit the nail on the head.* ❏ *Bob doesn't say much, but every now and then he hits the nail right on the head.*

hit the spot być dokładnie tym, czego potrzeba; być czymś odświeżającym. ❏ *This cool drink really hits the spot.* ❏ *That was a delicious meal, dear. It hit the spot.*

hold one's end (of the bargain) up AND **hold up one's end (of the bargain)** wykonać swoją część tak, jak było uzgodnione; działać zgodnie ze swoim zakresem odpowiedzialności, tak jak było uzgodnione. ❏ *Tom has to learn to cooperate. He must hold* *ı ı his end of the bargain.* ❏ *If you don't hold your end up, the v ıole project will fail.*

hold one's ground   Patrz pod   *stand one's ground.*

hold one's head up AND **hold up one's head**   mieć do siebie szacunek; zachować lub okazywać swą godność. ❏ *I've done nothing wrong. I can hold my head up in public.* ❏ *I'm so embarrassed and ashamed. I'll never be able to hold up my head again.*

hold one's own   działać równie dobrze jak kto inny. ❏ *I can hold my own in a footrace any day.* ❏ *She was unable to hold her own, and she had to quit.*

hold one's peace   milczeć. ❏ *Bill was unable to hold his peace any longer. "Don't do it!" he cried.* ❏ *Quiet, John. Hold your peace for a little while longer.*

hold one's temper   Patrz pod   *keep one's temper.*

hold one's tongue   powstrzymać się od mówienia; powstrzymać się od powiedzenia czegoś nieprzyjemnego. (Nie używane dosłownie.) ❏ *I felt like scolding her, but I held my tongue.* ❏ *Hold your tongue, John. You can't talk to me that way.*

Hold on to your hat!   Patrz pod   *Hang on to your hat!*

hold out the olive branch   zaproponować zakończenie sporu i przyjaźń; zaproponować pogodzenie się. (Gałązka oliwna jest symbolem pokoju i zgody. Nawiązanie do Biblii.) ❏ *Jill was the first to hold out the olive branch after our argument.* ❏ *I always try to hold out the olive branch to someone I have hurt. Life is too short for a person to bear grudges for very long.*

hold the fort   opiekować się jakimś miejscem, takim jak sklep czy dom. (Pochdzi z westernów.) ❏ *I'm going next door to visit Mrs. Jones. You stay here and hold the fort.* ❏ *You should open the store at eight o'clock and hold the fort until I get there at ten o'clock.*

hold true (w odniesieniu do czegoś) być prawdziwym; (w odniesieniu do czegoś) pozostawać prawdziwym. ❏ *Does this rule hold true all the time?* ❏ *Yes, it holds true no matter what.*

hold water, not Patrz *not hold water.*

hole in one **1.** przykład trafienia piłką golfową w dziurę już za pierwszą próbą. (Pochodzi z gry w golfa.) ❏ *John made a hole in one yesterday.* ❏ *I've never gotten a hole in one.* **2.** przykład sukcesu już za pierwszym razem. ❏ *It worked the first time I tried it – a hole in one.* ❏ *Bob got a hole in one on that sale. A lady walked in the door, and he sold her a car in five minutes.*

hole, in the Patrz *in the hole.*

hole, out of the Patrz *out of the hole.*

honeymoon is over, The. Patrz *The honeymoon is over.*

honor, on one's Patrz *on one's honor.*

honors, do the Patrz *do the honors.*

honor someone's check przyjąć czyjś osobisty czek. ❏ *The clerk at the store wouldn't honor my check. I had to pay cash.* ❏ *The bank didn't honor your check when I tried to deposit it. Please give me cash.*

hope against all hope mieć nadzieję, nawet jeśli sytuacja wydaje się beznadziejna. ❏ *We hope against all hope that she'll see the right thing to do and do it.* ❏ *There is little point in hoping against all hope, except that it makes you feel better.*

horizon, on the Patrz *on the horizon.*

horn in (on someone) próbować zmienić czyjąś decyzję lub przemieścić kogoś. ❏ *I'm going to ask Sally to the party. Don't you dare try to horn in on me!* ❏ *I wouldn't think of horning in.*

horns of a dilemma, on the Patrz *on the horns of a dilemma.*

horse of a different color   Patrz następne hasło.

horse of another color AND **horse of a different color**   całkowicie inna sprawa. ❑ *I was talking about the tree, not the bush. That's a horse of another color.* ❑ *Gambling is not the same as investing in the stock market. It's a horse of a different color.*

hot under the collar   bardzo rozgniewany. (Klisza.) ❑ *The boss was really hot under the collar when you told him you lost the contract.* ❑ *I get hot under the collar every time I think about it.*

hour, on the   Patrz *on the hour.*

house, on the   Patrz *on the house.*

huff, in a   Patrz *in a huff.*

hump, over the   Patrz *over the hump.*

hungry as a bear, as   Patrz *as hungry as a bear.*

I

(ifs, ands, or) buts about it, no   Patrz *no (ifs, ands, or) buts about it.*

If the shoe fits, wear it.   przysłowie mówiące, że powinieneś zwracać uwagę na coś, jeżeli to coś odnosi się do ciebie. ❑ *Some people here need to be quiet. If the shoe fits, wear it.* ❑ *This doesn't apply to everyone. If the shoe fits, wear it.*

if worst comes to worst   w najgorszej z możliwych sytuacji; jeżeli rzeczy naprawdę potoczą się źle. (Klisza.) ❑ *If worst comes to worst, we'll hire someone to help you.* ❑ *If worst comes to worst, I'll have to borrow some money.*

If you give one an inch, one will take a mile.   Patrz pod *Give one an inch, and one will take a mile.*

in a dead heat   kończąc wyścig w dokładnie takim samym czsie; powiązany. (Tutaj, *dead* oznacza "dokładny" albo "całkowity.") ❑ *The two horses finished the race in a dead heat.* ❑ *They ended the contest in a dead heat.*

in a flash   szybko; natychmiast. ❑ *I'll be there in a flash.* ❑ *It happened in a flash. Suddenly my wallet was gone.*

in a huff   gniewnie albo obraźliwie. (*In* można zastąpić *into*. Patrz przykłady.) ❑ *He heard what we had to say, then left in a huff.* ❑ *She came in a huff and ordered us to bring her something to eat.* ❑ *She gets into a huff very easily.*

in a mad rush w pośpiechu; w ogromnym pośpiechu. ❑ *I ran around all day today in a mad rush, looking for a present for Bill.* ❑ *Why are you always in a mad rush?*

in a (tight) spot w kłopocie; w trudnej sytuacji. (*In* można zastąpić *into.* Patrz przykłady.) ❑ *Look, John, I'm in a tight spot. Can you lend me twenty dollars?* ❑ *I'm in a spot too. I need $300.* ❑ *I have never gotten into a tight spot.*

in a vicious circle w sytuacji, w której rozwiązanie jednego problemu powoduje problem następny, zaś rozwiązanie tego z kolei problemu powoduje powrót do problemu pierwszego, etc. (*In* można zastąpić *into.* Patrz przykłady.) ❑ *Life is so strange. I seem to be in a vicious circle most of the time.* ❑ *I put lemon in my tea to make it sour, then sugar to make it sweet. I'm in a vicious circle.* ❑ *Don't let your life get into a vicious circle.*

in a world of one's own wyniosły; oderwany; skupiony na sobie. (*In* można zastąpić *into.* Patrz przykłady.) ❑ *John lives in a world of his own. He has very few friends.* ❑ *Mary walks around in a world of her own, but she's very intelligent.* ❑ *When she's thinking, she drifts into a world of her own.*

in bad faith nieszczerze; ze złym lub nieuczciwym zamiarem; obłudnie. ❑ *It appears that you acted in bad faith and didn't live up to the terms of our agreement.* ❑ *If you do things in bad faith, you'll get a bad reputation.*

in bad sorts w złym humorze. ❑ *Bill is in bad sorts today. He's very grouchy.* ❑ *I try to be extra nice to people when I'm in bad sorts.*

in bad taste AND **in poor taste** ordynarny; wulgarny; nieprzyzwoity. ❑ *Mrs. Franklin felt that your joke was in bad taste.* ❑ *We found the play to be in poor taste, so we walked out in the middle of the second act.*

in black and white oficjalny, na piśmie. (Używane w odniesieniu np. do umów lub oświadczeń, które zostały utrwalone na piśmie. *In* można zastąpić *into.* Patrz przykłady.) ❑ *I have it in black and white that I'm entitled to three weeks of vacation each year.* ❑ *It*

says right here in black and white that oak trees make acorns.
❏ *Please put the agreement into black and white.*

in broad daylight na widoku publicznym, w biały dzień. ❏ *The thief stole the car in broad daylight.* ❏ *There they were, selling drugs in broad daylight.*

inch by inch cal po calu; po trochu. ❏ *Traffic moved along inch by inch.* ❏ *Inch by inch, the snail moved across the stone.*

inch of one's life, within an Patrz *within an inch of one's life.*

in creation Patrz pod *on earth.*

in deep water w niebezpiecznej lub delikatnej sytuacji; w poważnej sytuacji; w kłopocie. (Jakby ktoś płynął lub wpadł do wody zakrywającej mu głowę. *In* można zastąpić *into.* Patrz przykłady.) ❏ *John is having trouble with his taxes. He's in deep water.* ❏ *Bill is in deep water in algebra class. He's almost failing.* ❏ *He really got himself into deep water.*

in fine feather w dobrym humorze; w dobrym zdrowiu. (Klisza. *In* można zastąpić *into.* Patrz przykłady. Nawiązuje do zdrowego, i dlatego pięknego, ptaka.) ❏ *Hello, John. You appear to be in fine feather.* ❏ *Of course I'm in fine feather. I get lots of sleep.* ❏ *Good food and lots of sleep put me into fine feather.*

in full swing w trakcie; pracujący lub biegnący bez przeszkód. (*In* można zastąpić *into.* Patrz przykłady.) ❏ *We can't leave now! The party is in full swing.* ❏ *Our program to help the starving people is in full swing. You should see results soon.* ❏ *Just wait until our project gets into full swing.*

in good condition Patrz następne hasło.

in good shape AND **in good condition** fizycznie i funkcjonalnie w dobrym stanie. (Używane w odniesieniu zarówno do ludzi, jak rzeczy. *In* można zastąpić *into.* Patrz przykłady.) ❏ *This car isn't in good shape.* ❏ *I'd like to have one that's in better condition.* ❏ *Mary is in good condition. She works hard to keep healthy.* ❏ *You have to make an effort to get into good shape.*

in heat w okresie seksualnego podniecenia; w okresie godowym. (Jest to taki okres, kiedy samice są najbardziej chętne do rozrodu. Patrz również *in season*. Wyrażenie to jest zwykle używane w odniesieniu do zwierząt. W odniesieniu do ludzi - żartobliwie. *In* można zastąpić *into*. Patrz przykłady.) ❑ *Our dog is in heat.* ❑ *She goes into heat every year at this time.* ❑ *When my dog is in heat, I have to keep her locked in the house.*

in less than no time bardzo szybko. ❑ *I'll be there in less than no time.* ❑ *Don't worry. This won't take long. It'll be over with in less than no time.*

in mint condition w doskonałej kondycji. (Nawiązuje do doskonałego stanu monety, która właśnie wyszła z mennicy. *In* można zastąpić *into*. Patrz przykłady.) ❑ *This is a fine car. It runs well and is in mint condition.* ❑ *We went through a house in mint condition and decided to buy it.* ❑ *We put our house into mint condition before we sold it.*

in name only nominalnie; nie w rzeczywistości, tylko z nazwy. ❑ *The president is head of the country in name only. Congress makes the laws.* ❑ *Mr. Smith is the boss of the Smith Company in name only. Mrs. Smith handles all the business affairs.*

innocent as a lamb, as Patrz *as innocent as a lamb.*

in no mood to do something nie mieć nastroju do zrobienia czegoś; mieć życzenie czegoś nie robić. ❑ *I'm in no mood to cook dinner tonight.* ❑ *Mother is in no mood to put up with our arguing.*

in nothing flat natychmiast. ❑ *Of course I can get there in a hurry. I'll be there in nothing flat.* ❑ *We covered the distance between New York and Philadelphia in nothing flat.*

in one ear and out the other [w odniesieniu do czegoś, co ma nastąpić] zignorowany; [w odniesieniu do czegoś, co ma nastąpić] nie usłyszany i nie zauważony. (Klisza. *In* can można zastąpić *into*. Patrz przykłady.) ❑ *Everything I say to you goes into one ear and out the other!* ❑ *Bill just doesn't pay attention. Everything is in one ear and out the other.*

in one fell swoop Patrz pod *at one fell swoop.*

in one's birthday suit nagi. (W "ubraniu", w którym przyszło się na świat. *In* można zastąpić *into*. Patrz przykłady.) ❑ *I've heard that John sleeps in his birthday suit.* ❑ *We used to go down to the river and swim in our birthday suits.* ❑ *You have to get into your birthday suit to bathe.*

in one's mind's eye w głowie. (Odnosi się do wizualizowania czegoś w głowie.) ❑ *In my mind's eye, I can see trouble ahead.* ❑ *In her mind's eye, she could see a beautiful building beside the river. She decided to design such a building.*

in one's or its prime u szczytu możliwości lub w najlepszym czasie. ❑ *Our dog – that is in its prime – is very active.* ❑ *The program ended in its prime when we ran out of money.* ❑ *I could work long hours when I was in my prime.*

in one's right mind zdrowy na umyśle; racjonalny o rozsądny. (Często w formie przeczącej.) ❑ *That was a stupid thing to do. You're not in your right mind.* ❑ *You can't be in your right mind! That sounds crazy!*

in one's second childhood zainteresowany rzeczami lub ludźmi, którymi normalnie interesuje się w dzieciństwie. ❑ *My father bought himself a toy train, and my mother said he was in his second childhood.* ❑ *Whenever I go to the river and throw stones, I feel as though I'm in my second childhood.*

in one's spare time w wolnym czasie; w czasie nie zarezerwowanym na robienie czegoś innego. ❑ *I write novels in my spare time.* ❑ *I'll try to paint the house in my spare time.*

in over one's head sprawiający trudności ponad możliwości poradzenia sobie z nimi. ❑ *Calculus is very hard for me. I'm in over my head.* ❑ *Ann is too busy. She's really in over her head.*

in poor taste Patrz *in bad taste.*

in print [w odniesieniu do książki] w sprzedaży. (Porównaj z *out of print*.) ❏ I think I can get that book for you. It's still in print. ❏ This is the only book in print on this subject.

in rags w znoszonej i porwanej odzieży. ❏ *Oh, look at my clothing. I can't go to the party in rags!* ❏ *I think the new casual fashions make you look as if you're in rags.*

in round figures Patrz następne hasło.

in round numbers AND **in round figures** w określonej liczbie; liczba, która została zaokrąglona do najbliższej pełnej liczby. (*In* można zastąpić *into*. Patrz przykłady.) ❏ *Please tell me in round numbers what it'll cost.* ❏ *I don't need the exact amount. Just give it to me in round figures.*

ins and outs of something prawidłowy i efektywny sposób zrobienia czegoś; szczególne rzeczy, które ktoś powinien wiedzieć, aby prawidłowo coś wykonać. ❏ *I don't understand the ins and outs of politics.* ❏ *Jane knows the ins and outs of working with computers.*

in season **1.** obecnie dostępny w sprzedaży. (Niektóre artykuły żywnościowe i inne rzeczy dostępne są tylko sezonowo. *In* można zastąpić *into*, zwłaszcza jeżeli chcemy użyć *come*. Patrz przykłady.) ❏ *Oysters are available in season.* ❏ *Strawberries aren't in season in January.* ❏ *When do strawberries come into season?* **2.** legalnie dozwolone do odłowienia lub upolowania. ❏ *Catfish are in season all year round.* ❏ *When are salmon in season?* **3.** [w odniesieniu do psów] w okresie godowym; *in heat.* ❏ *My dog is in season every year at this time.* ❏ *When my dog is in season, I have to keep her locked in the house.*

in seventh heaven bardzo szczęśliwy. (Klisza. Jest to najwyższy poziom nieba, tam, gdzie przebywa Bóg.) ❏ *Ann was really in seventh heaven when she got a car of her own.* ❏ *I'd be in seventh heaven if I had a million dollars.*

in short order bardzo szybko. ❏ *I can straighten out this mess in short order.* ❏ *The people came in and cleaned the place up in short order.*

in short supply   rzadko dostępny. (*In* można zastąpić *into*. Patrz przykłady.) ❑ *Fresh vegetables are in short supply in the winter.* ❑ *Yellow cars are in short supply because everyone likes them and buys them.* ❑ *At this time of the year, fresh vegetables go into short supply.*

in stock   dostępne, jak towary w magazynie. ❑ *I'm sorry, I don't have that in stock. I'll have to order it for you.* ❑ *We have all our Christmas merchandise in stock now.*

in the air   wszędzie wokół. (Używane również dosłownie.) ❑ *There is such a feeling of joy in the air.* ❑ *We felt a sense of tension in the air.*

in the bargain   w dodatku do czegoś, co zostało uzgodnione. (*In* można zastąpić *into*. Patrz przykłady.) ❑ *I bought a car, and they threw an air conditioner into the bargain.* ❑ *When I bought a house, I asked the seller to include the furniture in the bargain.*

in the black   bez długów; w korzystnej sytuacji finansowej. (Odnosi się do pisania cyfr raczej w czarnym kolorze niż w czerwonym, który oznacza dług. Patrz również *in the red*. *In* można zastąpić *into*. Patrz przykłady.) ❑ *I wish my accounts were in the black.* ❑ *Sally moved the company into the black.*

in the blood AND **in one's blood**   wbudowane w osobowość lub charakter. (W rzeczywistości w genach, nie we krwi.) ❑ *John's a great runner. It's in his blood.* ❑ *The whole family is very athletic. It's in the blood.*

in the bullpen   [w odniesieniu do gry w baseball] na specjalnym miejscu w pobliżu boiska, gdzie odbywa się rozgrzewka. (*In* można zastąpić *into*. Patrz przykłady.) ❑ *You can tell who is pitching next by seeing who is in the bullpen.* ❑ *Our best pitcher just went into the bullpen. He'll be pitching soon.*

in the cards   w przyszłości. ❑ *Well, what do you think is in the cards for tomorrow?* ❑ *I asked the boss if there was a raise in the cards for me.*

in the doghouse w kłopotach; w niełasce. (*In* można zastąpić *into*. Patrz przykłady. Tak jakby kogoś wyrzucić z domu za złe zachowanie, niczym psa do budy.) ❏ *I'm really in the doghouse. I was late for an appointment.* ❏ *I hate being in the doghouse all the time. I don't know why I can't stay out of trouble.*

in the doldrums leniwy; mało aktywny; w marnym nastroju. (*In* można zastąpić *into*. Patrz przykłady.) ❏ *He's usually in the doldrums in the winter.* ❏ *I had some bad news yesterday, which put me into the doldrums.*

in the flesh we własnej osobie. ❏ *I've heard that the queen is coming here in the flesh.* ❏ *Is she really here? In the flesh?* ❏ *I've wanted a color television for years, and now I've got one right here in the flesh.*

in the gutter [w odniesieniu do kogoś] na dolnych szczeblach społecznej drabiny; zdeprawowany. (*In* można zastąpić *into*. Patrz przykłady.) ❏ *You had better straighten out your life, or you'll end up in the gutter.* ❏ *His bad habits put him into the gutter.*

in the hole w długach. (*In* można zastąpić *into*. Patrz przykłady. Używane również dosłownie.) ❏ *I'm $200 in the hole.* ❏ *Our finances end up in the hole every month.*

in the know posiadający wiedzę, erudyta. (*In* można zastąpić *into*. Patrz przykłady.) ❏ *Let's ask Bob. He's in the know.* ❏ *I have no knowledge of how to work this machine. I think I can get into the know very quickly though.*

in the lap of luxury w luksusowym otoczeniu. (Klisza. *In* można zastąpić *into*. Patrz przykłady.) ❏ *John lives in the lap of luxury because his family is very wealthy.* ❏ *When I retire, I'd like to live in the lap of luxury.*

in the limelight AND **in the spotlight** w centrum uwagi. (*In* można zastąpić *into*. Patrz przykłady. Używane również dosłownie. *Limelight* to przestarzały typ reflektorów, i słowo to występuje tylko w tym wyrażeniu.) ❏ *John will do almost anything to get himself into the limelight.* ❏ *I love being in the spotlight.* ❏ *All elected officials spend a lot of time in the limelight.*

in the line of duty jako część obowiązków (wojskowych lub policyjnych), wykonania których się oczekuje. ❑ *When soldiers fight people in a war, it's in the line of duty.* ❑ *Police officers have to do things they may not like in the line of duty.*

in the long run w długim okresie czasu; ostatecznie. (Klisza.) ❑ *We'd be better off in the long run buying one instead of renting one.* ❑ *In the long run, we'd be happier in the South.*

in the money 1. bogaty. ❑ *John is really in the money. He's worth millions.* ❑ *If I am ever in the money, I'll be generous.* **2.** jako zwycięzca w wyścigu lub w zawodach. (Tak jakby ktoś wygrał nagrodę pieniężną.) ❑ *I knew when Jane came around the final turn that she was in the money.* ❑ *The horses coming in first, second, and third are said to be in the money.*

in the nick of time dokładnie na czas; w ostatnim możliwym momencie; tuż zanim stało się za późno. (Klisza.) ❑ *The doctor arrived in the nick of time. The patient's life was saved.* ❑ *I reached the airport in the nick of time.*

in the pink (of condition) w bardzo dobrym zdrowiu; w bardzo dobrej kondycji, zarówno fizycznej, jak i psychicznej. (*In* można zastąpić *into.* Patrz przykłady.) ❑ *The garden is lovely. All the flowers are in the pink of condition.* ❑ *Jane has to exercise hard to get into the pink of condition.* ❑ *I'd like to be in the pink, but I don't have the time.*

in the prime of life w najlepszym i najbardziej produktywnym okresie życia. (*In* można zastąpić *into.* Patrz przykłady.) ❑ *The good health of one's youth can carry over into the prime of life.* ❑ *He was struck down by a heart attack in the prime of life.*

in the public eye publicznie; widoczny dla wszystkich; jasny. (*In* można zastąpić *into.* Patrz przykłady.) ❑ *Elected officials find themselves constantly in the public eye.* ❑ *The mayor made it a practice to get into the public eye as much as possible.*

in the red w długach. (Odnosi się do zwyczaju pisania kwot długów na czerwono raczej niż na czarno. Patrz również *in the black.* *In* można zastąpić *into.* Patrz przykłady.) ❑ *My accounts are in the* *red at the end of every month.* ❑ *It's easy to get into the red if you don't pay close attention to the amount of money you spend.*

in the right po właściwej z punktu widzenia moralnego i prawnego stronie; po właściwej stronie. ❑ *I felt I was in the right, but the judge ruled against me.* ❑ *It's hard to argue with Jane. She always believes that she's in the right.*

in the same boat w tej samej sytuacji; mający ten sam problem. (Klisza. *In* można zastąpić *into.* Patrz przykłady.) ❑ *TOM: I'm broke. Can you lend me twenty dollars? BILL: Sorry. I'm in the same boat.* ❑ *Jane and Mary are in the same boat. They both have been called for jury duty.*

in the same breath [stwierdzone lub powiedziane] prawie w tym samym czasie; jako część tej samej myśli lub rozmowy. ❑ *He told me I was lazy, but then in the same breath he said I was doing a good job.* ❑ *The teacher said that the students were working hard and, in the same breath, that they were not working hard enough.*

in the spotlight Patrz pod *in the limelight.*

in the twinkling of an eye bardzo szybko. (Pochodzi z Biblii.) ❑ *In the twinkling of an eye, the deer had disappeared into the forest.* ❑ *I gave Bill ten dollars and, in the twinkling of an eye, he spent it.*

in the wind mający się wydarzyć. (Używane również dosłownie.) ❑ *There are some major changes in the wind. Expect these changes to happen soon.* ❑ *There is something in the wind. We'll find out what it is soon.*

in the world Patrz pod *on earth.*

in the wrong po niesłusznej lub bezprawnej stronie; winny lub w błędzie. ❑ *I felt she was in the wrong, but the judge ruled in her favor.* ❑ *It's hard to argue with Jane. She always believes that everyone else is in the wrong.*

in two shakes of a lamb's tail bardzo szybko. (Klisza.) ❏ *I'll be there in two shakes of a lamb's tail.* ❏ *In two shakes of a lamb's tail, the bird flew away.*

itchy palm, have an Patrz *have an itchy palm.*

It never rains but it pours. przysłowie mówiące, że wiele złych rzeczy często zdarza się razem. ❏ *The car won't start, the stairs broke, and the dog died. It never rains but it pours.* ❏ *Everything seems to be going wrong at the same time. It never rains but it pours.*

128

J

Johnny-come-lately ktoś, kto przyłącza sie do czegoś już w trakcie trwania. ❑ *Don't pay any attention to Sally. She's just a Johnny-come-lately and doesn't know what she's talking about.* ❑ *We've been here for thirty years. Why should some Johnny-come-lately tell us what to do?*

Johnny-on-the-spot ktoś, kto jest na właściwym miejscu we właściwym czsie. ❑ *Here I am, Johnny-on-the-spot. I told you I would be here at 12:20.* ❑ *Bill is late again. You can hardly call him Johnny-on-the-spot.*

jump off the deep end Patrz pod *go off the deep end.*

jump on the bandwagon Patrz pod *get on the bandwagon.*

jump out of one's skin silnie zareagować na szok lub niespodziankę. (Zwykle z *nearly, almost,* etc. Nigdy nie używane dosłownie.) ❑ *Oh! You really scared me. I nearly jumped out of my skin.* ❑ *Bill was so startled he almost jumped out of his skin.*

jump the gun zacząć przed sygnałem startu. (Początkowo używane w zawodach sportowych rozpoczynanych strzałem.) ❑ *We all had to start the race again because Jane jumped the gun.* ❑ *When we took the test, Tom jumped the gun and started early.*

jump the track **1.** [w odniesieniu do czegoś] spaść lub stoczyć się z szyn lub z trakcji. (Zwykle w odniesieniu do pociągów.) ❑ *The train jumped the track, causing many injuries to the passengers.* ❑ *The engine jumped the track, but the other cars stayed on.* **2.** nagle zmienić jedną rzecz, myśl, plan lub działanie na inny. ❑ *The entire project jumped the track, and we finally had to give*

129

up. ❑ *John's mind jumped the track while he was in the play, and he forgot his lines.*

just what the doctor ordered dokładnie to, o co poproszono, zwłaszcza jeśli chodzi o zdrowie lub wygodę. (Klisza.) ❑ *That meal was delicious, Bob. Just what the doctor ordered.* ❑ BOB: *Would you like something to drink?* MARY: *Yes, a cold glass of water would be just what the doctor ordered.*

K

keep a civil tongue (in one's head) mówić uczciwie i grzecznie. (Również z *have*.) ❑ *Please, John. Don't talk like that. Keep a civil tongue in your head.* ❑ *John seems unable to keep a civil tongue.* ❑ *He'd be welcome here if he had a civil tongue in his head.*

keep an eye out (for someone or something) Patrz pod *have an eye out (for someone or something)*.

keep a stiff upper lip być chłodnym i niewzruszonym w stosunku do niepojących zdarzeń. (Również z *have*. Patrz notatka przy *keep a straight face*.) ❑ *John always keeps a stiff upper lip.* ❑ *Now, Billy, don't cry. Keep a stiff upper lip.* ❑ *Bill can take it. He has a stiff upper lip.*

keep a straight face powstrzymać się od śmiechu. (*Keep* można zastąpić *have*. Uwaga: *Keep* implikuje wysiłek, zaś *have* po prostu sposób, który się na to ma.) ❑ *It's hard to keep a straight face when someone tells a funny joke.* ❑ *I knew it was John who played the trick. He couldn't keep a straight face.* ❑ *John didn't have a straight face.*

keep body and soul together wyżywić się, ubrać i utrzymać mieszkanie. (Klisza.) ❑ *I hardly have enough money to keep body and soul together.* ❑ *How the old man was able to keep body and soul together is beyond me.*

keep late hours siedzieć do późna w nocy; pracować do późna. ❑ *I'm always tired because I keep late hours.* ❑ *If I didn't keep late hours, I wouldn't sleep so late in the morning.*

keep one's ear to the ground Patrz pod *have one's ear to the ground.*

keep one's eye on the ball **1.** uważnie śledzić piłkę lub podążać za nią, zwłaszcza w grach z użyciem piłki; starannie dostosowywać się do szczegółów gry w piłkę. ❑ *John, if you can't keep your eye on the ball, I'll have to take you out of the game.* ❑ *"Keep your eye on the ball," the coach roared at the players.* **2.** pozostawać czujnym w stosunku do zdarzeń mających miejsce wokół. ❑ *If you want to get along in this office, you're going to have to keep your eye on the ball.* ❑ *Bill would do better in his classes if he would just keep his eye on the ball.*

keep one's feet on the ground Patrz pod *get one's feet on the ground.*

keep one's head above water Patrz pod *get one's head above water.*

keep one's nose to the grindstone Patrz pod *put one's nose to the grindstone.*

keep one's temper AND **hold one's temper** powstrzymać gniew: nie okazywać gniewu. ❑ *She should have learned to keep her temper when she was a child.* ❑ *Sally got thrown off the team because she couldn't hold her temper.*

keep one's weather eye open oczekiwać, że coś się zdarzy; być czujnym (w stosunku do czegoś); strzec się. ❑ *Some trouble is brewing. Keep your weather eye open.* ❑ *Try to be more alert. Learn to keep your weather eye open.*

keep one's word dotrzymać obietnicy. ❑ *I told her I'd be there to pick her up, and I intend to keep my word.* ❑ *Keeping one's word is necessary in the legal profession.*

keep someone in stitches bardzo kogoś rozśmieszać, raz za razem. (Również z *have*. Patrz uwaga przy *keep a straight face.*) ❑ *The comedian kept us in stitches for nearly an hour.* ❑ *The teacher kept the class in stitches, but the students didn't learn anything.*

keep someone on tenterhooks trzymać kogoś w zawieszeniu lub w stanie zmartwienia. (Również z *have*. Patrz uwaga przy *keep a straight face.*) ❑ *Please tell me now. Don't keep me on tenterhooks any longer!* ❑ *Now that we have her on tenterhooks, shall we let her worry, or shall we tell her?*

keep someone or something hanging in midair Patrz *leave someone or something hanging in midair.*

keep someone or something in mind AND **bear someone or something in mind** pamiętać i myśleć o kimś lub o czymś. ❑ *When you're driving a car, you must bear this in mind at all times: Keep your eyes on the road.* ❑ *As you leave home, keep your family in mind.*

keep someone posted przekazywać komuś aktualne informacje (o tym, co się dzieje). ❑ *If the price of corn goes up, I need to know. Please keep me posted.* ❑ *Keep her posted about the patient's status.*

keep something to oneself trzymać coś w tajemnicy. (Zauważ użycie *but* w przykładach.) ❑ *I'm quitting my job, but please keep that to yourself.* ❑ *Keep it to yourself, but I'm quitting my job.* ❑ *John is always gossiping. He can't keep anything to himself.*

keep something under one's hat trzymać coś w tajemnicy; trzymać coś w głowie (tylko). (Jeżeli tajemnica pozostanie pod kapeluszem, pozostanie tylko w twojej głowie. Zauważ użycie *but* w przykładach.) ❑ *Keep this under your hat, but I'm getting married.* ❑ *I'm getting married, but keep it under your hat.*

keep something under wraps trzymać coś w ukryciu (do jakiegoś momentu w przyszłości). ❑ *We kept the plan under wraps until after the election.* ❑ *The automobile company kept the new model under wraps until most of the old models had been sold.*

keep the home fires burning utrzymywać sprawy w toku w domu lub w jakimś innym centralnym punkcie. (Klisza.) ❑ *My uncle kept the home fires burning when my sister and I went to school.* ❑ *The manager stays at the office and keeps the home fires burning while I'm out selling our products.*

keep the wolf from the door utrzymywać się na jakimś minimalnym poziomie, wolnym od głodu, zimna etc. (Klisza.) ❑ *I don't make a lot of money, just enough to keep the wolf from the door.* ❑ *We have a small amount of money saved, hardly enough to keep the wolf from the door.*

keep up (with the Joneses) finansowo pozostawać na poziomie takim samym jak rówieśnicy; ciężko pracować, by mieć ten sam poziom dóbr materialnych, co przyjaciele czy sąsiedzi. ❑ *Mr. and Mrs. Brown bought a new car simply to keep up with the Joneses.* ❑ *Keeping up with the Joneses can take all your money.*

keep up (with the times) dotrzymywać kroku modzie; posiadać aktualny poziom informacji; być współczesnym lub nowoczesnym. ❑ *I try to keep up with the times. I want to know what's going on.* ❑ *I bought a whole new wardrobe because I want to keep up with the times.* ❑ *Sally learns all the new dances. She likes to keep up.*

kick up a fuss AND **kick up a row; kick up a storm** być dokuczliwym; źle się zachowywać lub przeszkadzać (komuś). (*Row* rymuje się z *cow*. Zauważ zróżnicowanie w przykładach.) ❑ *The customer kicked up such a fuss about the food that the manager came to apologize.* ❑ *I kicked up such a row that they kicked me out.*

kick up a row Patrz poprzednie hasło.

kick up a storm Patrz pod *kick up a fuss.*

kick up one's heels zachowywać się swawolnie; zachowywać się żywo i wesoło. ❑ *I like to go to an old-fashioned square dance and really kick up my heels.* ❑ *For an old man, your uncle is really kicking up his heels.*

kill the fatted calf przygotowywać wyszukany bankiet (na czyjąjś cześć). (Pochodzi z biblijnej przypowieści o powrocie syna marnotrawnego). ❑ *When Bob got back from college, his parents killed the fatted calf and threw a great party.* ❑ *Sorry, this meal isn't much, John. We didn't have time to kill the fatted calf.*

kill the goose that laid the golden egg przysłowie odwołujące się do niszczenia źródła swej fortuny. (Oparte na starej baśni.) ❏ *If you fire your best office worker, you'll be killing the goose that laid the golden egg.* ❏ *He sold his computer, which was like killing the goose that laid the golden egg.*

kill time tracić czas. ❏ *Stop killing time. Get to work!* ❏ *We went over to the record shop just to kill time.*

kill two birds with one stone rozwiązać dwa problemy za jednym zamachem. (Klisza.) ❏ *John learned the words to his part in the play while peeling potatoes. He was killing two birds with one stone.* ❏ *I have to cash a check and make a payment on my bank loan. I'll kill two birds with one stone by doing them both in one trip to the bank.*

kiss and make up przebaczyć komuś i znów być przyjaciółmi. (Używane również dosłownie.) ❏ *They were very angry, but in the end they kissed and made up.* ❏ *I'm sorry. Let's kiss and make up.*

kiss of death działanie kładące kres komuś lub czemuś. ❏ *The mayor's veto was the kiss of death for the new law.* ❏ *Fainting on stage was the kiss of death for my acting career.*

kiss something good-bye przewidzieć lub przeżyć stratę czegoś. (Nie używane dosłownie.) ❏ *If you leave your camera on a park bench, you can kiss it good-bye.* ❏ *You kissed your wallet good-bye when you left it in the store.*

knit one's brow zmarszczyć brew. ❏ *The woman knit her brow and asked us what we wanted from her.* ❏ *While he read his book, John knit his brow occasionally. He must not have agreed with what he was reading.*

knock on wood wyrażenie używane dla zaklęcia wyimaginowanego nieszczęścia. (To samo co brytyjskie "touch wood.") ❏ *My stereo has never given me any trouble – knock on wood.* ❏ *We plan to be in Florida by tomorrow evening – knock on wood.*

knock someone for a loop Patrz pod *throw someone for a loop.*

know all the tricks of the trade posiadać umiejętności i wiedzę konieczną do zrobienia czegoś. (Również bez *all*.) ❏ *Tom can repair car engines. He knows the tricks of the trade.* ❏ *If I knew all the tricks of the trade, I could be a better plumber.*

know enough to come in out of the rain, not Patrz *not know enough to come in out of the rain.*

know, in the Patrz *in the know.*

know one's ABCs znać alfabet; znać najbardziej podstawowe rzeczy (o czymś). ❏ *Bill can't do it. He doesn't even know his ABCs.* ❏ *You can't expect to write novels when you don't even know your ABCs.*

know someone by sight znać czyjeś nazwisko i rozpoznawać kogoś (z wyglądu). ❏ *I've never met the man, but I know him by sight.* ❏ BOB*: Have you ever met Mary?* JANE*: No, but I know her by sight.*

know someone from Adam, not Patrz *not know someone from Adam.*

know someone or something like a book Patrz pod *know someone or something like the palm of one's hand.*

know someone or something like the back of one's hand Patrz następne hasło.

know someone or something like the palm of one's hand AND **know someone or something like the back of one's hand; know someone or something like a book** znać kogoś lub coś bardzo dobrze. ❏ *Of course I know John. I know him like the back of my hand.* ❏ *I know him like a book.*

know something from memory znać coś tak dobrze, że nie trzeba odwoływać się do notatek; znać coś bardzo dobrze dlatego, że widziało się to coś bardzo często. ❏ *Mary didn't need the script because she knew the play from memory.* ❏ *The conductor went through the entire concert without music. He knew it from memory.*

know something in one's bones Patrz pod *feel something in one's bones.*

know something inside out znać coś dogłębnie; wiedzieć o czymś wszystko. ❏ *I know my geometry inside out.* ❏ *I studied and studied for my driver's test until I knew the rules inside out.*

know the ropes wiedzieć jak coś zrobić. ❏ *I can't do the job because I don't know the ropes.* ❏ *Ask Sally to do it. She knows the ropes.* ALSO: **show someone the ropes** powiedzieć lub pokazać komuś, jak coś powinno być zrobione. ❏ *Since this was my first day on the job, the manager spent a lot of time showing me the ropes.*

know the score AND **know what's what** znać fakty; znać fakty o życiu i jego problemach. (Używane również dosłownie.) ❏ *Bob is so naive. He sure doesn't know the score.* ❏ *I know what you're trying to do. Oh, yes, I know what's what.*

know what's what Patrz poprzednie hasło.

know which side one's bread is buttered on wiedzieć, co jest dla siebie najbardziej korzystne. (Klisza.) ❏ *He'll do it if his boss tells him to. He knows which side his bread is buttered on.* ❏ *Since John knows which side his bread is buttered on, he'll be there on time.*

L

land-office business, do a Patrz *do a land-office business.*

lap of luxury, in the Patrz *in the lap of luxury.*

last but not least ostatni w kolejności, ale nie ostatni, jeśli chodzi o znaczenie. (Nadużywana klisza. Często stosowana w prezentacjach.) ❑ *The speaker said, "And now, last but not least, I'd like to present Bill Smith, who will give us some final words." ❑ And last but not least, here is the loser of the race.*

last legs, on someone's or something's Patrz *on someone's or something's last legs.*

last minute, at the Patrz *at the last minute.*

laughing matter, no Patrz *no laughing matter.*

laugh out of the other side of one's mouth nagle zmienić nastrój ze szczęścia na smutek. (Klisza.) ❑ *Now that you know the truth, you'll laugh out of the other side of your mouth. ❑ He was so proud that he won the election. He's laughing out of the other side of his mouth since they recounted the ballots and found out that he lost.*

laugh up one's sleeve potajemnie śmiać się; śmiać się cicho do siebie. ❑ *Jane looked very serious, but I knew she was laughing up her sleeve. ❑ I told Sally that her dress was darling, but I was laughing up my sleeve because her dress was too small.*

law unto oneself ktoś, kto tworzy swoje własne prawa i reguły; ktoś, kto ustanawia swoje własne standardy zachowań. ❑ *You can't get Bill to follow the rules. He's a law unto himself.* ❑ *Jane is a law unto herself. She's totally unwilling to cooperate.*

lay a finger on someone or something dotknąć kogoś lub czegoś, nawet bardzo lekko, nawet tylko palcem. (Zwykle w formie przeczącej.) ❑ *Don't you dare lay a finger on my pencil. Go get your own!* ❑ *If you lay a finger on me, I'll scream.*

lay an egg bardzo źle zagrać. (Używane również dosłownie, ale tylko w odniesieniu do ptaków.) ❑ *The cast of the play really laid an egg last night.* ❑ *I hope I don't lay an egg when it's my turn to sing.*

lay down the law 1. potwierdzić stanowczo, jakie są zasady w (odniesieniu do czegoś). (Klisza.) ❑ *Before the meeting, the boss laid down the law. We all knew exactly what to do.* ❑ *The way she laid down the law means that I'll remember her rules.* **2.** zganić kogoś za złe zachowanie. ❑ *When the teacher caught us, he really laid down the law.* ❑ *Poor Bob. He really got it when his mother laid down the law.*

lay it on thick AND **pour it on thick; spread it on thick** przesadzona pochwała, wymówka lub nagana. ❑ *Sally was laying it on thick when she said that Tom was the best singer she had ever heard.* ❑ *After Bob finished making his excuses, Sally said that he was pouring it on thick.* ❑ *Bob always spreads it on thick.*

lay one's cards on the table Patrz pod *put one's cards on the table.*

lay something on the line Patrz pod *put something on the line.*

lay something to waste AND **lay waste to something** zniszczyć coś (dosłownie lub przenośnie). ❑ *The invaders laid the village to waste.* ❑ *The kids came in and laid waste to my clean house.*

lay waste to something Patrz poprzednie hasło.

lead a dog's life AND **live a dog's life** żyć nędznie. ❑ *Poor Jane really leads a dog's life.* ❑ *I've been working so hard. I'm tired of living a dog's life.*

lead someone down the garden path oszukać kogoś. (Klisza.) ❑ *Now, be honest with me. Don't lead me down the garden path.* ❑ *That cheater really led her down the garden path.*

lead someone on a merry chase poprowadzić kogoś na bezcelowe poszukiwania. ❑ *What a waste of time. You really led me on a merry chase.* ❑ *Jane led Bill on a merry chase trying to find an antique lamp.*

lead the life of Riley żyć w luksusie. (Nikt nie wie, kto to Riley.) ❑ *If I had a million dollars, I could live the life of Riley.* ❑ *The treasurer took our money to Mexico, where he lived the life of Riley until the police caught him.*

leaps and bounds, by Patrz *by leaps and bounds.*

learn something from the bottom up nauczyć się czegoś dogłębnie, od samego początku; nauczyć się wszystkich nawet najbardziej nieważnych, aspektów czegoś. ❑ *I learned my business from the bottom up.* ❑ *I started out sweeping the floors and learned everything from the bottom up.*

leave a bad taste in someone's mouth [w odniesieniu do kogoś lub czegoś] pozostawić u kogoś złe uczucia lub wspomnienie. (Używane również dosłownie.) ❑ *The whole business about the missing money left a bad taste in his mouth.* ❑ *It was a very nice party, but something about it left a bad taste in my mouth.* ❑ *I'm sorry that Bill was there. He always leaves a bad taste in my mouth.*

leave a sinking ship Patrz pod *desert a sinking ship.*

leave no stone unturned szukać we wszystkich możliwych miejscach. (Klisza. Jakby ktoś mógł znaleźć coś pod skałą.) ❑ *Don't*

worry. We'll find your stolen car. We'll leave no stone unturned.
❑ *In searching for a nice place to live, we left no stone unturned.*

leave one to one's fate pozostawić kogoś na łaskę tego, co się może wydarzyć - być może śmierci lub jakiegoś innego nieprzyjemnego zdarzenia. ❑ *We couldn't rescue the miners, and we were forced to leave them to their fate.* ❑ *Please don't try to help. Just go away and leave me to my fate.*

leave someone for dead pozostawić kogoś myśląc, że umarł. (Porzucony człowiek w rzeczywistości może żyć.) ❑ *He looked so bad that they almost left him for dead.* ❑ *As the soldiers turned – leaving the enemy captain for dead – the captain fired at them.*

leave someone high and dry **1.** pozostawić kogoś bez pomocy i niezdolnego do wykonania jakiegoś manewru; zostawić kogoś bezradnym. (Nawiązuje do łodzi, która utknęła na lądzie lub na rafie.) ❑ *All my workers quit and left me high and dry.* ❑ *All the children ran away and left Billy high and dry to take the blame for the broken window.* **2.** zostawić kogoś zupenie bez pieniędzy. ❑ *Mrs. Franklin took all the money out of the bank and left Mr. Franklin high and dry.* ❑ *Paying the bills always leaves me high and dry.*

leave someone holding the bag zostawić kogoś tak, by musiał całą winę wziąć na siebie; zostawić kogoś tak, by wydawał się winny. ❑ *They all ran off and left me holding the bag. It wasn't even my fault.* ❑ *It was the mayor's fault, but he wasn't left holding the bag.*

leave someone in peace przestać komuś zawracać głowę; odejść i zostawić kogoś w spokoju. (Niekoniecznie oznacza odejście od danej osoby.) ❑ *Please go – leave me in peace.* ❑ *Can't you see that you're upsetting her? Leave her in peace.*

leave someone in the lurch pozostawiać kogoś w oczekiwaniu, że coś zrobisz, lub przewidującego, że to zrobisz. ❑ *Where were you, John? You really left me in the lurch.* ❑ *I didn't mean to leave you in the lurch. I thought we had canceled our meeting.*

leave someone or something hanging in midair zawiesić jakieś sprawy z kimś lub czymś; zostawić kogoś lub coś w oczekiwaniu na kontynuację. (Używane również dosłownie.) ❑ *She left her sentence hanging in midair.* ❑ *She left us hanging in midair when she paused.* ❑ *Tell me the rest of the story. Don't leave me hanging in midair.* ❑ *Don't leave the story hanging in midair.* ALSO: **keep someone or something hanging in midair** pozostawić kogoś lub coś w oczekiwaniu na zakończenie lub kontynuację. ❑ *Please don't keep us hanging in midair.*

left field, out in Patrz *out in left field.*

leg to stand on, not have a Patrz *not have a leg to stand on.*

lend an ear (to someone) wysłuchać kogoś. ❑ *Lend an ear to John. Hear what he has to say.* ❑ *I'd be delighted to lend an ear. I find great wisdom in everything John has to say.*

lend oneself or itself to something [w odniesieniu do kogoś lub czegoś] dającym się do czegoś przystosować; [w odniesieniu do kogoś lub czegoś] być do czegoś użytecznym. ❑ *This room doesn't lend itself to bright colors.* ❑ *John doesn't lend himself to casual conversation.*

less than no time, in Patrz *in less than no time.*

Let bygones be bygones. przysłowie mówiące, że należy zapomnieć o problemach z przeszłości. (Również klisza.) ❑ *Okay, Sally, let bygones be bygones. Let's forgive and forget.* ❑ *Jane was unwilling to let bygones be bygones. She still won't speak to me.*

let grass grow under one's feet nic nie robić; stać w miejscu. (Klisza.) ❑ *Mary doesn't let the grass grow under her feet. She's always busy.* ❑ *Bob is too lazy. He's letting the grass grow under his feet.*

let off steam AND **blow off steam** wypuścić nadmiar energii lub gniewu. (Używane również dosłownie.) ❑ *Whenever John gets a* *little angry, he blows off steam.* ❏ *Don't worry about John. He's just letting off steam.*

let one's hair down AND **let down one's hair** pozwolić sobie na większą bliskość i zacząć mówić szczerze. ❏ *Come on, Jane, let your hair down and tell me all about it.* ❏ *I have a problem. Do you mind if I let down my hair?*

Let sleeping dogs lie. przysłowie mówiące, że nie należy szukać kłopotów lub że należy pozostawić coś w spokoju. (Klisza.) ❏ *Don't mention that problem with Tom again. It's almost forgotten. Let sleeping dogs lie.* ❏ *You'll never be able to reform Bill. Leave him alone. Let sleeping dogs lie.*

let someone off (the hook) zwolnić kogoś z odpowiedzialności. ❏ *Please let me off the hook for Saturday. I have other plans.* ❏ *Okay, I'll let you off.*

let something slide zlekceważyć coś. ❏ *John let his lessons slide.* ❏ *Jane doesn't let her work slide.*

let something slide by Patrz następne hasło.

let something slip by AND **let something slide by** **1.** zapomnieć o ważnej dacie lub opuścić ważne spotkanie. ❏ *I'm sorry I just let your birthday slip by.* ❏ *I let it slide by accidentally.* **2.** stracić jakiś czas. ❏ *You wasted the whole day by letting it slip by.* ❏ *We were having fun, and we let the time slide by.*

let the cat out of the bag AND **spill the beans** przypadkowo wyjawić tajemnicę lub powiedzieć o niespodziance. (Dwie klisze.) ❏ *When Bill glanced at the door, he let the cat out of the bag. We knew then that he was expecting someone to arrive.* ❏ *We are planning a surprise party for Jane. Don't let the cat out of the bag.* ❏ *It's a secret. Try not to spill the beans.*

let the chance slip by stracić okazję zrobienia czegoś. ❏ *When I was younger, I wanted to become a doctor, but I let the chance slip by.* ❏ *Don't let the chance slip by. Do it now!*

level, on the Patrz *on the level.*

lie through one's teeth kłamać śmiało, w sposób oczywisty i bez wyrzutów sumienia. (Klisza.) ❏ *I knew she was lying through her teeth, but I didn't want to say so just then.* ❏ *I'm not lying through my teeth! I never do!*

life of the party ktoś bardzo żywy, kto pomaga sprawić, by impreza była zabawna i udana. ❏ *Bill is always the life of the party. Be sure to invite him.* ❏ *Bob isn't exactly the life of the party, but he's polite.*

light as a feather, as Patrz *as light as a feather.*

light, out like a Patrz *out like a light.*

like a bat out of hell z wielką siłą i szybkością. (Klisza. Słowa *hell* należy używać ostrożnie.) ❏ *Did you see her leave? She left like a bat out of hell.* ❏ *The car sped down the street like a bat out of hell.*

like a bolt out of the blue nagle i bez ostrzeżenia. (Klisza. Nawiązuje do błyskawicy na niebieskim niebie.) ❏ *The news came to us like a bolt out of the blue.* ❏ *Like a bolt out of the blue, the boss came and fired us all.*

like a bump on a log nie reagujący; nieruchawy. (Klisza.) ❏ *I spoke to him, but he just sat there like a bump on a log.* ❏ *Don't stand there like a bump on a log. Give me a hand!*

like a fish out of water dziwny; w obcym lub niezwykłym otoczeniu. (Klisza.) ❏ *At a formal dance, John is like a fish out of*

144

water. ❏ *Mary was like a fish out of water at the bowling tournament.*

like a sitting duck AND **like sitting ducks** niestrzeżony; nie podejrzewający i nieświadomy. (Klisza. Drugie wyrażenie występuje w formie liczby mnogiej. Nawiązuje raczej do pływających niż latających kaczek.) ❏ *He was waiting there like a sitting duck– a perfect target for a mugger.* ❏ *The soldiers were standing at the top of the hill like sitting ducks. It's a wonder they weren't all killed.*

like a three-ring circus chaotyczny; ekscytujący i ruchliwy. (Klisza.) ❏ *Our household is like a three-ring circus on Monday mornings.* ❏ *This meeting is like a three-ring circus. Quiet down and listen!*

like looking for a needle in a haystack zajęty beznadziejnym poszukiwaniem. (Klisza.) ❏ *Trying to find a white dog in the snow is like looking for a needle in a haystack.* ❏ *I tried to find my lost contact lens on the beach, but it was like looking for a needle in a haystack.*

likely as not, as Patrz *as likely as not.*

like water off a duck's back łatwo; bez widocznego wysiłku. (Klisza.) ❏ *Insults rolled off John like water off a duck's back.* ❏ *The bullets had no effect on the steel door. They fell away like water off a duck's back.*

limelight, in the Patrz *in the limelight.*

limit, go the Patrz *go the limit.*

line of duty, in the Patrz *in the line of duty.*

little bird told me, a Patrz *a little bird told me.*

little by little powoli, jeden kawałek na raz. ❑ *Little by little, he began to understand what we were talking about.* ❑ *The snail crossed the stone little by little.*

little knowledge is a dangerous thing, A. Patrz *A little knowledge is a dangerous thing.*

live a dog's life Patrz pod *lead a dog's life.*

live and let live nie wtrącać się w sprawy lub upodobania innych ludzi. (Klisza.) ❑ *I don't care what they do! Live and let live, I always say.* ❑ *Your parents are strict. Mine just live and let live.*

live beyond one's means wydać więcej pieniędzy niż można sobie na to pozwolić. ❑ *The Browns are deeply in debt because they are living beyond their means.* ❑ *I keep a budget so that I don't live beyond my means.*

live by one's wits przeżyć dzięki swej mądrości. ❑ *When you're in the kind of business I'm in, you have to live by your wits.* ❑ *John was orphaned at the age of ten and grew up living by his wits.*

live from hand to mouth żyć w biedzie. ❑ *When both my parents were out of work, we lived from hand to mouth.* ❑ *We lived from hand to mouth during the war. Things were very difficult.*

live in an ivory tower być ponad realia życia. (*Live* można zastąpić innymi wyrażeniami oznaczającymi mieszkać lub spędzać czas, tak jak w przykładach. Często się tak mówi o uczonych.) ❑ *If you didn't spend so much time in your ivory tower, you'd know what people really think!* ❑ *Many professors are said to live in ivory towers. They don't know what the real world is like.*

live off the fat of the land hodować dla siebie żywność; żyć ze zmagazynowanych środków lub ze środków powyżej potrzeb. (Klisza.) ❑ *If I had a million dollars, I'd invest it and live off the* *fat of the land.* ❑ *I'll be happy to retire soon and live off the fat of the land.* ❑ *Many farmers live off the fat of the land.*

live out of a suitcase mieszkać krótko w jakimś miejscu, nie rozpakowując walizki. ❑ *I hate living out of a suitcase. For my next vacation, I want to go to just one place and stay there the whole time.* ❑ *We were living out of suitcases in a motel while they repaired the damage the fire caused to our house.*

live within one's means nie wydawać więcej pieniędzy niż się ma. ❑ *We have to struggle to live within our means, but we manage.* ❑ *John is unable to live within his means.*

lock horns (with someone) wplątać się w kłótnię z kimś. (Tak jak walczące byki lub jelenie.) ❑ *Let's settle this peacefully. I don't want to lock horns with the boss.* ❑ *The boss doesn't want to lock horns either.*

lock, stock, and barrel wszystko. ❑ *We had to move everything out of the house – lock, stock, and barrel.* ❑ *We lost everything – lock, stock, and barrel – in the fire.*

loggerheads, at Patrz *at loggerheads.*

long for this world, not Patrz *not long for this world.*

long haul, over the Patrz *over the long haul.*

long run, in the Patrz *in the long run.*

Long time no see. nie widzieć kogoś przez długi czas. ❑ *Hello, John. Long time no see.* ❑ *When John and Mary met on the street, they both said, "Long time no see."*

look as if butter wouldn't melt in one's mouth wydawać się zimnym i nieczułym (mimo tego, iż wiadomo, że jest odwrotnie). ❑ *Sally looks as if butter wouldn't melt in her mouth. She can be so*

147

cruel. ❑ *What a sour face. He looks as if butter wouldn't melt in his mouth.*

look daggers at someone spojrzeć wrogo na kogoś. (Jak gdyby czyjaś linia wzroku przypominała skierowane na kogoś sztylety.) ❑ *Tom must have been mad at Ann from the way he was looking daggers at her.* ❑ *Don't you dare look daggers at me. Don't even look cross-eyed at me!*

looking for a needle in a haystack, like Patrz *like looking for a needle in a haystack.*

look like a million dollars wyglądać na bardzo bogatego. (Klisza.) ❑ *Oh, Sally, you look like a million dollars.* ❑ *Your new hairdo looks like a million dollars.*

look like the cat that swallowed the canary wyglądać jak gdyby się właśnie odniosło ogromny sukces. (Klisza. Koty czasem wyglądają, jakby się czuły winne po zrobieniu czegoś.) ❑ *After the meeting John looked like the cat that swallowed the canary. I knew he must have been a success.* ❑ *What happened? You look like the cat that swallowed the canary.*

look the other way celowo coś zignorować. (Również używane dosłownie.) ❑ *John could have prevented the problem, but he looked the other way.* ❑ *By looking the other way, he actually made the problem worse.*

loose ends, at Patrz *at loose ends.*

lord it over someone dominować nad kimś; kierować kimś i kontrolować go. ❑ *Mr. Smith seems to lord it over his wife.* ❑ *The boss lords it over everyone in the office.*

lose face utracić swój status; stać się mniej szanowanym. ❑ *John is more afraid of losing face than losing money.* ❑ *Things will go* *better if you can explain to him where he was wrong without making him lose face.*

lose heart stracić odwagę lub pewność siebie. ❏ *Now, don't lose heart. Keep trying.* ❏ *What a disappointment! It's enough to make one lose heart.*

lose one's grip **1.** puścić coś. ❏ *I'm holding on to the rope as tightly as I can. I hope I don't lose my grip.* ❏ *This hammer is slippery. Try not to lose your grip.* **2.** stracić kontrolę nad czymś. ❏ *I can't seem to run things the way I used to. I'm losing my grip.* ❏ *They replaced the board of directors because it was losing its grip.*

lose one's temper rozzłościć się. ❏ *Please don't lose your temper. It's not good for you.* ❏ *I'm sorry that I lost my temper.*

lose one's train of thought zapomnieć, o czym się mówiło lub myślało. ❏ *Excuse me, I lost my train of thought. What was I talking about?* ❏ *You made the speaker lose her train of thought.*

lost in thought zajęty myśleniem. ❏ *I'm sorry, I didn't hear what you said. I was lost in thought.* ❏ *Bill – lost in thought as always – went into the wrong room.*

lot going (for one), have a Patrz *have a lot going (for one).*

love at first sight miłość od pierwszego momentu, kiedy dwoje ludzi się spotkało. (Klisza.) ❏ *Bill was standing at the door when Ann opened it. It was love at first sight.* ❏ *It was love at first sight when they met, but it didn't last long.*

lovely weather for ducks deszczowa pogoda. (Klisza.) ❏ BOB: *Not very nice out today, is it?* BILL: *It's lovely weather for ducks.* ❏ *I don't like this weather, but it's lovely weather for ducks.*

low boiling point, have a Patrz *have a low boiling point.*

lower one's sights ustawić swoje cele na niższym poziomie. ❏ *Even though you get frustrated, don't lower your sights.* ❏ *I shouldn't lower my sights. If I work hard, I can do what I want.*

lower one's voice mówić ciszej. ❏ *Please lower your voice, or you'll disturb the people who are working.* ❏ *He wouldn't lower his voice, so everyone heard what he said.*

lower the boom on someone złajać lub surowo kogoś ukarać; huknąć na kogoś. (Wyrażenie żeglarskie.) ❏ *If Bob won't behave better, I'll have to lower the boom on him.* ❏ *The teacher lowered the boom on the whole class for misbehaving.*

low man on the totem pole najmniej ważna osoba. (Patrz również *high man on the totem pole*.) ❏ *I was the last to find out because I'm low man on the totem pole.* ❏ *I can't be of any help. I'm low man on the totem pole.*

luck, out of Patrz *out of luck.*

luck would have it, as Patrz *as luck would have it.*

lunch, out to Patrz *out to lunch.*

M

mad as a hatter, as Patrz *as mad as a hatter.*

mad as a hornet, as Patrz *as mad as a hornet.*

mad as a March hare, as Patrz *as mad as a March hare.*

mad as a wet hen, as Patrz *as mad as a wet hen.*

mad rush, in a Patrz *in a mad rush.*

make a beeline for someone or something kierować się prosto ku komuś lub czemuś. (Używane również dosłownie w odniesieniu do pszczelich lotów.) ❑ *Billy came into the kitchen and made a beeline for the cookies.* ❑ *After the game, we all made a beeline for John, who was serving cold drinks.*

make a clean breast of something wyznać coś. ❑ *You'll feel better if you make a clean breast of it. Now tell us what happened.* ❑ *I was forced to make a clean breast of the whole affair.*

make a go of it sprawić, żeby coś zadziałało. ❑ *It's a tough situation, but Ann is trying to make a go of it.* ❑ *We don't like living here, but we have to make a go of it.*

make a great show of something sprawić, by coś stało się widoczne; zrobić coś w demonstracyjny sposób. ❑ *Ann made a great show of wiping up the drink that John spilled.* ❑ *Jane displayed her irritation at our late arrival by making a great show of serving the cold dinner.*

make a hit (with someone or something) zadowalać kogoś. ❏ *The singer made a hit with the audience.* ❏ *She was afraid she wouldn't make a hit.* ❏ *John made a hit with my parents last evening.*

make a long story short doprowadzić opowiadanie do końca. (Klisza. Jest to formuła streszczenia opowiadania lub żartu.) ❏ *And – to make a long story short – I never got back the money that I lent him.* ❏ *If I can make a long story short, let me say that everything worked out fine.*

make a mountain out of a molehill zrobić problem z niczego; przesadzić jeżeli chodzi o ważność czegoś. (Klisza.) ❏ *Come on, don't make a mountain out of a molehill. It's not that important.* ❏ *Mary is always making mountains out of molehills.*

make a nuisance of oneself stale sprawiać kłopot. ❏ *I'm sorry to make a nuisance of myself, but I do need an answer to my question.* ❏ *Stop making a nuisance of yourself and wait your turn.*

make a run for it szybko biec, aby się skądś wydostać lub gdzieś dostać. ❏ *When the guard wasn't looking, the prisoner made a run for it.* ❏ *In the baseball game, the player on first base made a run for it, but he didn't make it to second base.*

make a silk purse out of a sow's ear stworzyć coś cennego z czegoś o żadnej wartości. (Klisza. Często używane w formie przeczącej.) ❏ *Don't bother trying to fix up this old bicycle. You can't make a silk purse out of a sow's ear.* ❏ *My mother made a lovely jacket out of an old coat. She succeeded in making a silk purse out of a sow's ear.*

make cracks (about someone or something) ośmieszać kogoś lub coś lub żartować z kogoś lub czegoś. ❏ *Please stop making cracks about my haircut. It's the new style.* ❏ *Some people can't help making cracks. They are just rude.*

make fast work of someone or something Patrz pod *make short work of someone or something.*

make free with someone or something Patrz pod *take liberties with someone or something.*

make good money zarobić dużo pieniędzy. (Tutaj *good* oznacza wiele.) ❏ *Ann makes good money at her job.* ❏ *I don't know what she does, but she makes good money.*

Make hay while the sun is shining. przysłowie mówiące, że powinieneś właściwy czas wykorzystać jak najlepiej. ❏ *There are lots of people here now. You should try to sell them soda pop. Make hay while the sun is shining.* ❏ *Go to school and get a good education while you're young. Make hay while the sun is shining.*

make life miserable for someone uczynić kogoś na długo nieszczęśliwym. ❏ *My shoes are tight, and they are making life miserable for me.* ❏ *Jane's boss is making life miserable for her.*

make light of something traktować coś jakby to było nieważne lub humorystyczne. ❏ *I wish you wouldn't make light of his problems. They're quite serious.* ❏ *I make light of my problems, and that makes me feel better.*

make oneself at home czuć się wygodnie, tak jakby o siebie w domu. ❏ *Please come in and make yourself at home.* ❏ *I'm glad you're here. During your visit, just make yourself at home.*

make short work of someone or something AND **make fast work of someone or something** skończyć szybko z kimś lub czymś. ❏ *I made short work of Tom so I could leave the office to play golf.* ❏ *Billy made fast work of his dinner so he could go out and play.*

make someone or something tick spowodować, by ktoś lub coś zaczęło działać lub funkcjonować. (Zwykle z *what.* Początkowo mówiło się tak w odniesieniu do zegarów lub zegarków.) ❏ *I don't know what makes it tick.* ❏ *What makes John tick? I just don't understand him.* ❏ *I took apart the radio to find out what made it tick.*

make someone's blood boil bardzo kogoś rozgniewać. ❏ *It just makes my blood boil to think of the amount of food that gets* *wasted around here.* ❏ *Whenever I think of that dishonest mess, it makes my blood boil.*

make someone's blood run cold zaszokować lub przerazić kogoś. ❏ *The terrible story in the newspaper made my blood run cold.* ❏ *I could tell you things about prisons that would make your blood run cold.*

make someone's hair stand on end bardzo kogoś przerazić. ❏ *The horrible scream made my hair stand on end.* ❏ *The ghost story made our hair stand on end.*

make someone's head spin Patrz następne hasło.

make someone's head swim AND **make someone's head spin 1.** oszołomić lub zdezorientować kogoś. ❏ *Riding in your car makes my head spin.* ❏ *Breathing the gas made my head swim.* **2.** zmieszać lub przytłoczyć kogoś. ❏ *All these numbers make my head swim.* ❏ *The physics lecture made my head spin.*

make someone's mouth water spowodować, by ktoś poczuł głód (na coś), spowodować, by pociekła mu ślinka. (Używane również dosłownie.) ❏ *That beautiful salad makes my mouth water.* ❏ *Talking about food makes my mouth water.*

make someone the scapegoat for something spowodować, by ktoś wziął winę na siebie. ❏ *They made Tom the scapegoat for the whole affair. It wasn't all his fault.* ❏ *Don't try to make me the scapegoat. I'll tell who really did it.*

make something from scratch zrobić coś zaczynając od podstawowych składników. ❏ *We made the cake from scratch, using no prepared ingredients.* ❏ *I didn't have a ladder, so I made one from scratch.*

make something up out of whole cloth AND **make up something out of whole cloth** stworzyć opowiadanie lub kłamstwo nie mając po temu żadnych faktów. (Klisza.) ❏ *I don't believe you. I think you made that up out of whole cloth.* ❏ *Ann* *made up her explanation out of whole cloth. There was not a bit of truth in it.*

make the feathers fly Patrz następne hasło.

make the fur fly AND **make the feathers fly** wywołać bójkę lub kłótnię. ❏ *When your mother gets home and sees what you've done, she'll really make the fur fly.* ❏ *When those two get together, they'll make the feathers fly. They hate each other.*

make the grade zadowalający; taki, jakiego oczekiwano. ❏ *I'm sorry, but your work doesn't exactly make the grade.* ❏ *This meal doesn't just make the grade. It is excellent.*

make up for lost time nadrobić coś; zrobić coś szybko. ❏ *Because we took so long eating lunch, we have to drive faster to make up for lost time. Otherwise we won't arrive on time.* ❏ *At the age of sixty, Bill learned to play golf. Now he plays every day. He's making up for lost time.*

march to a different drummer wierzyć w inny zestaw zasad. (Klisza.) ❏ *John is marching to a different drummer, and he doesn't come to our parties anymore.* ❏ *Since Sally started marching to a different drummer, she has had a lot of great new ideas.*

market, on the Patrz *on the market.*

means, beyond one's Patrz *beyond one's means.*

meet one's end umrzeć. ❏ *The dog met his end under the wheels of a car.* ❏ *I don't intend to meet my end until I'm 100 years old.*

meet one's match spotkać kogoś równego sobie. ❏ *John played tennis with Bill yesterday, and it looks as if John has finally met his match.* ❏ *Listen to Jane and Mary argue. I always thought that Jane was loud, but she has finally met her match.*

meet someone halfway zaproponować komuś kompromis. ❏ *No, I won't give in, but I'll meet you halfway.* ❏ *They settled the argument by agreeing to meet each other halfway.*

melt in one's mouth wspaniale smakować; [w odniesieniu do jedzenia] bardzo bogate i satysfakcjonujące. (Klisza.) ❑ *This cake is so good it'll melt in your mouth.* ❑ *John said that the food didn't exactly melt in his mouth.*

mend (one's) fences odnowić dobre stosunki (z kimś). (Również używane dosłownie.) ❑ *I think I had better get home and mend my fences. I had an argument with my daughter this morning.* ❑ *Sally called up her uncle to apologize and try to mend fences.*

mend, on the Patrz *on the mend.*

mention something in passing wspomnieć o czymś mimochodem; wspomnieć o czymś mówiąc o czymś innym. ❑ *He just happened to mention in passing that the mayor had resigned.* ❑ *John mentioned in passing that he was nearly eighty years old.*

mill, been through the Patrz *been through the mill.*

millstone about one's neck stały ciężar lub brak. ❑ *This huge and expensive house is a millstone about my neck.* ❑ *Bill's inability to read is a millstone about his neck.*

mind one's own business zajmować się tylko tym, co kogoś dotyczy. ❑ *Leave me alone, Bill. Mind your own business.* ❑ *I'd be fine if John would mind his own business.*

mind one's p's and q's uważać na dobre maniery; zwracać uwagę na drobne szczegóły zachowania. (Pochodzi od starej uwagi zwracanej dzieciom uczącym się alfabetu lub zecerom, którzy musieli uważać na różnice między p i q.) ❑ *When we go to the mayor's reception, please mind your p's and q's.* ❑ *I always mind my p's and q's when I eat at a restaurant with white tablecloths.*

mind, on one's Patrz *on one's mind.*

mind, out of one's Patrz *out of one's mind.*

mind's eye, in one's Patrz *in one's mind's eye.*

mint condition, in Patrz *in mint condition.*

Missouri, be from Patrz *be from Missouri.*

miss (something) by a mile bardzo daleko minąć cel. (Klisza.) ❑ *Ann shot the arrow and missed the target by a mile.* ❑ *"Good grief, you missed by a mile," shouted Sally.*

miss the point nie zrozumieć zasadniczej myśli, celu lub zamiaru. ❑ *I'm afraid you missed the point. Let me explain it again.* ❑ *You keep explaining, and I keep missing the point.*

mixed feelings (about someone or something), have Patrz *have mixed feelings (about someone or something).*

Money burns a hole in someone's pocket. ktoś wydaje tyle pieniędzy, ile tylko jest możliwe. (Tak jakby pieniądze bardzo się starały wydostać na zewnątrz.) ❑ *Sally can't seem to save anything. Money burns a hole in her pocket.* ❑ *If money burns a hole in your pocket, you never have any for emergencies.*

money, in the Patrz *in the money.*

money is no object nieważne, ile to kosztuje. ❑ *Please show me your finest automobile. Money is no object.* ❑ *I want the finest earrings you have. Don't worry about how much they cost because money is no object.*

Money is the root of all evil. przysłowie mówiące, że pieniądze są główną przyczyną wszelkiego zła. ❑ *Why do you work so hard to make money? It will just cause you trouble. Money is the root of all evil.* ❑ *Any thief in prison can tell you that money is the root of all evil.*

money talks pieniądze dają władzę i wpływają na to, by coś się stało lub rzeczy potoczyły się tak, jak ktoś chce. ❑ *Don't worry. I have a way of getting things done. Money talks.* ❑ *I can't compete against rich old Mrs. Jones. She'll get her way because money talks.*

money to burn, have Patrz *have money to burn.*

mood to do something, in no   Patrz *in no mood to do something.*

motions, go through the   Patrz *go through the motions.*

mouth, down in the   Patrz *down in the mouth.*

move heaven and earth to do something   zrobić ogromny wysiłek, żeby coś się stało. (Klisza. Nie używane dosłownie.) ❏ *"I'll move heaven and earth to be with you, Mary," said Bill.* ❏ *I had to move heaven and earth to get there on time.*

move, on the   Patrz *on the move.*

move up (in the world)   posunąć się naprzód i odnieść sukces. ❏ *The harder I work, the more I move up in the world.* ❏ *Keep your eye on John. He's really moving up.*

much ado about nothing   dużo hałasu o nic. (Klisza. Jest to tytuł sztuki Szekspira. Nie mylić *ado* z *adieu.*) ❏ *All the commotion about the new tax law turned out to be much ado about nothing.* ❏ *Your promises always turn out to be much ado about nothing.*

158

N

name only, in Patrz *in name only.*

nape of the neck, by the Patrz *by the nape of the neck.*

neck and neck dokładnie równy, zwłaszcza w odniesieniu do wyścigów lub konkursu. ❑ *John and Tom finished the race neck and
neck.* ❑ *Mary and Ann were neck and neck in the spelling contest.
Their scores were tied.*

neck (in something), up to one's Patrz *up to one's neck (in
something).*

neither fish nor fowl żadna dająca się rozpoznać rzecz. (Klisza.)
❑ *The car that they drove up in was neither fish nor fowl. It must
have been made out of spare parts.* ❑ *This proposal is neither fish
nor fowl. I can't tell what you're proposing.*

neither hide nor hair żadnego znaku ni wskazówki (kogoś lub
czegoś). (Klisza.) ❑ *We could find neither hide nor hair of him.
I don't know where he is.* ❑ *There has been no one here – neither
hide nor hair – for the last three days.*

nerve, of all the Patrz *of all the nerve.*

new lease on life odnowiony i na nowo ożywiony pogląd na życie; nowy start w życiu. (Klisza.) ❑ *Getting the job offer was a
new lease on life.* ❑ *When I got out of the hospital, I felt as if I had
a new lease on life.*

nick of time, in the Patrz *in the nick of time.*

nip and tuck prawie równy; niemal związany. ❑ *The horses ran nip and tuck for the first half of the race. Then my horse pulled a-head.* ❑ *In the football game last Saturday, both teams were nip and tuck throughout the game.*

nip something in the bud położyć kres czemuś we wczesnym stadium. (Klisza. Jakby ktoś nakłuwał pąk irytującej go rośliny.) ❑ *John is getting into bad habits, and it's best to nip them in the bud.* ❑ *There was trouble in the classroom, but the teacher nipped it in the bud.*

no (ifs, ands, or) buts about it absolutnie żadnej dyskusji, niezgody lub wątpliwości w odniesieniu do czegoś. (Klisza.) ❑ *I want you there exactly at eight, no ifs, ands, or buts about it.* ❑ *This is the best television set available for the money, no buts about it.*

no laughing matter poważna sprawa. (Klisza.) ❑ *Be serious. This is no laughing matter.* ❑ *This disease is no laughing matter. It's quite deadly.*

none the worse for wear nie gorzej, mimo wysiłku lub używania. ❑ *I lent my car to John. When I got it back, it was none the worse for wear.* ❑ *I had a hard day today, but I'm none the worse for wear.*

nosedive, go into a Patrz *go into a nosedive.*

nose in a book, have one's Patrz *have one's nose in a book.*

no skin off someone's nose Patrz następne hasło.

no skin off someone's teeth AND **no skin off someone's nose** żadnej trudności dla kogoś; żadnego problemu dla kogoś. (Klisza.) ❑ *It's no skin off my nose if she wants to act that way.* ❑ *She said it was no skin off her teeth if we wanted to sell the house.*

no spring chicken już niemłody. ❑ *I don't get around very well anymore. I'm no spring chicken, you know.* ❑ *Even though John is no spring chicken, he still plays tennis twice a week.*

not able to see the forest for the trees pozwolić na to, by zbyt wiele szczegółów zamazało istotę problemu. (Klisza. *Not able to* jest często zastępowane *can't*.) ❏ *The solution is obvious. You missed it because you can't see the forest for the trees.* ❏ *She suddenly realized that she hadn't been able to see the forest for the trees.*

not born yesterday doświadczony; wiedzący, jak to w świecie bywa. ❏ *I know what's going on. I wasn't born yesterday.* ❏ *Sally knows the score. She wasn't born yesterday.*

not have a leg to stand on [w dyspucie lub w sprawie] nie mieć żadnego poparcia. ❏ *You may think you're in the right, but you don't have a leg to stand on.* ❏ *My lawyer said I didn't have a leg to stand on, so I shouldn't sue the company.*

nothing but skin and bones AND **all skin and bones** bardzo chudy lub wynędzniały. ❏ *Bill has lost so much weight. He's nothing but skin and bones.* ❏ *That old horse is all skin and bones. I won't ride it.*

nothing flat, in Patrz *in nothing flat.*

Nothing ventured, nothing gained. przysłowie mówiące, że nie osiągniesz niczego, jeżeli nie spróbujesz. ❏ *Come on, John. Give it a try. Nothing ventured, nothing gained.* ❏ *I felt as if I had to take the chance. Nothing ventured, nothing gained.*

not hold water bez sensu; nielogiczne. (Używane w odniesieniu do pomysłów, argumentów, etc, nie zaś ludzi. Oznacza, że pomysł jest dziurawy.) ❏ *Your argument doesn't hold water.* ❏ *This scheme won't work because it won't hold water.*

not know enough to come in out of the rain bardzo głupi. (Klisza.) ❏ *Bob is so stupid he doesn't know enough to come in out of the rain.* ❏ *You can't expect very much from somebody who doesn't know enough to come in out of the rain.*

not know someone from Adam w ogóle kogoś nie znać. (Klisza.) ❏ *I wouldn't recognize John if I saw him. I don't know*

161

him from Adam. ❏ *What does she look like? I don't know her from Adam.*

not long for this world blisko śmierci. (Klisza.) ❏ *Our dog is nearly twelve years old and not long for this world.* ❏ *I'm so tired. I think I'm not long for this world.*

not open one's mouth AND **not utter a word** nie powiedzieć w ogóle nic; nic nie mówić (do nikogo). ❏ *Don't worry, I'll keep your secret. I won't even open my mouth.* ❏ *Have no fear. I won't utter a word.* ❏ *I don't know how they found out. I didn't even open my mouth.*

not set foot somewhere nie pójść gdzieś. ❏ *I wouldn't set foot in John's room. I'm very angry with him.* ❏ *He never set foot here.*

not show one's face nie pokazać się (gdzieś). ❏ *After what she said, she had better not show her face around here again.* ❏ *If I don't say I'm sorry, I'll never be able to show my face again.*

not sleep a wink w ogóle nie spać; nie zamknąć oczu nawet na tyle, ile trwa mrugnięcie. ❏ *I couldn't sleep a wink last night.* ❏ *Ann hasn't been able to sleep a wink for a week.*

not someone's cup of tea nie to, co ktoś lubi. (Klisza.) ❏ *Playing cards isn't her cup of tea.* ❏ *Sorry, that's not my cup of tea.*

not up to scratch AND **not up to snuff** niewystarczający. ❏ *Sorry, your paper isn't up to scratch. Please do it over again.* ❏ *The performance was not up to snuff.*

not up to snuff Patrz poprzednie hasło.

not utter a word Patrz pod *not open one's mouth.*

O

odd man out niezwykła lub nietypowa osoba lub rzecz. ❏ *I'm odd man out because I'm not wearing a tie.* ❏ *You had better learn to work a computer unless you want to be odd man out.*

odds to be against one, for the Patrz *for the odds to be against one.*

of all the nerve szokujące; jak śmiesz. (Mówiący wykrzykuje to wtedy, kiedy ktoś jest bardzo bezczelny lub ordynarny.) ❏ *How dare you talk to me that way! Of all the nerve!* ❏ *Imagine anyone coming to a formal dance in jeans. Of all the nerve!*

off base nierealistyczny; niedokładny; nieprawidłowy. (Używane również dosłownie w odniesieniu do baseballu.) ❏ *I'm afraid you're off base when you state that this problem will take care of itself.* ❏ *You're way off base!*

off-color **1.** niedokładny kolor (nie taki, jak ktoś chce). ❏ *The book cover used to be red, but now it's a little off-color.* ❏ *The wall was painted off-color. I think it was meant to be orange.* **2.** ordynarny, wulgarny lub niegrzeczny. ❏ *That joke you told was off-color and embarrassed me.* ❏ *The nightclub act was a bit off-color.*

off duty nie w pracy. ❏ *I'm sorry, I can't talk to you until I'm off duty.* ❏ *The police officer couldn't help me because he was off duty.*

off the air nie nadający (program radiowy lub telewizyjny). ❏ *The radio audience won't hear what you say when you're off the air.*

❏ *When the performers were off the air, the director told them how well they had done.*

off the record nieoficjalny; nieformalny. ❏ *This is off the record, but I disagree with the mayor on this matter.* ❏ *Although her comments were off the record, the newspaper published them anyway.*

off the top of one's head [powiedzieć coś] bez namysłu i bez przypominania sobie. ❏ *I can't think of the answer off the top of my head.* ❏ *Jane can tell you the correct amount off the top of her head.*

off to a running start z dobrym, szybkim początkiem, przodujące od startu. ❏ *I got off to a running start in math this year.* ❏ *The horses got off to a running start.*

of the first water najlepszego gatunku. (Pochodzi od mierzenia jakości pereł.) ❏ *This is a very fine pearl – a pearl of the first water.* ❏ *Tom is of the first water – a true gentleman.*

on active duty w walce lub gotowy do walki. (Wojskowe.) ❏ *The soldier was on active duty for ten months.* ❏ *That was a long time to be on active duty.*

on all fours na rękach i kolanach. ❏ *I dropped a contact lens and spent an hour on all fours looking for it.* ❏ *The baby can walk, but is on all fours most of the time anyway.*

on a waiting list [w odniesieniu do nzwiska] na liście ludzi oczekujących na możliwość zrobienia czegoś. (*A* może być zastąpione przez *the*.) ❏ *I couldn't get a seat on the plane, but I got on a waiting list.* ❏ *There is no room for you, but we can put your name on the waiting list.*

once in a blue moon bardzo rzadko. (Klisza.) ❏ *I seldom go to a movie – maybe once in a blue moon.* ❏ *I don't go into the city except once in a blue moon.*

on cloud nine   bardzo szczęśliwy. ❑ *When I got my promotion, I was on cloud nine.* ❑ *When the check came, I was on cloud nine for days.*

on duty   w pracy; aktualnie wykonujący pracę. ❑ *I can't help you now, but I'll be on duty in about an hour.* ❑ *Who is on duty here? I need some help.*

on earth AND **in creation; in the world**   zdumiewające; na Boga! (Używane dla zintensyfikowania wypowiedzi po *who, what, when, where, how, which*.) ❑ *What on earth do you mean?* ❑ *How in creation do you expect me to do that?* ❑ *Who in the world do you think you are?* ❑ *When on earth do you expect me to do this?*

one ear and out the other, go in   Patrz *go in one ear and out the other.*

one ear and out the other, in   Patrz *in one ear and out the other.*

One good turn deserves another.   przysłowie mówiące, że dobry uczynek powinien być odpłacony innym dobrym uczynkiem. ❑ *If he does you a favor, you should do him a favor. One good turn deserves another.* ❑ *Glad to help you out. One good turn deserves another.*

one in a hundred   Patrz pod *one in a thousand.*

one in a million   Patrz następne hasło.

one in a thousand AND **one in a hundred; one in a million**   jedyny w swoim rodzaju; jeden z nielicznych. ❑ *He's a great guy. He's one in million.* ❑ *Mary's one in a hundred – such a hard worker.*

One man's meat is another man's poison.   przysłowie mówiące, że upodobania jednego człowieka nie muszą być upodobaniami innego. ❑ *John just loves his new fur hat, but I think it is horrible. Oh, well, one man's meat is another man's poison.* ❑ *The neighbors are very fond of their dog even though it's ugly, loud, and smelly. I guess one man's meat is another man's poison.*

One's bark is worse than one's bite. przysłowie mówiące, że ktoś może grozić, ale nie musi wyrządzić krzywdy. ❏ *Don't worry about Bob. He won't hurt you. His bark is worse than his bite.* ❏ *She may scream and yell, but have no fear. Her bark is worse than her bite.*

one's better half czyjś współmałżonek. (Zwykle odosi się do żony.) ❏ *I think we'd like to come for dinner, but I'll have to ask my better half.* ❏ *I have to go home now to my better half. We are going out tonight.*

one's days are numbered [w odniesieniu do kogoś] stanąć twarzą w twarz ze śmiercią lub dymisją. (Klisza.) ❏ *If I don't get this contract, my days are numbered at this company.* ❏ *Uncle Tom has a terminal disease. His days are numbered.*

one's desk, away from Patrz *away from one's desk.*

one's eyes are bigger than one's stomach [w odniesieniu do kogoś] wziąć więcej jedzenia niż można zjeść. ❏ *I can't eat all this. I'm afraid that my eyes were bigger than my stomach.* ❏ *Try to take less food. Your eyes are bigger than your stomach at every meal.* ALSO: **have eyes bigger than one's stomach** chcieć więcej jedzenia niż ktoś ma możliwości zjeść. ❏ *I know I have eyes bigger than my stomach, so I won't take a lot of food.*

one's heart is in one's mouth Patrz pod *have one's heart in one's mouth.*

one's heart is set on something Patrz pod *have one's heart set on something.*

one's number is up przyszedł czyjś czas na śmierć lub na jakieś inne nieprzyjemne wydarzenie. ❏ *John is worried. He thinks his number is up.* ❏ *When my number is up, I hope it all goes fast.*

one's song and dance about something, go into Patrz pod *go into one's song and dance about something.*

one's tail is between one's legs Patrz *have one's tail between one's legs.*

one's words stick in one's throat   Patrz pod   *have one's words stick in one's throat.*

on one's feet   **1.** stojący; stojący na własnych nogach. ❑ *Get on your feet. They are playing the national anthem.* ❑ *I've been on my feet all day, and they hurt.* **2.** w dobrym zdrowiu, zwłaszcza po chorobie. ❑ *I hope to be back on my feet next week.* ❑ *I can help out as soon as I'm back on my feet.*

on one's honor   zgodnie z uroczystą przysięgą; szczerze obiecane. ❑ *On my honor, I'll be there on time.* ❑ *He promised on his honor that he'd pay me back next week.*

on one's mind   zajmujący czyjeś myśli; aktualnie w głowie. ❑ *You've been on my mind all day.* ❑ *Do you have something on your mind? You look so serious.*

on one's toes   czujny. ❑ *You have to be on your toes if you want to be in this business.* ❑ *My boss keeps me on my toes.*

on pins and needles   zmartwiony; w zawieszeniu. (Klisza.) ❑ *I've been on pins and needles all day, waiting for you to call with the news.* ❑ *We were on pins and needles until we heard that your plane landed safely.*

on second thought   pomyślawszy więcej o tym; znów coś rozważywszy. ❑ *On second thought, maybe you should sell your house and move into an apartment.* ❑ *On second thought, let's not go to a movie.*

on someone's doorstep   Patrz pod *at someone's doorstep.*

on someone's head   na kogoś. (Zwykle używany z *blame. On* można zastąpić *upon.*) ❑ *All the blame fell on their heads.* ❑ *I don't think that all the criticism should be on my head.*

on someone's or something's last legs   w odniesieniu do kogoś lub czegoś - prawie wykończony. ❑ *This building is on its last legs. It should be torn down.* ❑ *I feel as if I'm on my last legs. I'm really tired.*

on someone's say-so   w oparciu o czyjś autorytet; za czyimś przyzwoleniem. ❑ *I can't do it on your say-so. I'll have to get a written request.* ❑ BILL: *I canceled the contract with the A.B.C. Company.* BOB: *On whose say-so?*

on someone's shoulders   na kimś. (Używane zwykle z *responsibility. On* można zastąpić *upon.*) ❑ *Why should all the responsibility fall on my shoulders?* ❑ *She carries a tremendous amount of responsibility on her shoulders.*

on target   według planu; dokładnie jak zostało przewidziane. ❑ *Your estimate of the cost was right on target.* ❑ *My prediction was not on target.*

on the air   nadając (program radiowy lub telewizyjny). ❑ *The radio station came back on the air shortly after the storm.* ❑ *We were on the air for two hours.*

on the average   ogólnie; zwykle. ❑ *On the average, you can expect about a 10 percent failure.* ❑ *This report looks okay, on the average.*

on the bench   **1.** kierując posiedzeniem sądu. (Mówi się tak o sędziach.) ❑ *I have to go to court tomorrow. Who's on the bench?* ❑ *It doesn't matter who's on the bench. You'll get a fair hearing.* **2.** siedząc, czekając na szansę zagrania w grze. (W sporcie, takim jak basketball, football, soccer etc.) ❑ *Bill is on the bench now. I hope he gets to play.* ❑ *John played during the first quarter, but now he's on the bench.*

on the block   **1.** w miejskim bloku. ❑ *John is the biggest kid on the block.* ❑ *We had a party on the block last weekend.* **2.** w sprzedaży na aukcji; w aukcyjnym bloku. ❑ *We couldn't afford to keep up the house, so it was put on the block to pay the taxes.* ❑ *That's the finest painting I've ever seen on the block.*

on the button   idealnie prawidłowy; dokładnie na właściwym miejscu; dokładnie we właściwym czasie. ❑ *That's it! You're right on the button.* ❑ *He got here at one o'clock on the button.*

on the contrary odwrotnie. ❏ *I'm not ill. On the contrary, I'm very healthy.* ❏ *She's not in a bad mood. On the contrary, she's as happy as a lark.*

on the dot dokładnie we właściwym czasie. ❏ *I'll be there at noon on the dot.* ❏ *I expect to see you here at eight o'clock on the dot.*

on the go zajęty; w ruchu. ❏ *I'm usually on the go all day long.* ❏ *I hate being on the go all the time.*

on the heels of something wkrótce po czymś. ❏ *There was a rainstorm on the heels of the windstorm.* ❏ *The team held a victory celebration on the heels of their winning season.*

on the horizon coś, co ma nastąpić wkrótce. (Używane również dosłownie.) ❏ *Do you know what's on the horizon?* ❏ *Who can tell what's on the horizon?*

on the horns of a dilemma mający zdecydować się na wybór pomiędzy dwoma rzeczami, ludźmi, itp.; zawieszony pomiędzy jedną a drugą możliwością. ❏ *Mary found herself on the horns of a dilemma. She didn't know which to choose.* ❏ *I make up my mind easily. I'm not on the horns of a dilemma very often.*

on the hour co godzinę, o równej godzinie. ❏ *I have to take this medicine every hour on the hour.* ❏ *I expect to see you there on the hour, not one minute before and not one minute after.*

on the house coś, co jest rozdawane za darmo przez sprzedające-go. (Używane również dosłownie.) ❏ *"Here," said the waiter, "have a cup of coffee on the house."* ❏ *I went to a restaurant last night. I was the ten thousandth customer, so my dinner was on the house.*

on the level uczciwy; godny zaufania i otwarty. (Również z strictly.) ❏ *How can I be sure you're on the level?* ❏ *You can trust Sally. She's on the level.*

on the market dostępny dla sprzedaży; oferowany do sprzedaży. ❏ *I had to put my car on the market.* ❏ *This is the finest home computer on the market.*

on the mend dochodzący do zdrowia. ❑ *My cold was terrible, but I'm on the mend now.* ❑ *What you need is some hot chicken soup. Then you'll really be on the mend.*

on the move w ruchu; szczęśliwie dziejący się. ❑ *What a busy day. Things are really on the move at the store.* ❑ *When all the buffalo were on the move across the plains, it must have been very exciting.*

on the QT cicho; w tajemnicy. ❑ *The company president was making payments to his wife on the QT.* ❑ *The mayor accepted a bribe on the QT.*

on the spot **1.** dokładnie we właściwym miejscu; dokładnie we właściwym czasie. ❑ *It's noon, and I'm glad you're all here on the spot. Now we can begin.* ❑ *I expect you to be on the spot when and where trouble arises.* **2.** w kłopocie; w trudnej sytuacji. ❑ *There is a problem in the department I manage, and I'm really on the spot.* ❑ *I hate to be on the spot when it's not my fault.*

on the spur of the moment nagle; spontanicznie. ❑ *We decided to go on the spur of the moment.* ❑ *I had to leave town on the spur of the moment.*

on the tip of one's tongue prawie powiedziane; prawie przypomniane. (Jakby słowo miało zeskoczyć z czyjegoś języka i zostać wypowiedziane.) ❑ *I have his name right on the tip of my tongue. I'll think of it in a second.* ❑ *John had the answer on the tip of his tongue, but Ann said it first.*

on the wagon nie pijący alkoholu; już więcej nie pijący alkoholu. (Również używane dosłownie. Odnosi się do *"water wagon."*) ❑ *None for me, thanks. I'm on the wagon.* ❑ *Look at John. I don't think he's on the wagon anymore.*

on the wrong track idąc niewłaściwą drogą; postępując według niesłusznych założeń. (Używane również dosłownie w odniesieniu do pociągów, psów myśliwskich, etc.) ❑ *You'll never get the right answer. You're on the wrong track.* ❑ *They won't get it figured out because they are on the wrong track.*

on thin ice w ryzykownej sytuacji. ❑ *If you try that you'll really be on thin ice. That's too risky.* ❑ *If you don't want to find yourself on thin ice, you must be sure of your facts.* ALSO: **skate on thin ice** w ryzykownej sytuacji. (Używane również dosłownie.) ❑ *I try to stay well informed so I don't end up skating on thin ice when the teacher asks me a question.*

on tiptoe stojąc lub idąc na przedniej części stopy bez ciężaru na piętach. (Robi się tak, by się podnieść lub iść bardzo cicho.) ❑ *I had to stand on tiptoe in order to see over the fence.* ❑ *I came in late and walked on tiptoe so I wouldn't wake anybody up.*

on top zwycięsko; sławny lub znany z czegoś. ❑ *I have to study day and night to keep on top.* ❑ *Bill is on top in his field.*

on top of the world wspaniale się czujący; cudowny; ekstatyczny. (Klisza.) ❑ *Wow, I feel on top of the world.* ❑ *Since he got a new job, he's on top of the world.*

on trial sądzony w sądzie. ❑ *My sister is on trial today, so I have to go to court.* ❑ *They placed the suspected thief on trial.*

on vacation nieobecny, na wakacjach. ❑ *Where are you going on vacation this year?* ❑ *I'll be away on vacation for three weeks.*

open a can of worms rozpocząć serię problemów; stworzyć niepotrzebne komplikacje. (*Can of worms* oznacza "chaos". Również z *open up* i z różnymi przydawkami, takimi jak *new, whole, another*, jak w przykładach.) ❑ *Now you are opening a whole new can of worms.* ❑ *How about cleaning up this mess before you open up a new can of worms?*

open one's heart (to someone) wyjawić komuś swoje najbardziej skryte myśli. ❑ *I always open my heart to my spouse when I have a problem.* ❑ *It's a good idea to open your heart every now and then.*

open one's mouth, not Patrz *not open one's mouth.*

open Pandora's box rozpocząć serię nieoczekiwanych problemów. (Klisza.) ❑ *When I asked Jane about her problems, I didn't* *know I had opened Pandora's box.* ❑ *You should be cautious with people who are upset. You don't want to open Pandora's box.*

order, out of Patrz *out of order.*

other side of the tracks biedniejsza część miasta, często blisko szos. (Szczególnie z *from the* lub *live on the.*) ❑ *Who cares if she's from the other side of the tracks?* ❑ *I came from a poor family – we lived on the other side of the tracks.*

ounce of prevention is worth a pound of cure, An. Patrz *An ounce of prevention is worth a pound of cure.*

out and about zdolny do wyjścia i poruszania się; wystarczająco zdrowy, żeby móc wyjść. ❑ *Beth has been ill, but now she's out and about.* ❑ *As soon as I feel better, I'll be able to get out and about.*

out cold AND **out like a light** nieprzytomny. ❑ *I fell and hit my head. I was out cold for about a minute.* ❑ *Tom fainted! He's out like a light!*

out in left field niezwykły i ekscentryczny. ❑ *Sally is a lot of fun, but she's sort of out in left field.* ❑ *What a strange idea. It's really out in left field.*

out like a light Patrz pod *out cold.*

out of a clear blue sky AND **out of the blue** nagle; bez ostrzeżenia. (Klisza.) ❑ *Then, out of a clear blue sky, he told me he was leaving.* ❑ *Mary appeared on my doorstep out of the blue.*

out of all proportion w przesadzonej proporcji; w nierealistycznej proporcji w porównaniu do czegoś innego; (przenośnie) krzywy. (*all* można opuścić.) ❑ *This problem has grown out of all proportion.* ❑ *Yes, this thing is way out of proportion.* ALSO: **blow something out of all proportion** spowodować, by coś urosło do rozmiaru nieproporcjonalnego w stosunku do czegoś innego. (*all* można opuścić.) ❑ *The press has blown this issue out of all proportion.* ❑ *Let's be reasonable. Don't blow this thing out of proportion.*

out of circulation   **1.** niedostępne do użytku lub do pożyczenia. (Zwykle używane w odniesieniu do materiałów bibliotecznych.) ❑ *I'm sorry, but the book you want is temporarily out of circulation.* ❑ *How long will it be out of circulation?* **2.** nieaktywny towarzysko. ❑ *I don't know what's happening because I've been out of circulation for a while.* ❑ *My cold has kept me out of circulation for a few weeks.*

out of commission   **1.** [w odniesieniu do statków] aktualnie nie działający; nie pod komendą. ❑ *This vessel will remain out of commission for another month.* ❑ *The ship has been out of commission since repairs began.* **2.** zepsuty, nie działający, nie nadający się do użytku. ❑ *My watch is out of commission and is running slowly.* ❑ *I can't run in the marathon because my knees are out of commission.*

out of gas   **1.** nie mający więcej benzyny (w samochodzie, ciężarówce, etc.). ❑ *We can't go any farther. We're out of gas.* ❑ *This car will be completely out of gas in a few more miles.* **2.** zmęczony; wyczerpany; zużyty. ❑ *What a day! I've been working since morning, and I'm really out of gas.* ❑ *This electric clock is out of gas. I'll have to get a new one.* ALSO: **run out of gas** zużyć całą dostępną benzynę. ❑ *I hope we don't run out of gas.*

out of hand   natychmiast i bez konsultowania się z nikim; bezzwłocznie. ❑ *I can't answer that out of hand. I'll check with the manager and call you back.* ❑ *The offer was so good that I accepted it out of hand.*

out of luck   bez szczęścia; mający pecha. ❑ *If you wanted some ice-cream, you're out of luck.* ❑ *I was out of luck. I got there too late to get a seat.*

out of one's element   w nienaturalnej lub niewygodnej sytuacji. ❑ *When it comes to computers, I'm out of my element.* ❑ *Sally's out of her element in math.*

out of one's head   Patrz następne hasło.

out of one's mind AND **out of one's head; out of one's senses**   głupi i nierozsądny; szalony; nieracjonalny. ❑ *Why did* *you do that? You must be out of your mind!* ❏ *Good grief, Tom! You have to be out of your head!* ❏ *She's acting as if she were out of her senses.*

out of one's senses Patrz poprzednie hasło.

out of order 1. nie we właściwym porządku. ❏ *This book is out of order. Please put it in the right place on the shelf.* ❏ *You're out of order, John. Please get in line after Jane.* 2. nie postępujący według właściwej parlamentarnej procedury. ❏ *I was declared out of order by the president.* ❏ *Ann inquired, "Isn't a motion to table the question out of order at this time?"*

out of practice wykonujący coś źle ze względu na brak praktyki. ❏ *I used to be able to play the piano extremely well, but now I'm out of practice.* ❏ *The baseball players lost the game because they were out of practice.*

out of print [w odniesieniu do książek] nie być dłużej dostępny w sprzedaży. (Porównaj z *in print.*) ❏ *The book you want is out of print, but perhaps I can find a used copy for you.* ❏ *It was published nearly ten years ago, so it's probably out of print.*

out of season 1. niedostępny teraz w sprzedaży. ❏ *Sorry, oysters are out of season. We don't have any.* ❏ *Watermelon is out of season in the winter.* 2. prawnie zakazane do odłowienia lub polowania. ❏ *Are salmon out of season?* ❏ *I caught a trout out of season and had to pay a fine.*

out of service nie do użytku; nie działające. ❏ *Both elevators are out of service, so I had to use the stairs.* ❏ *The washroom is temporarily out of service.*

Out of sight, out of mind. przysłowie mówiące, że jeśli czegoś nie widzisz, to o tym nie myślisz. ❏ *When I go home, I put my schoolbooks away so I won't worry about doing my homework. After all, out of sight, out of mind.* ❏ *Jane dented the fender on her car. It's on the right side, so she doesn't have to look at it. Like they say, out of sight, out of mind.*

out of sorts nie czujący się dobrze; zgryźliwy i drażliwy. ❑ *I've been out of sorts for a day or two. I think I'm coming down with something.* ❑ *The baby is out of sorts. Maybe she's getting a tooth.*

out of the blue Patrz pod *out of a clear blue sky.*

out of the corner of one's eye [widząc coś] w przebłysku. ❑ *I saw someone do it out of the corner of my eye. It might have been Jane who did it.* ❑ *I only saw the accident out of the corner of my eye. I don't know who is at fault.*

out of the frying pan into the fire ze złej sytuacji w gorszą. (Klisza. Jeżeli na patelni jest gorąco, to w ogniu jeszcze goręcej.) ❑ *When I tried to argue about my fine for a traffic violation, the judge charged me with contempt of court. I really went out of the frying pan into the fire.* ❑ *I got deeply in debt. Then I really got out of the frying pan into the fire when I lost my job.*

out of the hole wyjść z długów. (Używane również dosłownie.) ❑ *I get paid next week, and then I can get out of the hole.* ❑ *I can't seem to get out of the hole. I keep spending more money than I earn.*

out of the question niemożliwe; niedozwolone. ❑ *I'm sorry, but it's out of the question.* ❑ *You can't go to Florida this spring. We can't afford it. It's out of the question.*

out of the red wyjść z długów. ❑ *This year our firm is likely to get out of the red before fall.* ❑ *If we can cut down on expenses, we can get out of the red fairly soon.*

out of the running już nie brany pod uwagę; wyeliminowany z zawodów. ❑ *After the first part of the diving meet, three members of our team were out of the running.* ❑ *After the scandal was made public, I was no longer in the running. I pulled out of the election.*

out of the woods po przejściu fazy krytycznej; wyść z nieznanego. ❑ *When the patient got out of the woods, everyone relaxed.* ❑ *I can give you a better prediction for your future health when you are out of the woods.*

out of thin air   znikąd. ❏ *Suddenly – out of thin air – the messenger appeared.* ❏ *You just made that up out of thin air.*

out of this world   cudowny; nadzwyczajny. (Klisza. Używane również dosłownie.) ❏ *This pie is just out of this world.* ❏ *Look at you! How lovely you look – simply out of this world.*

out of tune (with someone or something)   **1.** w muzycznej harmonii z kimś lub czymś. ❏ *The oboe is out of tune with the flute.* ❏ *The flute is out of tune with John.* ❏ *They are all out of tune.* **2.** (przenośnie) nie w harmonii i nie w zgodzie. ❏ *Your proposal is out of tune with my ideas of what we should be doing.* ❏ *Let's get all our efforts in tune.*

out of turn   nie we właściwym czasie; nie we właściwym porządku. ❏ *We were permitted to be served out of turn, because we had to leave early.* ❏ *Bill tried to register out of turn and was sent away.*

out on a limb   w niebezpiecznej pozycji; podejmując szansę. ❏ *I don't want to go out on a limb, but I think I'd agree to your request.* ❏ *She really went out on a limb when she agreed.*

out on the town   świętując w jednym lub więcej miejscach w mieście. ❏ *I'm really tired. I was out on the town until dawn.* ❏ *We went out on the town to celebrate our wedding anniversary.*

outside, at the   Patrz *at the outside.*

out to lunch   wychodząc na lunch poza miejsce pracy. ❏ *I'm sorry, but Sally Jones is out to lunch. May I take a message?* ❏ *She's been out to lunch for nearly two hours. When will she be back?*

overboard, go   Patrz *go overboard.*

over the hill   za stary, żeby coś zrobić. ❏ *Now that Mary's forty, she thinks she's over the hill.* ❏ *My grandfather was over eighty before he felt as if he was over the hill.*

over the hump   po najtrudniejszej części. ❏ *This is a difficult project, but we're over the hump now.* ❏ *I'm halfway through – over the hump – and it looks as if I may get finished after all.*

over the long haul   przez stosunkowo długi okres czasu. ❏ *Over the long haul, it might be better to invest in stocks.* ❏ *Over the long haul, everything will turn out all right.*

over the short haul   na najbliższą przszłość. ❏ *Over the short haul, you'd be better off to put your money in the bank.* ❏ *Over the short haul, you may wish you had done something different. But things will work out all right.*

over the top   osiągnąwszy więcej niż jeden cel. ❏ *Our fund-raising campaign went over the top by $3,000.* ❏ *We didn't go over the top. We didn't even get half of what we set out to collect.*

P

packed (in) like sardines bardzo ciasno zapakowany. (Klisza. Możliwych jest wiele odmian, jak w przykładach.) ❏ *It was terribly crowded there. We were packed in like sardines.* ❏ *The bus was full. The passengers were packed like sardines.* ❏ *They packed us in like sardines.*

paddle one's own canoe zrobić coś samemu; być samotnym. (Klisza. Może być też używane dosłownie.) ❏ *I've been left to paddle my own canoe too many times.* ❏ *Sally isn't with us. She's off paddling her own canoe.*

pad the bill dokładać niekonieczne elementy do rachunku po to, by cały koszt był wyższy. ❏ *The plumber had padded the bill with things we didn't need.* ❏ *I was falsely accused of padding the bill.*

paint the town red szalone nocne uroczystości w mieście. (Nie używane dosłownie.) ❏ *Let's all go out and paint the town red!* ❏ *Oh, do I feel awful. I was out all last night, painting the town red.*

pale, beyond the Patrz *beyond the pale.*

part and parcel Patrz pod *bag and baggage.*

part someone's hair podejść bardzo blisko do kogoś. (Zwykle z przesadą. Używane też dosłownie.) ❏ *That plane flew so low that* *it nearly parted my hair.* ❑ *He punched at me and missed. He only parted my hair.*

par, up to Patrz *up to par.*

pass the buck przerzucić winę na kogoś; przerzucić odpowiedzialność na kogoś. ❑ *Don't try to pass the buck! It's your fault, and everybody knows it.* ❑ *Some people try to pass the buck whenever they can.*

pass the hat starać się zebrać pieniądze na jakiś dobroczynny projekt. ❑ *Bob is passing the hat to collect money to buy flowers for Ann.* ❑ *He's always passing the hat for something.*

pay an arm and a leg (for something) AND **pay through the nose (for something)** za dużo za coś zapłacić. ❑ *I hate to have to pay an arm and a leg for a tank of gas.* ❑ *If you shop around, you won't have to pay an arm and a leg.* ❑ *Why should you pay through the nose?* ALSO: **cost an arm and a leg** kosztować zbyt dużo. ❑ *It cost an arm and a leg, so I didn't buy it.*

pay one's debt (to society) odbyć wyrok za przestępstwo, zwykle odsiedzieć w więzieniu. ❑ *The judge said that Mr. Simpson had to pay his debt to society.* ❑ *Mr. Brown paid his debt in state prison.*

pay one's dues **1.** zapłacić składki za przynależność do organizacji. ❑ *If you haven't paid your dues, you can't come to the club picnic.* ❑ *How many people have paid their dues?* **2.** zapracować prawo do czegoś ciężką pracą lub cierpieniem. ❑ *He worked hard to get to where he is today. He paid his dues and did what he was told.* ❑ *I have every right to be here. I paid my dues!*

pay the piper stanąć twarzą w twarz z rezultatami swoich działań; otrzymać karę za coś. (Klisza.) ❑ *You can put off paying your debts only so long. Eventually you'll have to pay the piper.* ❑ *You* *can't get away with that forever. You'll have to pay the piper someday.*

pay through the nose (for something) Patrz pod *pay an arm and a leg (for something)*.

penny saved is a penny earned, A. Patrz *A penny saved is a penny earned.*

penny-wise and pound-foolish przysłowie mówiące, że głupio jest tracić dużo pieniędzy po to, by zarobić niewiele. (Klisza.) ❑ *Sally shops very carefully to save a few cents on food, then charges the food to a charge card that costs a lot in annual interest. That's being penny-wise and pound-foolish.* ❑ *John drives thirty miles to buy gas for three cents a gallon less than it costs here. He's really penny-wise and pound-foolish.*

Perish the thought. Niech ci nawet nie przyjdzie do głowy myśleć o tym. (Literackie.) ❑ *If you should become ill – perish the thought – I'd take care of you.* ❑ *I'm afraid that we need a new car. Perish the thought.*

pick up the tab zapłacić rachunek. (Podnieść rachunek i zapłacić go.) ❑ *Whenever we go out, my father picks up the tab.* ❑ *Order whatever you want. The company is picking up the tab.*

pie in the sky przyszła nagroda, zwłaszcza po śmierci. (Klisza. Wzięte z dłuższego wyrażenia *"pie in the sky by and by when you die."*) ❑ *Are you nice to people just because of pie in the sky, or do you really like them?* ❑ *Don't hold out for a big reward, you know – pie in the sky.*

pillar to post, from Patrz *from pillar to post.*

pink (of condition), in the Patrz *in the pink (of condition).*

pins and needles, on Patrz *on pins and needles.*

pitch in (and help) weź się do pracy i pomóż. ❑ *Pick up a paint-brush and pitch in and help.* ❑ *Why don't some of you pitch in? We need all the help we can get.*

pitch someone a curve (ball) zaskoczyć kogoś niespodziewanym działaniem lub wydarzeniem. (Używane również dosłownie w odniesieniu do zaokrąglonej piłki w baseballu.) ❑ *You really pitched me a curve ball when you said I had done a poor job. I did my best.* ❑ *You asked Tom a hard question. You certainly pitched him a curve.*

plain as day, as Patrz *as plain as day.*

plain as the nose on one's face, as Patrz *as plain as the nose on one's face.*

play ball (with someone) **1.** zagrać z kimś w piłkę. (Zauważ specjalne użycie z odniesieniem do baseballu w drugim przykładzie.) ❑ *When will our team play ball with yours?* ❑ *Suddenly, the umpire shouted, "Play ball!" and the game began.* **2.** współpracować z kimś. ❑ *Look, friend, if you play ball with me, everything will work out all right.* ❑ *Things would go better for you if you'd learn to play ball.*

play both ends (against the middle) [w odniesieniu do kogoś] zagrać tak, by ustawić dwie strony przeciwko sobie (dla własnej korzyści.) ❑ *I told my brother that Mary doesn't like him. Then I told Mary that my brother doesn't like her. They broke up, so now I can have the car this weekend. I succeeded in playing both ends against the middle.* ❑ *If you try to play both ends, you're likely to get in trouble with both sides.*

play by ear Patrz pod *play something by ear.*

play cat and mouse (with someone) (dosłownie i w przenośni) chwytać i uwalniać kogoś raz po razie. (Klisza.) ❑ *The police played cat and mouse with the suspect until they had sufficient*

181

evidence to make an arrest. ❑ *Tom had been playing cat and mouse with Ann. Finally she got tired of it and broke up with him.*

play fast and loose (with someone or something) działać nieuważnie, bezmyślnie i nieodpowiedzialnie. ❑ *I'm tired of your playing fast and loose with me. Leave me alone.* ❑ *Bob got fired for playing fast and loose with the company's money.* ❑ *If you play fast and loose like that, you can get into a lot of trouble.*

play it safe być bezpiecznym lub działać bezpiecznie; robić coś bezpiecznie. ❑ *You should play it safe and take your umbrella.* ❑ *If you have a cold or the flu, play it safe and go to bed.*

play one's cards close to one's vest Patrz następne hasło.

play one's cards close to the chest AND **play one's cards close to one's vest** [w odniesieniu do kogoś] pracować lub negocjować w sposób ostrożny i prywatnie. (Nawiązuje do trzymania kart blisko siebie, tak by nikt nie zauważył, co ktoś trzyma w garści.) ❑ *It's hard to figure out what John is up to because he plays his cards close to his chest.* ❑ *Don't let them know what you're up to. Play your cards close to your vest.*

play second fiddle (to someone) być w pozycji podrzędnej do kogoś. ❑ *I'm tired of playing second fiddle to John.* ❑ *I'm better trained than he, and I have more experience. I shouldn't play second fiddle.*

play something by ear **1.** umieć zagrać jakiś fragment muzyczny po wysłuchaniu go kilka razy, bez zaglądania do nut. ❑ *I can play "Stardust" by ear.* ❑ *Some people can play Chopin's music by ear.* **2.** AND **play by ear** dobrze grać na jakimś instrumencie bez formalnego kształcenia w tej dziedzinie. ❑ *John can play the piano by ear.* ❑ *If I could play by ear, I wouldn't have to take lessons – or practice!*

play the field umawiać się z wieloma różnymi ludźmi raczej niż z jedną osobą. ❑ *When Tom told Ann good-bye, he said he wanted to* *play the field.* ❑ *He said he wanted to play the field while he was still young.*

play to the gallery grać a sposób, który uzyska silną akceptację publiczności; grać pod publiczność. ❑ *John is a competent actor, but he has a tendency to play to the gallery.* ❑ *When he made the rude remark, he was just playing to the gallery.*

play with fire podjąć duże ryzyko. (Również używane dosłownie.) ❑ *If you accuse her of stealing, you'll be playing with fire.* ❑ *I wouldn't try that if I were you – unless you like playing with fire.*

pocket, have someone in one's Patrz *have someone in one's pocket.*

poke fun (at someone) śmiać się z kogoś; ośmieszać kogoś. ❑ *Stop poking fun at me! It's not nice.* ❑ *Bob is always poking fun.*

poke one's nose in(to something) AND **stick one's nose in(to something)** wtrącać się w coś; pakować się w coś. (Nie u-żywane dosłownie.) ❑ *I wish you'd stop poking your nose into my business.* ❑ *She was too upset for me to stick my nose in and ask what was wrong.*

poles apart, be Patrz *be poles apart.*

poor as a church mouse, as Patrz *as poor as a church mouse.*

poor taste, in Patrz *in poor taste.*

pop the question oświadczyć się komuś. ❑ *I was surprised when he popped the question.* ❑ *I've been waiting for years for someone to pop the question.*

pot calling the kettle black, the Patrz *the pot calling the kettle black.*

pot, go to Patrz *go to pot.*

pound a beat zrobić obchód. (Zwykle mówi się tak o oficerach patroli policyjnych.) ❑ *The patrolman pounded the same beat for years and years.* ❑ *Pounding a beat will wreck your feet.*

pound the pavement chodzić po ulicach szukając zajęcia. ❑ *I spent two months pounding the pavement after the factory I worked for closed.* ❑ *Hey, Bob. You'd better get busy pounding those nails unless you want to be out pounding the pavement.*

pour cold water on something AND **dash cold water on something; throw cold water on something** zniechęcić do zrobienia czegoś; ochłodzić entuzjazm do czegoś. (W tym znaczeniu nie używane dosłownie.) ❑ *When my father said I couldn't have the car, he poured cold water on my plans.* ❑ *John threw cold water on the whole project by refusing to participate.*

pour it on thick Patrz pod *lay it on thick.*

pour money down the drain stracić pieniądze; wyrzucić pieniądze. ❑ *What a waste! You're just pouring money down the drain.* ❑ *Don't buy any more of that low-quality merchandise. That's just throwing money down the drain.*

pour oil on troubled water uspokoić sprawy. (Klisza. Olej wylany na morze podczas burzy nieco uspokaja wody.) ❑ *That was a good thing to say to John. It helped pour oil on troubled water. Now he looks happy.* ❑ *Bob is the kind of person who pours oil on troubled water.*

practice, out of Patrz *out of practice.*

practice what you preach robić to, co radzisz innym ludziom, aby robili. (Klisza.) ❑ *If you'd practice what you preach, you'd be better off.* ❑ *You give good advice. Why not practice what you preach?*

premium, at a Patrz *at a premium.*

press one's luck Patrz pod *push one's luck.*

press someone to the wall Patrz pod *push someone to the wall.*

pretty as a picture, as Patrz *as pretty as a picture.*

Pretty is as pretty does. powinieneś robić miłe rzeczy, jeśli chcesz być uważany za miłego. (Klisza.) ❑ *Now, Sally. Let's be nice. Pretty is as pretty does.* ❑ *My great-aunt always used to say "pretty is as pretty does" to my sister.*

price on one's head, have a Patrz *have a price on one's head.*

prick up one's ears uważnie nasłuchiwać. ❑ *At the sound of my voice, my dog pricked up her ears.* ❑ *I pricked up my ears when I heard my name mentioned.*

prime, in one's or its Patrz *in one's or its prime.*

prime of life, in the Patrz *in the prime of life.*

print, in Patrz *in print.*

print, out of Patrz *out of print.*

promise the moon (to someone) AND **promise someone the moon** robić komuś ekstrawaganckie obietnice. ❑ *Bill will promise you the moon, but he won't live up to his promises.* ❑ *My boss promised the moon, but only paid the minimum wage.*

proportion, out of all Patrz *out of all proportion.*

proud as a peacock, as Patrz *as proud as a peacock.*

public eye, in the Patrz *in the public eye.*

pull oneself up (by one's own bootstraps) osiągnąć coś dzięki swoim własnym wysiłkom. (Klisza.) ❏ *They simply don't have the resources to pull themselves up by their own bootstraps.* ❏ *If I could have pulled myself up, I'd have done it by now.*

pull someone's leg zażartować, zakpić z kogoś lub zrobić z kogoś głupca. ❏ *You don't mean that. You're just pulling my leg.* ❏ *Don't believe him. He's just pulling your leg.*

pull someone's or something's teeth zmniejszyć władzę kogoś lub czegoś. (Używane również dosłownie.) ❏ *The mayor tried to pull the teeth of the new law.* ❏ *The city council pulled the teeth of the new mayor.*

pull something out of a hat AND **pull something out of thin air** stworzyć coś jakby za pomocą czarów. ❏ *This is a serious problem, and we just can't pull a solution out of a hat.* ❏ *I'm sorry, but I don't have a pen. What do you want me to do, pull one out of thin air?*

pull something out of thin air Patrz poprzednie hasło.

pull the rug out (from under someone) sprawić, by ktoś stał się nieskuteczny. ❏ *The treasurer pulled the rug out from under the mayor.* ❏ *Things were going along fine until the treasurer pulled the rug out.*

pull the wool over someone's eyes oszukać kogoś. (Klisza.) ❏ *You can't pull the wool over my eyes. I know what's going on.* ❏ *Don't try to pull the wool over her eyes. She's too smart.*

pull up stakes przenieść się na inne miejsce. (Jakby przenosić kijki od namiotów.) ❏ *I've been here long enough. It's time to pull up stakes.* ❏ *I hate the thought of having to pull up stakes.*

push one's luck AND **press one's luck** oczekiwać stałego dobrego losu; oczekiwać stałej ucieczki od pecha. ❑ *You're okay so far, but don't push your luck.* ❑ *Bob pressed his luck too much and got into a lot of trouble.*

push someone to the wall AND **press someone to the wall** ustawić kogoś w pozycji, w której możliwy jest tylko jeden wybór; ustawić kogoś w pozycji defensywnej. (Używane również dosłownie.) ❑ *There was little else I could do. They pushed me to the wall.* ❑ *When we pressed him to the wall, he told us where the cookies were hidden.*

put a bee in someone's bonnet Patrz pod *have a bee in one's bonnet.*

put all one's eggs in one basket zaryzykować wszystko od razu. (Klisza. Często używane w formie przeczącej. Jeżeli koszyk się upuści, wszystkie jajka zostaną potłuczone.) ❑ *Don't put all your eggs in one basket. Then everything won't be lost if there is a catastrophe.* ❑ *John only applied to the one college he wanted to go to. He put all his eggs in one basket.*

put in a good word (for someone) powiedzieć coś komuś dla poparcia tego kogoś. ❑ *I hope you get the job. I'll put in a good word for you.* ❑ *Yes, I want the job. If you see the boss, please put in a good word.*

put in one's two cents (worth) dodać swoje komentarze (do czegoś). (Implikuje, że komentarze te nie muszą być wielkiej wartości, ale jednak powinny być dodane.) ❑ *Can I put in my two cents worth?* ❑ *Sure, go ahead – put your two cents in.*

put on airs zachowywać się wyniośle. ❑ *Stop putting on airs. You're just human like the rest of us.* ❑ *Ann is always putting on airs. You'd think she was a queen.*

put one's best foot forward działać lub ukazywać się z najlepszej strony; starać się zrobić najlepsze wrażenie. (Klisza.) ❑ *When you apply for a job, you should always put your best foot forward.*

187

❑ *I try to put my best foot forward whenever I meet someone for the first time.*

put one's cards on the table AND **lay one's cards on the table** odkryć wszystko; być z kimś szczerym i uczciwym. (Tak jakby ktoś w pewnym momencie gry w karty przedstawił wszystkie karty trzymane przez siebie.) ❑ *Come on, John, lay your cards on the table. Tell me what you really think.* ❑ *Why don't we both put our cards on the table?*

put one's dibs on something Patrz pod *have dibs on something.*

put one's foot in it Patrz następne hasło.

put one's foot in one's mouth AND **put one's foot in it; stick one's foot in one's mouth** powiedzieć coś, czego pożałowałeś; powiedzieć coś głupiego, obraźliwego lub krzywdzącego. ❑ *When I told Ann that her hair was more beautiful than I had ever seen it, I really put my foot in my mouth. It was a wig.* ❑ *I put my foot in it by telling John's secret.*

put one's hand to the plow zacząć wykonywać jakieś wielkie i ważne zadanie; podjąć jakiś wielki wysiłek. (Klisza. Rzadko używane dosłownie.) ❑ *If John would only put his hand to the plow, he could do an excellent job.* ❑ *You'll never accomplish anything if you don't put your hand to the plow.*

put one's nose to the grindstone zająć się pracą. (Nigdy nie używane dosłownie. Również z *have* i *get*, jak w przykładach.) ❑ *The boss told me to put my nose to the grindstone.* ❑ *I've had my nose to the grindstone ever since I started working here.* ❑ *If the other people in this office would get their noses to the grindstone, more work would get done.* ALSO: **keep one's nose to the grindstone** być stale zajętym przez jakiś czas. ❑ *The manager told me to keep my nose to the grindstone or be fired.*

put one's oar in AND **put in one's oar** udzielić pomocy; wtrącić się ze swoją radą; dodać swą pomoc do ogólnego wysiłku. ❏ *You don't need to put your oar in. I don't need your advice.* ❏ *I'm sorry. I shouldn't have put in my oar.*

put one's shoulder to the wheel zająć się pracą. (Nie używane dosłownie.) ❏ *You won't accomplish anything unless you put your shoulder to the wheel.* ❏ *I put my shoulder to the wheel and finished the job quickly.*

put one through one's paces sprawić, by ktoś zademonstrował, co potrafi; sprawić, by ktoś całościowo wykonał swą pracę. ❏ *The boss really put me through my paces today. I'm tired.* ❏ *I tried out for a part in the play, and the director really put me through my paces.*

put on one's thinking cap zacząć poważnie myśleć. (Klisza. Nie używane dosłownie. Zwykle w stosunku do dzieci.) ❏ *All right now, let's put on our thinking caps and do some arithmetic.* ❏ *It's time to put on our thinking caps, children.*

put someone or something out to pasture wysłać kogoś lub coś na emeryturę. (Początkowo mówiło się tak o koniach zbyt starych do pracy.) ❏ *Please don't put me out to pasture. I have lots of good years left.* ❏ *This car has reached the end of the line. It's time to put it out to pasture.*

put someone or something to bed **1.** [z *someone*] pomóc komuś – zwykle dziecku – pójść do łóżka. ❏ *Come on, Billy, it's time for me to put you to bed.* ❏ *I want grandpa to put me to bed.* **2.** [z *something*] skończyć pracę nad czymś i przesłać to do następnego etapu produkcji, zwłaszcza w wydawnictwach. ❏ *This edition is finished. Let's put it to bed.* ❏ *Finish the editing of this book and put it to bed.*

put someone or something to sleep **1.** zabić kogoś lub coś. (Eufemizm.) ❏ *We had to put our dog to sleep.* ❏ *The robber said he'd put us to sleep forever if we didn't cooperate.* **2.** uśpić kogoś lub coś, być może za pomocą medykamentów lub za pomocą anestezji. ❏ *The doctor put the patient to sleep before the operation.* ❏ *I put the cat to sleep by stroking its tummy.* **3.** [z *someone*] znudzić kogoś. (Dosłowne.) ❏ *That dull lecture put me to sleep.* ❏ *Her long story almost put me to sleep.*

put someone's nose out of joint obrazić kogoś; spowodować, by ktoś poczuł się zlekceważony lub obrażony. (Nie używane dosłownie.) ❏ *I'm afraid I put his nose out of joint by not inviting him to the picnic.* ❏ *There is no reason to put your nose out of joint. I meant no harm.*

put someone through the wringer utrudnić komuś życie. (Jakby ktoś wyżymał odzież w staromodnej wyżymaczce.) ❏ *They are really putting me through the wringer at school.* ❏ *The boss put Bob through the wringer over this contract.*

put someone to shame wprawić kogoś w zakłopotanie; zawstydzić kogoś. ❏ *Your excellent efforts put us all to shame.* ❏ *I put him to shame by telling everyone about his bad behavior.*

put someone to the test sprawdzić kogoś; zobaczyć, co ktoś może osiągnąć. ❏ *I think I can jump that far, but no one has ever put me to the test.* ❏ *I'm going to put you to the test right now!*

put something on ice AND **put something on the back burner** odwlec coś; zawiesić coś. (W tym znaczeniu żadne z tych wyrażeń nie jest używane dosłownie.) ❏ *I'm afraid that we'll have to put your project on ice for a while.* ❏ *Just put your idea on ice and keep it there till we get some money.*

put something on paper napisać coś; napisać lub wydrukować umowę. ❏ *You have a great idea for a novel. Now put it on paper.* ❏ *I'm sorry, I can't discuss your offer until I see something in writing. Put it on paper, and then we'll talk.*

put something on the back burner Patrz pod *put something on ice*.

put something on the cuff kupić coś na kredyt; dodać coś do swojego kredytowego bilansu. (Tak jakby ktoś notował zakup na mankiecie koszuli.) ❏ *I'll take two of those, and please put them on the cuff.* ❏ *I'm sorry, Tom. We can't put anything more on the cuff.*

put something on the line AND **lay something on the line** mówić zdecydowanie i bezpośrednio o czymś. (Być może odwołuje się do`linii frontu.) ❑ *She was very mad. She put it on the line, and we have no doubt about what she meant.* ❑ *All right, you kids! I'm going to lay it on the line. Don't ever do that again if you know what's good for you.*

put something through its paces zademonstrować, jak dobrze coś działa; zademonstrować wszystko, co coś może zdziałać. ❑ *I was down by the barn, watching Sally put her horse through its paces.* ❑ *This is an excellent can opener. Watch me put it through its paces.*

put the cart before the horse mieć sprawy poustawiane w złym porządku; mieć sprawy pomieszane. (Odwołuje się do wyimaginowanego zaprzęgnięcia konia do wozu w ten sposób, że wóz porusza się przed koniem, zamiast koń go ciągnąć. (Klisza. Również z *have*.) ❑ *You're eating your dessert! You've put the cart before the horse.* ❑ *Slow down and get organized. Don't put the cart before the horse!* ❑ *John has the cart before the horse in most of his projects.*

put two and two together wywnioskować coś z dostępnych informacji. (Klisza.) ❑ *Well, I put two and two together and came up with an idea of who did it.* ❑ *Don't worry. John won't figure it out. He can't put two and two together.*

put up a (brave) front wydawać się odważnym (nawet jeżeli się nie jest). ❑ *Mary is frightened, but she's putting up a brave front.* ❑ *If she weren't putting up a front, I'd be more frightened than I am.*

put words into someone's mouth mówić za kogoś bez pozwolenia. ❑ *Stop putting words into my mouth. I can speak for myself.* ❑ *The lawyer was scolded for putting words into the witness's mouth.*

Put your money where your mouth is! polecenie, by ktoś przestał się chwalić, a założył się. (Klisza. Nie używane dosłownie.) ❑ *I'm tired of your bragging about your skill at betting. Put your money where your mouth is!* ❑ *You talk about betting, but you don't bet. Put your money where your mouth is!*

Q

QT, on the Patrz *on the QT.*

quake in one's boots Patrz pod *shake in one's boots.*

question, out of the Patrz *out of the question.*

quick as a wink, as Patrz *as quick as a wink.*

quick on the draw Patrz następne hasło.

quick on the trigger AND **quick on the draw** **1.** szybki, jeśli chodzi o wyciąganie rewolweru i strzelanie. ❏ *Some of the old cowboys were known to be quick on the trigger.* ❏ *Wyatt Earp was particularly quick on the draw.* **2.** szybki w reakcji na coś. ❏ *John gets the right answer before anyone else. He's really quick on the trigger.* ❏ *Sally will probably win the quiz game. She's really quick on the draw.*

quick on the uptake szybki w rozumieniu (czegoś). ❏ *Just because I'm not quick on the uptake, it doesn't mean I'm stupid.* ❏ *Mary understands jokes before anyone else because she's so quick on the uptake.*

quiet as a mouse, as Patrz *as quiet as a mouse.*

R

rack and ruin, go to Patrz *go to rack and ruin.*

rack one's brain(s) bardzo się starać o czymś myśleć. ❏ *I racked my brains all afternoon, but couldn't remember where I put the book.* ❏ *Don't waste any more time racking your brain. Go borrow the book from the library.*

rags, in Patrz *in rags.*

rags to riches, from Patrz *from rags to riches.*

rain cats and dogs bardzo mocno padać. (Klisza. Nie używane dosłownie, oczywiście.) ❏ *It's raining cats and dogs. Look at it pour!* ❏ *I'm not going out in that storm. It's raining cats and dogs.*

rain or shine niezależnie, czy pada deszcz, czy świeci słońce. (Klisza.) ❏ *Don't worry. I'll be there rain or shine.* ❏ *We'll hold the picnic – rain or shine.*

rains but it pours, It never. Patrz *It never rains but it pours.*

raise one's sights postwić sobie wysokie cele. ❏ *When you're young, you tend to raise your sights too high.* ❏ *On the other hand, some people need to raise their sights.*

raise some eyebrows lekko kogoś zaszokować lub zaskoczyć (zrobiwszy lub powiedziwawszy coś). (*Some* można zastąpić *a few, someone's, a lot of*, ect.) ❏ *What you just said may raise* *some eyebrows, but it shouldn't make anyone really angry.* ❏ *John's sudden marriage to Ann raised a few eyebrows.*

rake someone over the coals AND **haul someone over the coals** bardzo ostro kogoś złajać. ❏ *My mother hauled me over the coals for coming in late last night.* ❏ *The manager raked me over the coals for being late again.*

reach first base (with someone or something) Patrz pod *get to first base (with someone or something).*

read between the lines wywnioskować coś (z czegoś); próbować zrozumieć, co oznacza coś, co nie jest napisane jasno lub otwarcie. (Zwykle używane przenośnie. Niekoniecznie odnosi się do informacji na piśmie.) ❏ *After listening to what she said, if you read between the lines, you can begin to see what she really means.* ❏ *Don't believe everything you hear. Learn to read between the lines.*

read someone like a book bardzo dobrze kogoś rozumieć. ❏ *I've got John figured out. I can read him like a book.* ❏ *Of course I understand you. I read you like a book.*

read someone the riot act ostro kogo złajać. ❏ *The manager read me the riot act for coming in late.* ❏ *The teacher read the students the riot act for their failure to do their assignments.*

record, for the Patrz *for the record.*

record, off the Patrz *off the record.*

red, in the Patrz *in the red.*

red, out of the Patrz *out of the red.*

regular as clockwork, as Patrz *as regular as clockwork.*

return mail, by Patrz *by return mail.*

ride, go along for the Patrz *go along for the ride.*

ride roughshod over someone or something traktować kogoś lub coś z lekceważeniem lub pogardą. ❑ *Tom seems to ride roughshod over his friends.* ❑ *You shouldn't have come into our town to ride roughshod over our laws and our traditions.*

ride the gravy train żyć w luksusie. ❑ *If I had a million dollars, I sure could ride the gravy train.* ❑ *I wouldn't like loafing. I don't want to ride the gravy train.*

riding for a fall ryzykując porażkę lub wypadek, zwykle z powodu zbytniego zadufania. ❑ *Tom drives too fast, and he seems too sure of himself. He's riding for a fall.* ❑ *Bill needs to eat better and get more sleep. He's riding for a fall.*

right, in the Patrz *in the right.*

right mind, in one's Patrz *in one's right mind.*

right off the bat natychmiast; pierwsza rzecz. (Wydaje się, że wyrażenie nawiązuje do piłki i kija w baseballu, ale pierwotnie prawdopodobnie odnosiło się do kija krykietowego.) ❑ *When he was learning to ride a bicycle, he fell on his head right off the bat.* ❑ *The new manager demanded new office furniture right off the bat.*

right-of-way, have the Patrz *have the right-of-way.*

ring in the new year obchodzić początek nowego roku o północy 31 grudnia. (Jak gdyby głos kościelnych dzwonów świętował nadejście Nowego Roku.) ❑ *We are planning a big party to ring in the new year.* ❑ *How did you ring in the new year?*

risk one's neck (to do something) ryzykować fizyczną szkodę po to, by coś osiągnąć. ❑ *Look at that traffic! I refuse to risk my neck just to cross the street to buy a paper.* ❑ *I refuse to risk my neck at all.*

rob Peter to pay Paul zabrać jednemu by dać drugiemu. (Klisza.) ❑ *Why borrow money to pay your bills? That's just robbing Peter to pay Paul.* ❑ *There's no point in robbing Peter to pay Paul. You still will be in debt.*

rob the cradle poślubić lub spotykać się z kimś znacznie młodszym. (Jak gdyby ktoś zadawał się z niemowlęciem.) ❑ *I hear that Bill is dating Ann. Isn't that sort of robbing the cradle? She's much younger than he is.* ❑ *Uncle Bill – who is nearly eighty – married a thirty-year-old woman. That is really robbing the cradle.*

rock and a hard place, between a Patrz *between a rock and a hard place.*

rock the boat spowodować niepotrzebny kłopot; zakłócić stabilną i zadowalającą sytuację. (Często w formie przeczącej.) ❑ *Look, Tom, everything is going fine here. Don't rock the boat!* ❑ *You can depend on Tom to mess things up by rocking the boat.*

rolling stone gathers no moss, A. Patrz *A rolling stone gathers no moss.*

roll out the red carpet for someone Patrz pod *get the red-carpet treatment.*

Rome wasn't built in a day. ważne rzeczy nie stają się w ciągu jednej nocy. (Klisza.) ❑ *Don't expect a lot to happen right away. Rome wasn't built in a day, you know.* ❑ *Don't be anxious about how fast you are growing. Rome wasn't built in a day.*

roof, go through the Patrz *go through the roof.*

round figures, in Patrz *in round figures.*

round numbers, in Patrz *in round numbers.*

rub elbows with someone AND **rub shoulders with someone** blisko z kimś współpracować. ❑ *I don't care to rub elbows* *with someone who acts like that!* ❑ *I rub shoulders with John at work. We are good friends.*

rub shoulders with someone Patrz poprzednie hasło.

rub someone's fur the wrong way AND **rub someone the wrong way** zirytować kogoś. (Tak jakby ktoś głaskał ulubione zwierzę pod włos, w ten sposób je drażniąc. Drugie hasło wywodzi się z pierwszego.) ❑ *I'm sorry I rubbed your fur the wrong way. I didn't mean to upset you.* ❑ *Don't rub her the wrong way!*

rub someone the wrong way Patrz poprzednie hasło.

rule the roost przewodzić, zwłaszcza w domu. ❑ *Who rules the roost at your house?* ❑ *Our new office manager really rules the roost.*

run a fever AND **run a temperature** mieć wyższą niż normalnie temperaturę; mieć gorączkę. ❑ *I ran a fever when I had the flu.* ❑ *The baby is running a temperature and is grouchy.*

run (around) in circles Patrz następne hasło.

run around like a chicken with its head cut off AND **run (around) in circles** biegać szaleńczo i bezcelowo; być w stanie chaosu. (Klisza.) ❑ *I spent all afternoon running around like a chicken with its head cut off.* ❑ *If you run around in circles, you'll never get anything done.* ❑ *Get organized and stop running in circles.*

run a taut ship Patrz pod *run a tight ship.*

run a temperature Patrz pod *run a fever.*

run a tight ship AND **run a taut ship** prowadzić statek lub organizację w sposób porządny i zdyscyplinowany. (*Taut* i *tight* znaczą to samo. *Taut* jest poprawnym wyrażeniem żeglarskim.) ❑ *The* *new office manager really runs a tight ship.* ❏ *Captain Jones is known for running a taut ship.*

run for one's life uciec by ratować swe życie. ❏ *The dam has burst! Run for your life!* ❏ *The captain told us all to run for our lives.*

run in the family [o charakterystycznej cesze] występować u wszystkich lub u większości członków rodziny. ❏ *My grand-parents lived well into their nineties, and it runs in the family.* ❏ *My brothers and I have red hair. It runs in the family.*

run into a stone wall dojść do bariery dalszego postępu. (Używane również dosłownie.) ❏ *We've run into a stone wall in our investigation.* ❏ *Algebra was hard for Tom, but he really ran into a stone wall with geometry.*

running, out of the Patrz *out of the running.*

running start, off to a Patrz *off to a running start.*

run out of gas Patrz pod *out of gas.*

run someone ragged przebiegać ostro i szybko dla kogoś; być przepracowanym. ❏ *This busy season is running us all ragged at the store.* ❏ *What a busy day. I ran myself ragged.*

run to seed AND **go to seed** zniszczony i zaniedbany. (Mówi się tak zwłaszcza o trawnikach, które potrzebują opieki.) ❏ *Look at that lawn. The whole thing has run to seed.* ❏ *Pick things up around here. This place is going to seed. What a mess!*

S

safe and sound bezpieczny i cały lub zdrowy. (Klisza.) ❏ *It was a rough trip, but we got there safe and sound.* ❏ *I'm glad to see you here safe and sound.*

same boat, in the Patrz *in the same boat.*

same breath, in the Patrz *in the same breath.*

same token, by the Patrz *by the same token.*

save something for a rainy day zarezerwować coś – zwykle pieniądze – na jakieś przyszłe potrzeby. (Klisza. Również używane dosłownie. *Save something* można zastąpić *put something aside, hold something back, keep something,* itd.) ❏ *I've saved a little money for a rainy day.* ❏ *Keep some extra candy for a rainy day.*

save the day osiągnąć dobry wynik wtedy, kiedy oczekiwano złego. ❏ *The team was expected to lose, but Sally made many points and saved the day.* ❏ *Your excellent speech saved the day.*

say Jack Robinson, before you can Patrz *before you can say Jack Robinson.*

say-so, on someone's Patrz *on someone's say-so.*

scarce as hens' teeth, as Patrz *as scarce as hens' teeth.*

scarcer than hens' teeth Patrz pod *as scarce as hens' teeth.*

scot-free, go Patrz *go scot-free.*

scrape the bottom of the barrel wybrać wśród najgorszych; wybrać z tego, co pozostało. (Jakby się ktoś zdecydował na ostatnią i najgorszą możliwość.) ❑ *You've bought a bad-looking car. You really scraped the bottom of the barrel to get that one.* ❑ *The worker you sent over was the worst I've ever seen. Send me another – and don't scrape the bottom of the barrel.*

scrape (with someone or something), have a Patrz *have a scrape (with someone or something).*

scratch, not up to Patrz *not up to scratch.*

scratch the surface właśnie zaczynać czegoś dociekać; zbadać tylko powierzchowny aspekt czegoś. ❑ *The investigation of the governor's staff revealed some suspicious dealing. It is thought that the investigators have just scratched the surface.* ❑ *We don't know how bad the problem is. We've only scratched the surface.*

scream bloody murder Patrz pod *cry bloody murder.*

screw up one's courage nabierać odwagi. ❑ *I guess I have to screw up my courage and go to the dentist.* ❑ *I spent all morning screwing up my courage to take my driver's test.*

sea (about something), at Patrz *at sea (about something).*

search something with a fine-tooth comb Patrz pod *go over something with a fine-tooth comb.*

season, in Patrz *in season.*

season, out of Patrz *out of season.*

seat of one's pants, by the Patrz *by the seat of one's pants.*

second childhood, in one's Patrz *in one's second childhood.*

second nature to someone łatwy i naturalny dla kogoś. ❑ *Swimming is second nature to Jane.* ❑ *Driving is no problem for Bob. It's second nature to him.*

second thought, on Patrz *on second thought.*

seed, go to Patrz *go to seed.*

see eye to eye (about something) AND **see eye to eye on something** spoglądać na coś w ten sam sposób co ktoś inny. ❏ *John and Ann see eye to eye about the new law. Neither of them likes it.* ❏ *That's interesting because they rarely see eye to eye.*

see eye to eye on something Patrz poprzednie hasło.

see the forest for the trees, not able to Patrz *not able to see the forest for the trees.*

see the (hand)writing on the wall wiedzieć, że coś na pewno się wydarzy. (Klisza.) ❏ *If you don't improve your performance, they'll fire you. Can't you see the writing on the wall?* ❏ *I know I'll get fired. I can see the handwriting on the wall.*

see the light (at the end of the tunnel) przewidzieć koniec kłopotów po jakimś długim okresie czasu. ❏ *I had been horribly ill for two months before I began to see the light at the end of the tunnel.* ❏ *I began to see the light one day in early spring. At that moment, I knew I'd get well.*

see the light, begin to Patrz *begin to see the light.*

see the light (of day) dotrzeć do końca bardzo zapracowanego czasu. ❏ *Finally, when the holiday season was over, we could see the light of day. We had been so busy!* ❏ *When business lets up for a while, we'll be able to see the light.*

sell like hot cakes [w odniesieniu do czegoś] być bardzo szybko sprzedanym. ❏ *The delicious candy sold like hot cakes.* ❏ *The fancy new cars were selling like hot cakes.*

sell someone a bill of goods spowodować, by ktoś uwierzył w coś, co jest nieprawdą; oszukać kogoś. ❏ *Don't pay any attention to what John says. He's just trying to sell you a bill of goods.* ❏ *I'm not selling you a bill of goods. What I say is true.*

sell someone or something short nie doceniać kogoś lub czegoś; nie widzieć dobrych cech kogoś lub czegoś. ❑ *This is a very good restaurant. Don't sell it short.* ❑ *When you say that John isn't interested in music, you're selling him short. Did you know he plays the violin quite well?*

send one about one's business odesłać kogoś, zwykle w sposób mało przyjazny. ❑ *Is that annoying man on the telephone again? Please send him about his business.* ❑ *Ann, I can't clean up the house with you running around. I'm going to have to send you about your business.*

send someone packing odesłać kogoś; zdymisjonować kogoś, prawdopodobnie szorstko. ❑ *I couldn't stand him anymore, so I sent him packing.* ❑ *The maid proved to be so incompetent that I had to send her packing.*

send someone to the showers odsunąć gracza od gry i odesłać go z pola, boiska etc. (Sportowe.) ❑ *John played so badly that the coach sent him to the showers after the third quarter.* ❑ *After the fist fight, the coaches sent both players to the showers.*

senses, out of one's Patrz *out of one's senses.*

separate the men from the boys odseparować kogoś kompetentnego od mniej kompetentnych. ❑ *This is the kind of task that separates the men from the boys.* ❑ *This project requires a lot of thinking. It'll separate the men from the boys.*

separate the sheep from the goats podzielić ludzi na dwie grupy. ❑ *Working in a place like this really separates the sheep from the goats.* ❑ *We can't go on with the game until we separate the sheep from the goats. Let's see who can jump the farthest.*

serve as a guinea pig [w odniesieniu do kogoś] służyć jako obiekt eksperymentów; pozwolić przeprowadzać na sobie jakieś testy. (Klisza.) ❑ *Try it on someone else! I don't want to serve as a guinea pig!* ❑ *Jane agreed to serve as a guinea pig. She'll be the one to try out the new flavor of ice-cream.*

serve someone right [w odniesieniu do jakiegoś aktu lub wydarzenia] sprawiedliwie kogoś ukarać za zrobienie czegoś. ❑ *John copied off my test paper. It would serve him right if he fails the test.* ❑ *It'd serve John right if he got arrested.*

service, out of Patrz *out of service.*

set foot somewhere pójść gdzieś lub wejść gdzieś. (Często w formie przeczącej.) ❑ *If I were you, I wouldn't set foot in that town.* ❑ *I wouldn't set foot in her house! Not after the way she spoke to me.*

set foot somewhere, not Patrz *not set foot somewhere.*

set great store by someone or something mieć pozytywne oczekiwania w stosunku do kogoś lub czegoś; mieć duże nadzieje w odniesieniu do kogoś lub czegoś. ❑ *I set great store by my computer and its ability to help me in my work.* ❑ *We set great store by John because of his quick mind.*

set one back on one's heels zaskoczyć, zaszokować lub przytłoczyć kogoś. ❑ *Her sudden announcement set us all back on our heels.* ❑ *The manager scolded me, and that really set me back on my heels.*

set one's heart on something Patrz pod *have one's heart set on something.*

set one's sights on something wybrać coś jako swój cel. ❑ *I set my sights on a master's degree from the state university.* ❑ *Don't set your sights on something you cannot possibly do.*

set someone's teeth on edge **1.** [W odniesieniu do kwaśnego lub gorzkiego smaku] podrażnić podniebienie i mieć w związku z tym zabawne uczucie. ❑ *Have you ever eaten a lemon? It'll set your teeth on edge.* ❑ *I can't stand food that sets my teeth on edge.* **2.** [w odniesieniu do człowieka lub do hałasu] drażnić lub działać na nerwy. ❑ *Please don't scrape your fingernails on the blackboard! It sets my teeth on edge!* ❑ *Here comes Bob. He's so annoying. He really sets my teeth on edge.*

set the world on fire robić ekscytujące, przynoszące sławę i chwałę rzeczy. (Nie używane dosłownie. Często w formie przeczącej.) ❑ *I'm not very ambitious. I don't want to set the world on fire.* ❑ *You don't have to set the world on fire. Just do a good job.*

seventh heaven, in Patrz *in seventh heaven.*

shake in one's boots AND **quake in one's boots** przestraszyć się; trząść się ze strachu. ❑ *I was shaking in my boots because I had to go see the manager.* ❑ *Stop quaking in your boots, Bob. I'm not going to fire you.*

Shape up or ship out. albo się poprawić (w pracy lub w zachowaniu), albo odejść lub zrezygnować. (Klisza.) ❑ *Okay, Tom. That's the end. Shape up or ship out!* ❑ *John was late again, so I told him to shape up or ship out.*

shed crocodile tears ronić fałszywe łzy; udawać, że się płacze. ❑ *The child wasn't hurt, but she shed crocodile tears anyway.* ❑ *He thought he could get his way if he shed crocodile tears.*

shoe fits, wear it, If the. Patrz *If the shoe fits, wear it.*

shoe is on the other foot, The. Patrz *The shoe is on the other foot.*

shoe on the other foot, have the Patrz *have the shoe on the other foot.*

shoot from the hip **1.** wystrzelić z rewolweru trzymanego przy boku, zwykle przy biodrze. (Zwiększa to szybkość wystrzału.) ❑ *When I lived at home on the farm, my father taught me to shoot from the hip.* ❑ *I quickly shot the snake before it bit my horse. I'm glad I learned to shoot from the hip.* **2.** mówić otwarcie i szczerze. ❑ *John has a tendency to shoot from the hip, but he generally speaks the truth.* ❑ *Don't pay any attention to John. He means no harm. It's just his nature to shoot from the hip.*

short haul, over the Patrz *over the short haul.*

short order, in Patrz *in short order.*

short supply, in Patrz *in short supply.*

shot in the arm podnieta; coś co dodaje energii. ❏ *Thank you for cheering me up. It was a real shot in the arm.* ❏ *Your friendly greeting card was just what I needed – a real shot inthe arm.*

shoulders, on someone's Patrz *on someone's shoulders.*

should have stood in bed powinien pozostać w łóżku. (Nie ma nic wspólnego ze staniem.) ❏ *What a horrible day! I should have stood in bed.* ❏ *The minute I got up and heard the news this morning, I knew I should have stood in bed.*

show one's face, not Patrz *not show one's face.*

show one's (true) colors pokazać, co się rzeczywiście lubi lub myśli. ❏ *Whose side are you on, John? Come on. Show your colors.* ❏ *It's hard to tell what Mary is thinking. She never shows her true colors.*

show someone the ropes Patrz pod *know the ropes.*

sick as a dog, as Patrz *as sick as a dog.*

sight, out of mind, Out of. Patrz *Out of sight, out of mind.*

signed, sealed, and delivered formalnie i oficjalnie podpisane; [w odniesieniu do oficjalnego dokumentu] wyegzekwowany. (Klisza.) ❏ *Here is the deed to the property – signed, sealed, and delivered.* ❏ *I can't begin work on this project until I have the contract signed, sealed, and delivered.*

sign one's own death warrant (przenośnie) podpisać papier skazujący siebie na śmierć. (Klisza.) ❏ *I wouldn't ever gamble a large sum of money. That would be signing my own death warrant.* ❏ *The killer signed his own death warrant when he walked into the police station and gave himself up.*

sign on the dotted line umieścić swój podpis na kontrakcie lub innym ważnym dokumencie. (Klisza.) ❏ *This agreement isn't* *properly concluded until we both sign on the dotted line.* ❑ *Here are the papers for the purchase of your car. As soon as you sign on the dotted line, that beautiful, shiny automobile will be all yours!*

sink one's teeth into something (Klisza.) **1.** ugryźć coś, zwłaszcza coś specjalnego. ❑ *I can't wait to sink my teeth into a nice juicy steak.* ❑ *Look at that chocolate cake! Don't you want to sink your teeth into that?* **2.** zdobyć szansę zrobienia czegoś, nauczenia się czegoś lub kontrolowania czegoś. ❑ *That appears to be a very challenging assignment. I can't wait to sink my teeth into it.* ❑ *Being the manager of this department is a big task. I'm very eager to sink my teeth into it.*

sink or swim odnieść sukces lub porażkę. (Klisza.) ❑ *After I've studied and learned all I can, I have to take the test and sink or swim.* ❑ *It's too late to help John now. It's sink or swim for him.*

sit on one's hands nic nie zrobić; nie pomóc. (Nie używane dosłownie.) ❑ *When we needed help from Mary, she just sat on her hands.* ❑ *We need the cooperation of everyone. You can't sit on your hands!* ALSO: **sit on its hands** [dla publiczności] odmówić oklasków. (Nie używane dosłownie.) ❑ *We saw a very poor performance of the play. The audience sat on its hands for the entire play.*

sit tight czekać; czekać cierpliwie. (Niekoniecznie odnosi się do siedzenia.) ❑ *Just relax and sit tight. I'll be right with you.* ❑ *We were waiting in line for the gates to open when someone came out and told us to sit tight because it wouldn't be much longer before we could go in.*

sitting duck, like a Patrz *like a sitting duck.*

sitting on a powder keg w ryzykownej i wybuchowej sytuacji; w sytuacji, kiedy w każdej chwili może się zdarzyć coś niebezpiecznego. (Nie używane dosłownie. Beczka prochu to beczka z prochem strzelniczym.) ❑ *Things are very tense at work. The whole office is sitting on a powder keg.* ❑ *The fire at the oil field seems* *to be under control for now, but all the workers there are sitting on a powder keg.*

sit up and take notice być czujnym i uważać. ❏ *A loud noise from the front of the room caused everyone to sit up and take notice.* ❏ *The company wouldn't pay any attention to my complaints. When I had my lawyer write them a letter, they sat up and took notice.*

sixes and sevens, at Patrz *at sixes and sevens.*

six of one and half a dozen of the other wszystko jedno w jaki sposób. (Klisza.) ❏ *It doesn't matter to me which way you do it. It's six of one and half a dozen of the other.* ❏ *What difference does it make? They're both the same − six of one and half a dozen of the other.*

skate on thin ice Patrz pod *on thin ice.*

skeleton in the closet ukryta i szokująca tajemnica; ukryty fakt o kimś. (Często w liczbie mnogiej. Jakby ktoś ukrył w komórce ponury fakt morderstwa.) ❏ *You can ask anyone about how reliable I am. I don't mind. I don't have any skeletons in the closet.* ❏ *My uncle was in jail for a day once. That's our family's skeleton in the closet.*

skin off someone's nose, no Patrz *no skin off someone's nose.*

skin off someone's teeth, no Patrz *no skin off someone's teeth.*

skin of one's teeth, by the Patrz *by the skin of one's teeth.*

sleep a wink, not Patrz *not sleep a wink.*

sleep like a log bardzo mocno spać. (Klisza. Oczywiście, nie używane dosłownie.) ❏ *Nothing can wake me up. I usually sleep like a* *log.* ❏ *Everyone in our family sleeps like a log, so no one heard the fire engines in the middle of the night.*

sleep on something przemyśleć coś w nocy; ważyć decyzję w nocy. ❏ *I don't know whether I agree to do it. Let me sleep on it.* ❏ *I slept on it, and I've decided to accept your offer.*

slip of the tongue błąd w mówieniu, kiedy słowo nie jest poprawnie wypowiedziane, lub kiedy mówiący powiedział coś, czego powiedzieć nie chciał. (Tak jakby język zrobił fałszywy krok.) ❏ *I didn't mean to tell her that. It was a slip of the tongue.* ❏ *I failed to understand the instructions because the speaker made a slip of the tongue at an important point.*

slip one's mind [o czymś, co miało być zapamiętane] zapomniane. (Tak jakby myśl uciekła komuś z głowy.) ❏ *I meant to go to the grocery store on the way home, but it slipped my mind.* ❏ *My birthday slipped my mind. I guess I wanted to forget it.*

slippery as an eel, as Patrz *as slippery as an eel.*

slip through someone's fingers umknąć od kogoś; zgubić ślad (kogoś lub czegoś). ❏ *I had a copy of the book you want, but somehow it slipped through my fingers.* ❏ *There was a detective following me, but I managed to slip through his fingers.*

Slow and steady wins the race. przysłowie mówiące, że konsekwencja i zdecydowanie poprowadzą do sukcesu, lub (dosłownie), w rozsądnym tempie zwycięża się wyścig. ❏ *I worked my way through college in six years. Now I know what they mean when they say, "Slow and steady wins the race."* ❏ *Ann won the race because she started off slowly and established a good pace. The other runners tried to sprint the whole distance, and they tired out before the final lap. Ann's trainer said, "You see! I told you! Slow and steady wins the race."*

smack-dab in the middle dokładnie pośrodku. ❏ *I want a big helping of mashed potatoes with a glob of butter smack-dab in the* *middle.* ❏ *Tom and Sally were having a terrible argument, and I was trapped – smack-dab in the middle.*

smart as a fox, as Patrz *as smart as a fox.*

smoke, go up in Patrz *go up in smoke.*

snail's pace, at a Patrz *at a snail's pace.*

snuff, not up to Patrz *not up to snuff.*

snug as a bug in a rug, as Patrz *as snug as a bug in a rug.*

sober as a judge, as Patrz *as sober as a judge.*

soft as a baby's bottom, as Patrz *as soft as a baby's bottom.*

soft spot in one's heart for someone or something, have a Patrz *have a soft spot in one's heart for someone or something.*

soil one's hands Patrz pod *get one's hands dirty.*

soon as possible, as Patrz *as soon as possible.*

so quiet you could hear a pin drop Patrz *so still you could hear a pin drop.*

sorts, out of Patrz *out of sorts.*

so still you could hear a pin drop AND **so quiet you could hear a pin drop** bardzo cichy. (Klisza. Występuje również z *can.*) ❏ *When I came into the room, it was so still you could hear a pin drop. Then everyone shouted, "Happy birthday!"* ❏ *Please be quiet. Be so quiet you can hear a pin drop.*

sow one's wild oats robić w młodości szalone i głupie rzeczy. (Często rozumiane w podtekście seksualnym, przy czym *wild oats* oznacza nasienie młodego człowieka.) ❑ *Dale was out sowing his wild oats last night, and he's in jail this morning.* ❑ *Mrs. Smith told Mr. Smith that he was too old to be sowing his wild oats.*

spare, have something to Patrz *have something to spare.*

spare time, in one's Patrz *in one's spare time.*

speak of the devil używane wtedy, kiedy ktoś, kogo imię właśnie wspomniano, pojawia się lub jest od niego jakaś wiadomość. (Klisza.) ❑ *Well, speak of the devil! Hello, Tom. We were just talking about you.* ❑ *I had just mentioned Sally when – speak of the devil – she walked in the door.*

spill the beans Patrz pod *let the cat out of the bag.*

spit and image of someone, be the Patrz *be the spit and image of someone.*

spitting image of someone, be the Patrz *be the spit and image of someone.*

split the difference podzielić różnicę (z kimś). ❑ *You want to sell for $120, and I want to buy for $100. Let's split the difference and close the deal at $110.* ❑ *I don't want to split the difference. I want $120.*

spot, in a (tight) Patrz *in a (tight) spot.*

spotlight, in the Patrz *in the spotlight.*

spot, on the Patrz *on the spot.*

spread it on thick Patrz pod *lay it on thick.*

spread like wildfire rozprzestrzeniać się szeroko i poza kontrolą. (Klisza.) ❑ *The epidemic is spreading like wildfire. Everyone is* *getting sick.* ❑ *John told a joke that was so funny it spread like wildfire.*

spread oneself too thin robić tyle rzeczy, że żadnej z nich nie można zrobić dobrze; zbyt szeroko rozdzielać wysiłki i uwagę. ❑ *It's a good idea to get involved in a lot of activities, but don't spread yourself too thin.* ❑ *I'm too busy these days. I'm afraid I've spread myself too thin.*

spring chicken, no Patrz *no spring chicken.*

spur of the moment, on the Patrz *on the spur of the moment.*

square peg in a round hole niedopasowanie. (Klisza.) ❑ *John can't seem to get along with the people he works with. He's just a square peg in a round hole.* ❑ *I'm not a square peg in a round hole. It's just that no one understands me.*

squeak by (someone or something) prześliznąć się obok czegoś lub kogoś. ❑ *The guard was almost asleep, so I squeaked by him.* ❑ *I wasn't very well prepared for the test, and I just squeaked by.*

stab someone in the back zdradzić kogoś. (Również używane dosłownie.) ❑ *I thought we were friends! Why did you stab me in the back?* ❑ *You don't expect a person whom you trust to stab you in the back.*

stage (of the game), at this Patrz *at this stage (of the game).*

stag, go Patrz *go stag.*

stand one's ground AND **hold one's ground** trwać przy swoich prawach; odeprzeć atak. ❑ *The lawyer tried to confuse me when I was giving testimony, but I managed to stand my ground.* ❑ *Some people were trying to crowd us off the beach, but we held our ground.*

stand on one's own two feet być niezależnym i samowystarczalnym, nie zaś utrzymywanym przez kogoś. ❑ *I'll be glad when I* *have a good job and can stand on my own two feet.* ❑ *When Jane gets out of debt, she'll be able to stand on her own two feet again.*

stand up and be counted oświadczyć o swym poparciu dla kogoś lub czegoś; wyjść naprzeciw komuś lub czemuś. ❑ *If you believe in more government help for farmers, write your representative – stand up and be counted.* ❑ *I'm generally in favor of what you propose, but not enough to stand up and be counted.*

start from scratch zacząć od początku; zacząć z niczego. ❑ *Whenever I bake a cake, I start from scratch. I never use a cake mix in a box.* ❑ *I built every bit of my own house. I started from scratch and did everything with my own hands.*

start (off) with a clean slate zacząć na nowo; zignorować przeszłość i zacząć od nowa. ❑ *I plowed under all last year's flowers so I could start with a clean slate next spring.* ❑ *If I start off with a clean slate, then I'll know exactly what each plant is.*

start to finish, from Patrz *from start to finish.*

steal a base przebiec od jednej podstawy do drugiej w baseballu. ❑ *The runner stole second base, but he nearly got put out on the way.* ❑ *Tom runs so slowly that he never tries to steal a base.*

steal a march (on someone) niezauważalnie uzyskać jakąś przewagę nad kimś. ❑ *I got the contract because I was able to steal a march on my competitor.* ❑ *You have to be clever and fast – not dishonest – to steal a march.*

steal someone's thunder zmniejszyć czyjąś siłę lub autorytet. (Nie używane dosłownie.) ❑ *What do you mean by coming in here and stealing my thunder? I'm in charge here!* ❑ *Someone stole my thunder by leaking my announcement to the press.*

steal the show Patrz następne hasło.

steal the spotlight AND **steal the show** najlepiej zagrać w widowisku, sztuce, lub na jakiejś imprezie; zwrócić na siebie uwagę. ❑ *The lead in the play was very good, but the butler stole the* *show.* ❑ *Ann always tries to steal the spotlight when she and I make a presentation.*

steam, under one's own Patrz *under one's own steam.*

stem to stern, from Patrz *from stem to stern.*

step on it Patrz pod *step on the gas.*

step on someone's toes AND **tread on someone's toes** wtrącić się w coś lub obrazić kogoś. (Używane również dosłownie. Zwróć uwagę na przykłady z *anyone.*) ❑ *When you're in public office, you have to avoid stepping on anyone's toes.* ❑ *Ann trod on someone's toes during the last campaign and lost the election.*

step on the gas AND **step on it** pospieszyć się. ❑ *I'm in a hurry, driver. Step on it!* ❑ *I can't step on the gas, mister. There's too much traffic.*

step out of line 1. wysunąć się nieco z kolejki, w której ktoś stoi. (Dosłowne.) ❑ *I stepped out of line for a minute and lost my place.* ❑ *It's better not to step out of line if you aren't sure you can get back in again.* **2.** niewłaściwie się zachować; zachować się obraźliwie w stosunku do kogoś. ❑ *I'm terribly sorry. I hope I didn't step out of line.* ❑ *John is a lot of fun to go out with, but he has a tendency to step out of line.*

stew in one's own juice być pozostawionym samemu sobie z gniewem lub rozczarowaniem. ❑ *John has such a terrible temper. When he got mad at us, we just let him go away and stew in his own juice.* ❑ *After John stewed in his own juice for a while, he decided to come back and apologize to us.*

stick one's foot in one's mouth Patrz pod *put one's foot in one's mouth.*

stick one's neck out podjąć ryzyko. ❑ *Why should I stick my neck out to do something for her? What's she ever done for me?* ❑ *He made a risky investment. He stuck his neck out because he thought he could make some money.*

stick one's nose in(to something) Patrz pod *poke one's nose in(to something).*

stick to one's guns pozostać wiernym swoim przekonaniom; upominać się o swoje prawa. ❑ *I'll stick to my guns on this matter. I'm sure I'm right.* ❑ *Bob can be persuaded to do it our way. He probably won't stick to his guns on this point.*

Still waters run deep. przysłowie mówiące, że ktoś małomówny prawdopodobnie głęboko o czymś rozmyśla lub myśli o ważnych sprawach. ❑ *Jane is so quiet. She's probably thinking. Still waters run deep, you know.* ❑ *It's true that still waters run deep, but I think that Jane is really half asleep.*

stir up a hornet's nest stworzyć kłopoty lub trudności. ❑ *What a mess you have made of things. You've really stirred up a hornet's nest.* ❑ *Bill stirred up a hornet's nest when he discovered the theft.*

stock, have something in Patrz *have something in stock.*

stock, in Patrz *in stock.*

stone's throw away, a Patrz *a stone's throw away.*

straight from the horse's mouth z autorytatywnego lub godnego zaufania źródła. (Klisza. Nie używane dosłownie.) ❑ *I know it's true! I heard it straight from the horse's mouth!* ❑ *This comes straight from the horse's mouth, so it has to be believed.*

straight from the shoulder otwarcie; szczerze; nie trzymając nic w zanadrzu. (Klisza.) ❑ *Sally always speaks straight from the shoulder. You never have to guess what she really means.* ❑ *Bill gave a good presentation – straight from the shoulder and brief.*

strike a happy medium AND **hit a happy medium** znaleźć rozwiązanie kompromisowe; znaleźć rozwiązanie pomiędzy dwoma nie do zaakceptowania punktami krańcowymi. ❑ *Ann likes very spicy food, but Bob doesn't care for spicy food at all. We are trying to find a restaurant that strikes a happy medium.* ❑ *Tom is either very happy or very sad. He can't seem to hit a happy medium.*

strike a match zapalić zapałkę. ❑ *Mary struck a match and lit a candle.* ❑ *When Sally struck a match to light a cigarette, Jane said quickly, "No smoking, please."*

strike a sour note AND **hit a sour note** oznaczać coś nieprzy-jemnego. ❑ *Jane's sad announcement struck a sour note at the annual banquet.* ❑ *News of the crime hit a sour note in our holiday celebration.*

strike, go (out) on Patrz *go (out) on strike.*

strike it rich nagle zdobyć bogactwo. ❑ *If I could strike it rich, I wouldn't have to work anymore.* ❑ *Sally ordered a dozen oysters and found a huge pearl in one of them. She struck it rich!*

strike someone funny wydawać się komuś zabawnym. ❑ *Sally has a great sense of humor. Everything she says strikes me funny.* ❑ *Why are you laughing? Did something I said strike you funny?*

strike someone's fancy trafić komuś w upodobania. ❑ *I'll have some ice-cream, please. Chocolate strikes my fancy right now.* ❑ *Why don't you go to the store and buy a record album that strikes your fancy?*

strike up a friendship zaprzyjaźnić się (z kimś). ❑ *I struck up a friendship with John while we were on a business trip together.* ❑ *If you're lonely, you should go out and try to strike up a friendship with someone you like.*

strike while the iron is hot robić coś w możliwie najlepszym czasie; robić coś, kiedy jest po temu czas. (Klisza.) ❑ *He was in a good mood, so I asked for a loan of $200. I thought I'd better strike while the iron was hot.* ❑ *Please go to the bank and settle this matter now! They are willing to be reasonable. You've got to strike while the iron is hot.*

strings attached, with no Patrz *with no strings attached.*

strings attached, without any Patrz *without any strings attached.*

strong as an ox, as Patrz *as strong as an ox.*

stubborn as a mule, as Patrz *as stubborn as a mule.*

stuff and nonsense nonsens. ❑ *Come on! Don't give me all that stuff and nonsense!* ❑ *I don't understand this book. It's all stuff and nonsense as far as I am concerned.*

stuff the ballot box włożyć fałszywe kartki z głosami do urny; oszukiwać w naliczaniu głosów w wyborach. ❑ *The election judge was caught stuffing the ballot box in the election yesterday.* ❑ *Election officials are supposed to guard against stuffing the ballot box.*

suit someone to a T AND **fit someone to a T** bardzo komś odpowiadać. ❑ *This kind of job suits me to a T.* ❑ *This is Sally's kind of house. It fits her to a T.*

sweat of one's brow, by the Patrz *by the sweat of one's brow.*

sweet tooth, have a Patrz *have a sweet tooth.*

swim against the current Patrz następne hasło.

swim against the tide AND **swim against the current** robić coś odwrotnie niż wszyscy inni; iść pod prąd. ❑ *Bob tends to do what everybody else does. He isn't likely to swim against the tide.* ❑ *Mary always swims against the current. She's a very contrary person.*

T

table, under the Patrz *under the table.*

tail between one's legs, have one's Patrz *have one's tail between one's legs.*

tailspin, go into a Patrz *go into a tailspin.*

tail wagging the dog sytuacja, w której mała grupa kontroluje wszystko. ❏ *John was just hired yesterday, and today he's bossing everyone around. It's a case of the tail wagging the dog.* ❏ *Why is this small matter so important? Now the tail is wagging the dog!*

take a backseat (to someone) ulec komuś; oddać komuś kontrolę. ❏ *I decided to take a backseat to Mary and let her manage the project.* ❏ *I had done the best I could, but it was time to take a backseat and let someone else run things.*

take a leaf out of someone's book zachowywać się lub robić coś w taki sposób, w jaki zrobiłby to kto inny. (*A leaf* oznacza stronę.) ❏ *When you act like that, you're taking a leaf out of your sister's book, and I don't like it!* ❏ *You had better do it your way. Don't take a leaf out of my book. I don't do it well.*

take a load off one's feet Patrz pod *get a load off one's feet.*

take a nosedive Patrz pod *go into a nosedive.*

take cold Patrz pod *catch cold.*

take forty winks zdrzemnąć się; iść spać. ❑ *I think I'll go to bed and take forty winks. See you in the morning.* ❑ *Why don't you go take forty winks and call me in about an hour?*

take it or leave it zaakceptować coś takie, jakie jest lub zapomnieć o tym. ❑ *This is my last offer. Take it or leave it.* ❑ *It's not much, but it's the only food we have. You can take it or leave it.*

take liberties with someone or something AND **make free with someone or something** zużywać coś lub nadużywać kogoś lub czegoś. ❑ *You are overly familiar with me, Mr. Jones. One might think you were taking liberties with me.* ❑ *I don't like it when you make free with my lawn mower. You should at least ask when you want to borrow it.*

take one's death of cold Patrz pod *catch one's death (of cold).*

take one's medicine zaakceptować karę lub zły los, na który się zasłużyło. (Używane również dosłownie.) ❑ *I know I did wrong, and I know I have to take my medicine.* ❑ *Billy knew he was going to get spanked, and he didn't want to take his medicine.*

take someone or something by storm przytłoczyć kogoś lub coś; przyciągnąć wiele uwagi. (Klisza.) ❑ *Jane is madly in love with Tom. He took her by storm at the office party, and they've been together ever since.* ❑ *The singer took the world of opera by storm with her performance in La Boheme.*

take someone or something for granted zaakceptować kogoś lub coś – bez uczucia wdzięczności – jako coś normalnego i codziennego. ❑ *We tend to take a lot of things for granted.* ❑ *Mrs. Franklin complained that Mr. Franklin takes her for granted.*

take someone's breath away **1.** sprawić, by ktoś stracił oddech z powodu szoku lub intensywnych ćwiczeń. ❑ *Walking this fast takes my breath away.* ❑ *Mary frightened me and took my breath away.* **2.** przytłoczyć kogoś pięknem lub wspaniałością. ❑ *The magnificent painting took my breath away.* ❑ *Ann looked so beautiful that she took my breath away.*

take someone under one's wing(s) przejąć nad kimś opiekę. ❏ *John wasn't doing well in geometry until the teacher took him under her wing.* ❏ *I took the new workers under my wings, and they learned the job in no time.*

take something at face value zaakceptować coś tak jak zostało zaprezentowane. ❏ *John said he wanted to come to the party, and I took that at face value. I'm sure he'll arrive soon.* ❏ *He made us a promise, and we took his word at face value.*

take something in stride zaakceptować coś jako naturalne lub oczekiwane. ❏ *The argument surprised him, but he took it in stride.* ❏ *It was a very rude remark, but Mary took it in stride.*

take something lying down wytrzymać coś nieprzyjemnego bez kontrataku. ❏ *He insulted me publicly. You don't expect me to take that lying down, do you?* ❏ *I'm not the kind of person who'll take something like that lying down.*

take something on faith przyjąć coś lub uwierzyć w coś na podstawie znikomych lub żadnych dowodów. ❏ *Please try to believe what I'm telling you. Just take it on faith.* ❏ *Surely you can't expect me to take a story like that on faith.*

take something on the chin doświadczyć lub wytrzymać bezpośrednie (przenośnie lub dosłownie) uderzenie lub atak. ❏ *The bad news was a real shock, and John took it on the chin.* ❏ *The worst luck comes my way, and I always end up taking it on the chin.*

take something with a pinch of salt AND **take something with a grain of salt** wysłuchać opowiadania lub wyjaśnienia ze znaczną dozą wątpliwości. ❏ *You must take anything she says with a grain of salt. She doesn't always tell the truth.* ❏ *They took my explanation with a pinch of salt. I was sure they didn't believe me.*

take the bitter with the sweet zaakceptować złe rzeczy wraz z dobrymi. (Klisza.) ❏ *We all have disappointments. You have to learn to take the bitter with the sweet.* ❏ *There are good days and bad days, but every day you take the bitter with the sweet. That's life.*

take the bull by the horns przyjąć wyzwanie. (Klisza.) ❏ *If we are going to solve this problem, someone is going to have to take the bull by the horns.* ❏ *This threat isn't going to go away by itself. We are going to take the bull by the horns and settle this matter once and for all.*

take the law into one's own hands próbować zarządzać prawem; postąpić jak sędzia i ława przysięgłych w stosunku do kogoś, kto postąpił źle. ❏ *Citizens don't have the right to take the law into their own hands.* ❏ *The shopkeeper took the law into his own hands when he tried to arrest the thief.*

take the stand występować w sądzie jako świadek. ❏ *I was in court all day, waiting to take the stand.* ❏ *The lawyer asked the witness to take the stand.*

take the words out of one's mouth [w odniesieniu do kogoś innego] powiedzieć coś, co ty zamierzałeś powiedzieć. (Również z *right*, jak w przykładzie niżej.) ❏ *John said exactly what I was going to say. He took the words out of my mouth.* ❏ *I agree with you, and I wanted to say the same thing. You took the words right out of my mouth.*

take to one's heels uciec. ❏ *The little boy said hello and then took to his heels.* ❏ *The man took to his heels to try to get to the bus stop before the bus left.*

take up one's abode somewhere osiąść gdzieś i mieszkać tam. (Literackie.) ❏ *I took up my abode downtown near my office.* ❏ *We decided to take up our abode in a warmer climate.*

talk a blue streak mówić dużo i bardzo szybko. ❏ *Billy didn't talk until he was six, and then he started talking a blue streak.* ❏ *I can't understand anything Bob says. He talks a blue streak, and I can't follow his thinking.*

talk in circles mówić w sposób chaotyczny lub okrężny. ❏ *I couldn't understand a thing he said. All he did was talk in circles.* ❏ *We argued for a long time and finally decided that we were talking in circles.*

talk shop rozmawiać o sprawach zawodowych na spotkaniu towarzyskim (tam, gdzie taka rozmowa jest nie na miejscu). ❑ *All right, everyone, we're not here to talk shop. Let's have a good time.* ❑ *Mary and Jane stood by the punch bowl, talking shop.*

talk through one's hat opowiadać bzdury; chwalić się. ❑ *John isn't really as good as he says. He's just talking through his hat.* ❑ *Stop talking through your hat and start being sincere!*

talk until one is blue in the face mówić aż do momentu, kiedy ktoś jest wykończony. ❑ *I talked until I was blue in the face, but I couldn't change her mind.* ❑ *She had to talk until she was blue in the face in order to convince him.*

target, on Patrz *on target.*

teacher's pet, be the Patrz *be the teacher's pet.*

tear one's hair być zmartwionym, sfrustrowanym lub złościć się. (Nie używane dosłownie.) ❑ *I was so nervous, I was about to tear my hair.* ❑ *I had better get home. My parents will be tearing their hair.*

tell one to one's face powiedzieć coś komuś prosto z mostu. ❑ *I'm sorry that Sally feels that way about me. I wish she had told me to my face.* ❑ *I won't tell Tom that you're mad at him. You should tell him to his face.*

tell tales out of school wyjawiać sekrety lub szerzyć plotki. ❑ *I wish that John would keep quiet. He's telling tales out of school again.* ❑ *If you tell tales out of school a lot, people won't know when to believe you.*

tempest in a teapot hałas o nic. (Klisza.) ❑ *This isn't a serious problem – just a tempest in a teapot.* ❑ *Even a tempest in a teapot can take a lot of time to get settled.*

thank one's lucky stars być wdzięcznym za swoje szczęście. (Klisza.) ❑ *You can thank your lucky stars that I was there to help* *you.* ❏ *I thank my lucky stars that I studied the right things for the test.*

That's the last straw. AND **That's the straw that broke the camel's back.** To ostatnia rzecz, która się mogła wydarzyć. (Klisza.) ❏ *Now it's raining! That's the last straw. The picnic is canceled!* ❏ *When Sally came down sick, that was the straw that broke the camel's back.*

That's the straw that broke the camel's back. Patrz poprzednie hasło.

That's the ticket. Jest to dokładnie coś, co ktoś potrzebował. (Klisza.) ❏ *That's the ticket, John. You're doing it just the way it should be done.* ❏ *That's the ticket! I knew you could do it.*

That takes care of that. To postanowione. (Klisza.) ❏ *That takes care of that, and I'm glad it's over.* ❏ *I spent all morning dealing with this matter, and that takes care of that.*

The coast is clear. Nie ma widocznego niebezpieczeństwa. ❏ *I'm going to stay hidden here until the coast is clear.* ❏ *You can come out of your hiding place now. The coast is clear.*

The early bird gets the worm. przysłowie mówiące, że osoba przychodząca wcześniej dostanie nagrodę. ❏ *Don't be late again! Don't you know that the early bird gets the worm?* ❏ *I'll be there before the sun is up. After all, the early bird gets the worm.*

The fat is in the fire. przysłowie mówiące, że wyniknął poważny kłopot. ❏ *Now that Mary is leaving, the fat is in the fire. How can we get along without her?* ❏ *The fat's in the fire! There's $3,000 missing from the office safe.*

The honeymoon is over. Przyjemny początek się skończył. (Klisza.) ❏ *Okay, the honeymoon is over. It's time to settle down* *and do some hard work.* ❏ *I knew the honeymoon was over when they started yelling at me to work faster.*

the pot calling the kettle black przykład kogoś posiadającego jakąś przywarę i oskarżającego kogoś innego o posiadanie tej samej przywary. (Klisza.) ❏ *Ann is always late, but she was rude enough to tell everyone when I was late. Now that's the pot calling the kettle black!* ❏ *You're calling me thoughtless? That's really a case of the pot calling the kettle black.*

There are plenty of other fish in the sea Są inne możliwości. (Klisza. Używane w odniesieniu do ludzi.) ❏ *When John broke up with Ann, I told her not to worry. There are plenty of other fish in the sea.* ❏ *It's too bad that your secretary quit, but there are plenty of other fish in the sea.*

There's more than one way to skin a cat. Przysłowie mówiące, że istnieje więcej niż jeden sposób zrobienia czegoś. ❏ *If that way won't work, try another way. There's more than one way to skin a cat.* ❏ *Don't worry, I'll figure out a way to get it done. There's more than one way to skin a cat.*

There's no accounting for taste. przysłowie mówiące, że nie istnieje żadne wyjaśnienie dla ludzkich gustów. ❏ *Look at that purple and orange car! There's no accounting for taste.* ❏ *Some people seemed to like the music, although I thought it was worse than noise. There's no accounting for taste.*

There will be the devil to pay. Będzie mnóstwo kłopotów. ❏ *If you damage my car, there will be the devil to pay.* ❏ *Bill broke a window, and now there will be the devil to pay.*

The shoe is on the other foot. przysłowie mówiące, że ktoś doświadcza tych samych rzeczy, których doświadczenie spowodował komuś innemu. (Zauważ zróżnicowanie w przykładach.) ❏ *The teacher is taking a course in summer school and is finding out what it's like when the shoe is on the other foot.* ❏ *When the* *policeman was arrested, he learned what it was like to have the shoe on the other foot.*

thick and thin, through Patrz *through thick and thin.*

thick as pea soup, as Patrz *as thick as pea soup.*

thick as thieves, as Patrz *as thick as thieves.*

thin air, out of Patrz *out of thin air.*

thin ice, on Patrz *on thin ice.*

think on one's feet myśleć podczas mówienia. ❑ *If you want to be a successful teacher, you must be able to think on your feet.* ❑ *I have to write out everything I'm going to say, because I can't think on my feet too well.*

thorn in someone's side, be a Patrz *be a thorn in someone's side.*

three-ring circus, like a patrz *like a three-ring circus.*

through thick and thin w dobrych i złych czasach. (Klisza.) ❑ *We've been together through thick and thin and we won't desert each other now.* ❑ *Over the years, we went through thick and thin and enjoyed every minute of it.*

throw a monkey wrench in the works spowodować problemy w realizacji czyichś planów. ❑ *I don't want to throw a monkey wrench in the works, but have you checked your plans with a lawyer?* ❑ *When John refused to help us, he really threw a monkey wrench in the works.*

throw caution to the wind postąpić bardzo lekkomyślnie. (Klisza.) ❑ *Jane, who is usually cautious, threw caution to the wind and went windsurfing.* ❑ *I don't mind taking a little chance now and then, but I'm not the type of person who throws caution to the wind.*

throw cold water on something Patrz pod *pour cold water on something.*

throw down the gauntlet rzucić wyzwanie komuś do kłótni lub (przenośnie) walki. ❏ *When Bob challenged my conclusions, he threw down the gauntlet. I was ready for an argument.* ❏ *Frowning at Bob is the same as throwing down the gauntlet. He loves to get into a fight about something.*

throw good money after bad stracić dodatkowo jakieś pieniądze już po jednej stracie. (Klisza.) ❏ *I bought a used car and then had to spend $300 on repairs. That was throwing good money after bad.* ❏ *The Browns are always throwing good money after bad. They bought an acre of land that turned out to be swamp, and then had to pay to have it filled in .*

throw in the sponge Patrz następne hasło.

throw in the towel AND **throw in the sponge** zrezygnować z robienia czegoś. ❏ *When John could stand no more of Mary's bad temper, he threw in the towel and left.* ❏ *Don't give up now! It's too soon to throw in the sponge.*

throw oneself at someone's feet skłonić się pokornie do czyichś stóp. (Używane zarówno dosłownie, jak i przenośnie). ❏ *Do I have to throw myself at your feet in order to convince you that I'm sorry?* ❏ *I love you sincerely, Jane. I'll throw myself at your feet and await your command. I'm your slave!*

throw oneself on the mercy of the court AND **throw oneself at the mercy of the court** błagać o łaskę sędziego w sądzie. ❏ *Your honor, please believe me, I didn't do it on purpose. I throw myself on the mercy of the court and beg for a light sentence.* ❏ *Jane threw herself at the mercy of the court and hoped for the best.*

throw someone a curve **1.** rzucić komuś piłkę w baseballu. ❏ *The pitcher threw John a curve, and John swung wildly against thin air.* ❏ *During that game, the pitcher threw everyone a curve at least once.* **2.** zamieszać komuś w głowie przez zrobienie czegoś nieoczekiwanego. ❏ *When you said house you threw me a curve.*

225

The password was supposed to be home. ❏ *John threw me a curve when we were making our presentation, and I forgot my speech.*

throw someone for a loop AND **knock someone for a loop** zmieszać lub zaszokować kogoś. ❏ *When Bill heard the news, it threw him for a loop.* ❏ *The manager knocked Bob for a loop by firing him on the spot.*

throw someone to the wolves (przenośnie) poświęcić kogoś. (Klisza. Nie używane dosłownie.) ❏ *The press was demanding an explanation, so the mayor blamed the mess on John and threw him to the wolves.* ❏ *I wouldn't let them throw me to the wolves! I did nothing wrong, and I won't take the blame for their errors.*

throw something into the bargain włączyć coś do układu. ❏ *To encourage me to buy a new car, the car dealer threw a free radio into the bargain.* ❏ *If you purchase three pounds of chocolates, I'll throw one pound of salted nuts into the bargain.*

thumb a ride AND **hitch a ride** być podwiezionym przez przejeżdżającego kierowcę; dawać znaki kciukiem, że prosi się o podwiezienie. ❏ *My car broke down on the highway, and I had to thumb a ride to get back to town.* ❏ *Sometimes it's dangerous to hitch a ride with a stranger.*

thumb one's nose at someone or something (przenośnie lub dosłownie) wykonać wulgarny gest oznaczający niesmak kciukiem na nosie. ❏ *The tramp thumbed his nose at the lady and walked away.* ❏ *You can't just thumb your nose at people who give you trouble. You've got to learn to get along.*

tickle someone's fancy zainteresować kogoś; zaciekawić kogoś. ❏ *I have an interesting problem here that I think will tickle your fancy.* ❏ *This doesn't tickle my fancy at all. This is dull and boring.*

tied to one's mother's apron strings zdominowany przez matkę; zależny od matki. ❏ *Tom is still tied to his mother's apron strings.* ❏ *Isn't he a little old to be tied to his mother's apron strings?*

tie someone in knots zdenerwować się lub zmartwić się. ❏ *John tied himself in knots worrying about his wife during the operation.* ❏ *This waiting and worrying really ties me in knots.*

tie someone's hands nie dopuścić do zrobienia czegoś przez kogoś. (Używane również dosłownie.) ❏ *I'd like to help you, but my boss has tied my hands.* ❏ *Please don't tie my hands with unnecessary restrictions. I'd like the freedom to do whatever is necessary.*

tie the knot ożenić się lub wyjść za mąż. ❏ *Well, I hear that you and John are going to tie the knot.* ❏ *My parents tied the knot almost forty years ago.*

tight as a tick, as Patrz *as tight as a tick.*

tight as Dick's hatband, as Patrz *as tight as Dick's hatband.*

tighten one's belt starać się wydawać mniej pieniędzy. ❏ *Things are beginning to cost more and more. It looks like we'll all have to tighten our belts.* ❏ *Times are hard, and prices are high. I can tighten my belt for only so long.*

tilt at windmills walczyć z wyimaginowanymi wrogami; walczyć przeciwko mało znaczącym wrogom lub sprawom. (Podobnie jak fikcyjna postać, Don Kiszot, który walczył z wiatrakami.) ❏ *Aren't you too smart to go around tilting at windmills?* ❏ *I'm not going to fight this issue. I've wasted too much of my life tilting at windmills.*

Time hangs heavy on someone's hands. Czas biegnie powoli, kiedy się nie ma nic do roboty. (Nie używane dosłownie. Zauważ zróżnicowanie w przykładach.) ❏ *I don't like it when time hangs so heavily on my hands.* ❏ *John looks so bored. Time hangs heavy on his hands.*

Time is money. [Mój] czas jest cenny, więc go nie trać. ❏ *I can't afford to spend a lot of time standing here talking. Time is money, you know!* ❏ *People who keep saying time is money may be working too hard.*

time of one's life, have the Patrz *have the time of one's life.*

227

tip of one's tongue, on the Patrz *on the tip of one's tongue.*

tip the scales at something ważyć jakąś ilość. ❏ *Tom tips the scales at nearly 200 pounds.* ❏ *I'll be glad when I tip the scales at a few pounds less.*

tiptoe, on Patrz *on tiptoe.*

toes, on one's Patrz *on one's toes.*

toe the line Patrz następne hasło.

toe the mark AND **toe the line** robić to, czego się od kogoś oczekuje; postępować zgodnie z zasadami. ❏ *You'll get ahead, Sally. Don't worry. Just toe the mark, and everything will be okay.* ❏ *John finally got fired. He just couldn't learn to toe the line.*

tongue-in-cheek nieszczery; żartujący. ❏ *Ann made a tongue-in-cheek remark to John, and he got mad because he thought she was serious.* ❏ *The play seemed very serious at first, but then everyone saw that it was tongue-in-cheek, and they began laughing.*

too good to be true prawie nie do wiary; zbyt dobre, by było prawdziwe. (Klisza.) ❏ *The news was too good to be true.* ❏ *When I finally got a big raise, it was too good to be true.*

Too many cooks spoil the broth. Patrz następne hasło.

Too many cooks spoil the stew. AND **Too many cooks spoil the broth.** przysłowie mówiące, że jeśli zbyt wiele ludzi próbuje czymś zarządzać, po prostu to psuje. ❏ *Let's decide who is in charge around here. Too many cooks spoil the stew.* ❏ *Everyone is giving orders, but no one is following them! Too many cooks spoil the broth.*

too many irons in the fire, have Patrz *have too many irons in the fire.*

to one's heart's content tak jak ktoś chce. ❏ *John wanted a week's vacation so he could go to the lake and fish to his heart's content.* ❏ *I just sat there, eating chocolate to my heart's content.*

toot one's own horn AND **blow one's own horn** wychwalać się. ❏ *Tom is always tooting his own horn. Is he really as good as he says he is?* ❏ *I find it hard to blow my own horn, but I manage.*

top of one's head, off the Patrz *off the top of one's head.*

top of one's lungs, at the Patrz *at the top of one's lungs.*

top of one's voice, at the Patrz *at the top of one's voice.*

top of the world, on Patrz *on top of the world.*

top, on Patrz *on top.*

top, over the Patrz *over the top.*

top to bottom, from patrz *from top to bottom.*

toss one's hat into the ring oświadczyć, że bierze się udział w wyborach. ❏ *Jane wanted to run for treasurer, so she tossed her hat into the ring.* ❏ *The mayor never tossed his hat into the ring. Instead he announced his retirement.*

to the ends of the earth do najdalszych i najbardziej niedostępnych części ziemi. ❏ *I'll pursue him to the ends of the earth.* ❏ *We've almost explored the whole world. We've traveled to the ends of the earth trying to learn about our world.*

To the victors belong the spoils. przysłowie mówiące, że zwycięzcy zdobywają władzę i majątek. ❏ *The mayor took office and immediately fired many workers and hired new ones. Everyone said, "To the victors belong the spoils."* ❏ *The office of president includes the right to live in the White House and at Camp David. To the victors belong the spoils.*

tough act to follow trudne zadanie prezentacji lub wystąpienia po jakiejś innej prezentacji. (Klisza.) ❑ *Bill's speech was excellent. It was a tough act to follow, but my speech was good also.* ❑ *In spite of the fact that I had a tough act to follow, I did my best.*

tough row to hoe trudne do wykonania zadanie. (Klisza.) ❑ *It was a tough row to hoe, but I finally got a college degree.* ❑ *Getting the contract signed is going to be a tough row to hoe, but I'm sure I can do it.*

town, go to Patrz *go to town.*

town, out on the Patrz *out on the town.*

tread on someone's toes Patrz pod *step on someone's toes.*

trial, on Patrz *on trial.*

true to one's word dotrzymywanie obietnicy. ❑ *True to his word, Tom showed up at exactly eight o'clock.* ❑ *We'll soon know if Jane is true to her word. We'll see if she does what she promised.*

try one's wings (out) AND **try out one's wings** próbować zrobić coś, do czego się właśnie uzyskało kwalifikacje. (Podobnie jak młody ptak próbuje swych skrzydeł podrywając się do lotu.) ❑ *John just got his driver's license and wants to borrow the car to try out his wings.* ❑ *I learned to skin dive, and I want to go to the seaside to try out my wings.* ❑ *You've read about it enough. It's time to try your wings.*

try someone's patience zrobić coś irytującego, co może spowodować, że ktoś straci cierpliwość; zirytować kogoś. ❑ *Stop whistling. You're trying my patience. Very soon I'm going to lose my temper.* ❑ *Some students think it's fun to try the teacher's patience.*

tune (with someone or something), out of Patrz *out of tune (with someone or something).*

turn a blind eye to someone or something zignorować coś i udawać, że się tego nie widzi. ❑ *The usher turned a blind eye to* *the little boy who sneaked into the theater.* ❏ *How can you turn a blind eye to all those starving children?*

turn a deaf ear (to something) zignorować to, co ktoś widzi; zignorować wołanie o pomoc. ❏ *How can you just turn a deaf ear to their cries for food and shelter?* ❏ *The government has turned a deaf ear.*

turn on a dime skręcić na bardzo wąskim zakręcie. ❏ *This car handles very well. It can turn on a dime.* ❏ *The speeding car turned on a dime and headed in the other direction.*

turn one's nose up at someone or something AND **turn up one's nose at someone or something** prychnąć na kogoś lub coś; odrzucić kogoś lub coś. ❏ *John turned his nose up at Ann, and that hurt her feelings.* ❏ *I never turn up my nose at dessert, no matter what it is.*

turn, out of Patrz *out of turn.*

turn over a new leaf zacząć znowu z zamiarem robienia lepiej; zacząć znowu, ignorując przeszłe błędy. (Klisza.) ❏ *Tom promised to turn over a new leaf and do better from now on.* ❏ *After a minor accident, Sally decided to turn over a new leaf and drive more carefully.*

turn over in one's grave [w odniesieniu do zmarłego] zaszokowany lub przerażony. (Klisza. Oczywiście, nie używane dosłownie.) ❏ *If Beethoven heard Mary play one of his sonatas, he'd turn over in his grave.* ❏ *If Aunt Jane knew what you were doing with her favorite chair, she would turn over in her grave.*

turn someone's stomach spowodować czyjąś chorobę (dosłownie lub w przenośni). ❏ *This milk is spoiled. The smell of it turns my stomach.* ❏ *The play was so bad that it turned my stomach.*

turn something to one's advantage odnieść z czegoś korzyść dla siebie (z czegoś, co w innym przypadku byłoby niekorzyścią). ❏ *Sally found a way to turn the problem to her advantage.* ❏ *The* *ice-cream store manager was able to turn the hot weather to her advantage.*

turn the other cheek zignorować nadużycie lub obrazę. (Biblijne.) ❑ *When Bob got mad at Mary and yelled at her, she just turned the other cheek.* ❑ *Usually I turn the other cheek when someone is rude to me.*

turn the tide odwrócić kierunek zdarzeń; odwrócić kierunek opinii publicznej. ❑ *It looked as if the team was going to lose, but near the end of the game, our star player turned the tide.* ❑ *At first, people were opposed to our plan. After a lot of discussion, we were able to turn the tide.*

twiddle one's thumbs zabijać czas bawiąc się palcami. ❑ *What am I supposed to do while waiting for you? Sit here and twiddle my thumbs?* ❑ *Don't sit around twiddling your thumbs. Get busy!*

twinkling of an eye, in the Patrz *in the twinkling of an eye.*

twist someone around one's little finger manipulować kimś i kontrolować go. (Klisza.) ❑ *Bob really fell for Jane. She can twist him around her little finger.* ❑ *Billy's mother has twisted him around her little finger. He's very dependent on her.*

twist someone's arm zmusić kogoś do czegoś lub wyperswadować komuś coś. ❑ *At first she refused, but after I twisted her arm a little, she agreed to help.* ❑ *I didn't want to run for mayor, but everyone twisted my arm.*

two shakes of a lamb's tail, in Patrz *in two shakes of a lamb's tail.*

U

under a cloud (of suspicion) być podejrzanym o zrobienie czegoś. ❑ *Someone stole some money at work, and now everyone is under a cloud of suspicion.* ❑ *Even the manager is under a cloud.*

under construction w budowie lub remoncie. ❑ *We cannot travel on this road because it's under construction.* ❑ *Our new home has been under construction all summer. We hope to move in next month.*

under fire podczas ataku. ❑ *There was a scandal in city hall, and the mayor was forced to resign under fire.* ❑ *John is a good lawyer because he can think under fire.*

under one's own steam własnymi siłami lub własnym wysiłkiem. ❑ *I missed my ride to class, so I had to get there under my own steam.* ❑ *John will need some help with this project. He can't do it under his own steam.*

under the counter [w odniesieniu do czegoś, co ma być kupione lub sprzedane] w tajemnicy lub bezprawnie. (Używane również dosłownie.) ❑ *The drugstore owner was arrested for selling liquor under the counter.* ❑ *This owner was also selling dirty books under the counter.*

under the table w tajemnicy, jak przy dawaniu łapówki. (Używane również dosłownie.) ❑ *The mayor had been paying money to the* *construction company under the table.* ❑ *Tom transferred the deed to the property to his wife under the table.*

under the weather chory. ❑ *I'm a bit under the weather today, so I can't go to the office.* ❑ *My head is aching, and I feel a little under the weather.*

under the wire w ostatniej sekundzie. ❑ *I turned in my report just under the wire.* ❑ *Bill was the last person to get in the door. He got in under the wire.*

up a blind alley w ślepym zaułku; na drodze, która donikąd nie prowadzi. ❑ *I have been trying to find out something about my ancestors, but I'm up a blind alley. I can't find anything.* ❑ *The police are up a blind alley in their investigation of the crime.*

up in arms podnosząc się w gniewie; (przenośnie lub dosłownie) uzbrojony. ❑ *My father was really up in arms when he got his tax bill this year.* ❑ *The citizens were up in arms, pounding on the gates of the palace, demanding justice.*

up in the air niezdecydowany; niepewny. (Używane również dosłownie.) ❑ *I don't know what Sally plans to do. Things were sort of up in the air the last time we talked.* ❑ *Let's leave this question up in the air until next week.*

upset the apple cart wprowadzić chaos lub zniszczyć coś. ❑ *Tom really upset the apple cart by telling Mary the truth about Jane.* ❑ *I always knew he'd upset the apple cart.*

up to one's ears (in something) Patrz następne hasło.

up to one's neck (in something) AND **up to one's ears (in something)** bardzo w coś zaangażowany. ❑ *I can't come to the meeting. I'm up to my neck in these reports.* ❑ *Mary is up to her ears in her work.*

up to par dobry w tym stopniu co standardowy lub przeciętny; zbliżony do wymagań standardowych. ❑ *I'm just not feeling up to par today. I must be coming down with something.* ❑ *The manager said that the report was not up to par and gave it back to Mary to do over again.*

use every trick in the book zastosować każdą możliwą metodę. ❑ *I used every trick in the book, but I still couldn't manage to get a ticket to the game Saturday.* ❑ *Bob tried to use every trick in the book, but he still failed.*

utter a word, not Patrz *not utter a word.*

V

vacation, on Patrz *on vacation.*

vanish into thin air zniknąć bez pozostawiania śladu. ❑ *My money gets spent so fast. It seems to vanish into thin air.* ❑ *When I came back, my car was gone. I had locked it, and it couldn't have vanished into thin air!*

Variety is the spice of life. przysłowie mówiące, że różnice i zmiana sprawiają, iż życie staje się interesujące. ❑ *Mary reads all kinds of books. She says variety is the spice of life.* ❑ *The Franklins travel all over the world so they can learn how different people live. After all, variety is the spice of life.*

vicious circle, in a Patrz *in a vicious circle.*

victors belong the spoils, To the. Patrz *To the victors belong the spoils.*

virtue of something, by Patrz *by virtue of something.*

vote a straight ticket głosować na wszystkich członków tej samej partii politycznej. ❑ *I'm not a member of any political party, so I never vote a straight ticket.* ❑ *I usually vote a straight ticket because I believe in the principles of one party and not in the other's.*

W

wagon, on the Patrz *on the wagon.*

wait-and-see attitude stanowisko sceptyczne; stanowisko nie-pewne, kiedy ktoś po prostu czeka, by zobaczyć, co się stanie. ❏ *John thought that Mary couldn't do it, but he took a wait-and-see attitude.* ❏ *His wait-and-see attitude didn't influence me at all.*

waiting list, on a Patrz *on a waiting list.*

wait on someone hand and foot bardzo dobrze komuś służyć, dbając o wszystkie jego osobiste potrzeby. ❏ *I don't mind bringing you your coffee, but I don't intend to wait on you hand and foot.* ❏ *I don't want anyone to wait on me hand and foot. I can take care of myself.*

walk a tightrope znaleźć się w sytuacji, w której musi się być bardzo ostrożnym. (Używane również dosłownie.) ❏ *I've been walking a tightrope all day. I need to relax.* ❏ *Our business is about to fail. We've been walking a tightrope for three months.*

walk on air być bardzo szczęśliwym; być w euforii. (Nigdy nie używane dosłownie.) ❏ *Ann was walking on air when she got the job.* ❏ *On the last day of school, all the children are walking on air.*

walk on eggs być bardzo ostrożnym. (Nigdy nie używane do-słownie.) ❏ *The manager is very hard to deal with. You really* *have to walk on eggs.* ❏ *I've been walking on eggs ever since I started working here.*

walk the floor nerwowo się przechadzać czekając. ❏ *While Bill waited for news of the operation, he walked the floor for hours on end.* ❏ *Walking the floor won't help. You might as well sit down and relax.*

wall, go to the Patrz *go to the wall.*

walls have ears ktoś może nas podsłuchać. (Klisza.) ❏ *Let's not discuss this matter here. Walls have ears, you know.* ❏ *Shhh. Walls have ears. Someone may be listening.*

warm the bench [w odniesieniu do graczy] nie grać podczas zawodów – pozostawać na ławce. ❏ *John spent the whole game warming the bench.* ❏ *Mary never warms the bench. She plays from the beginning to the end.*

warm the cockles of someone's heart sprawić, by ktoś się czuł przytulnie i szczęśliwie. (Klisza.) ❏ *It warms the cockles of my heart to hear you say that.* ❏ *Hearing that old song again warmed the cockles of her heart.*

wash one's hands of someone or something zakończyć swoje stosunki z kimś lub czymś. ❏ *I washed my hands of Tom. I wanted no more to do with him.* ❏ *That car was a real headache. I washed my hands of it long ago.*

waste one's breath tracić czas mówiąc; mówić na próżno. ❏ *Don't waste your breath talking to her. She won't listen.* ❏ *You can't persuade me. You're just wasting your breath.*

watched pot never boils, A. Patrz *A watched pot never boils.*

water off a duck's back, like Patrz *like water off a duck's back.*

water under the bridge   przeszły i zapomniany. (Klisza.)
❑ *Please don't worry about it anymore. It's all water under the bridge.* ❑ *I can't change the past. It's water under the bridge.*

weak as a kitten, as   Patrz *as weak as a kitten.*

weakness for someone or something, have a   Patrz *have a weakness for someone or something.*

wear more than one hat   być odpowiedzialnym za więcej niż jedną sprawę; piastować więcej niż jeden urząd. ❑ *The mayor is also the police chief. She wears more than one hat.* ❑ *I have too much to do to wear more than one hat.*

wear out one's welcome   pozostawać gdzieś zbyt długo (na imprezie, na którą się było zaproszonym); odwiedzać kogoś zbyt często. (Klisza.) ❑ *Tom visited the Smiths so often that he wore out his welcome.* ❑ *At about midnight, I decided that I had worn out my welcome, so I went home.*

weather, under the   Patrz *under the weather.*

well-fixed   Patrz następne hasło.

well-heeled   AND **well-fixed; well-off**   bogaty; z wystarczającą ilością pieniędzy. ❑ *My uncle can afford a new car. He's well-heeled.* ❑ *Everyone in his family is well-off.*

well-off   Patrz poprzednie hasło.

well-to-do   bogaty i w dobrej pozycji towarzyskiej. (Często z *quite,* jak w przykładach.) ❑ *The Jones family is quite well-to-do.* ❑ *There is a gentleman waiting for you at the door. He appears quite well-to-do.*

were, as it   Patrz *as it were.*

wet behind the ears młody i niedoświadczony. ❏ *John's too young to take on a job like this! He's still wet behind the ears!* ❏ *He may be wet behind the ears, but he's well trained and totally competent.*

What is sauce for the goose is sauce for the gander. przysłowie mówiące, że jeśli coś jest właściwe dla jednej osoby, jest również właściwe dla innej. ❏ *If John gets a new coat, I should get one, too. After all, what is sauce for the goose is sauce for the gander.* ❏ *If I get punished for breaking the window, so should Mary. What is sauce for the goose is sauce for the gander.*

what makes someone tick to, co kogoś motywuje; coś, co powoduje, że ktoś się zachowuje w ten, a nie inny sposób. ❏ *William is sort of strange. I don't know what makes him tick.* ❏ *When you get to know people, you find out what makes them tick.*

When in Rome, do as the Romans do. przysłowie mówiące, że należy się tak zachowywać, jak zachowują się ludzie miejscowi. ❏ *I don't usually eat lamb, but I did when I went to Australia. When in Rome, do as the Romans do.* ❏ *I always carry an umbrella when I visit London. When in Rome, do as the Romans do.*

When the cat's away the mice will play. Niektórzy ludzie zaczynają postępować źle, kiedy się ich nie obserwuje. (Klisza.) ❏ *The students behaved very badly for the substitute teacher. When the cat's away the mice will play.* ❏ *John had a wild party at his house when his parents were out of town. When the cat's away the mice will play.*

when the time is ripe dokładnie we właściwym czasie. ❏ *I'll tell her the good news when the time is ripe.* ❏ *When the time is ripe, I'll bring up the subject again.*

Where there's a will there's a way. przysłowie mówiące, że ktoś jest w stanie coś zrobić, jeżeli chce tego wystarczająco mocno. ❏ *Don't give up, Ann. You can do it. Where there's a will there's a way.* ❏ *They told John he'd never walk again after his* *accident. He worked at it, and he was able to walk again! Where there's a will there's a way.*

Where there's smoke there's fire. przysłowie mówiące, że jeśli są jakieś wskazówki mówiące o tym, że problem istnieje, to prawdopodobnie on istnieje. ❑ *There is a lot of noise coming from the classroom. There is probably something wrong. Where there's smoke there's fire.* ❑ *I think there is something wrong at the house on the corner. The police are there again. Where there's smoke there's fire.*

whisker, by a Patrz *by a whisker.*

white as the driven snow, as Patrz *as white as the driven snow.*

wide of the mark 1. daleko od celu. ❑ *Tom's shot was wide of the mark.* ❑ *The pitch was quite fast, but wide of the mark.* **2.** niewystarczający; daleki od tego, czego się wymaga lub oczekuje. ❑ *Jane's efforts were sincere, but wide of the mark.* ❑ *He failed the course because everything he did was wide of the mark.*

wild-goose chase bezwartościowe poszukiwanie; daremne dążenia. ❑ *I wasted all afternoon on a wild-goose chase.* ❑ *John was angry because he was sent out on a wild-goose chase.*

win by a nose zwyciężyć bardzo drobną różnicą. (Podobnie jak w wyścigach konnych koń wyprzedza drugiego tylko o długość swojego nosa.) ❑ *I ran the fastest race I could, but I only won by a nose.* ❑ *Sally won the race, but she only won by a nose.*

wind, in the Patrz *in the wind.*

wire, down to the Patrz *down to the wire.*

wire, under the Patrz *under the wire.*

wise as an owl, as Patrz *as wise as an owl.*

with all one's heart and soul bardzo szczerze. (Klisza.) ❑ *Oh, Bill, I love you with all my heart and soul, and I always will!* ❑ *She thanked us with all her heart and soul for the gift.*

with both hands tied behind one's back Patrz pod *with one hand tied behind one's back.*

wither on the vine AND **die on the vine** [w odniesieniu do czegoś] uwiędnąć lub zaniknąć we wczesnej fazie rozwoju. (Również używane dosłownie w odniesieniu do winogron lub innych owoców.) ❑ *You have a great plan, Tom. Let's keep it alive. Don't let it wither on the vine.* ❑ *The whole project died on the vine when the contract was canceled.*

with every (other) breath [mówiąc coś] ciągle lub co chwilę. ❑ *Bob was out in the yard, raking leaves and cursing with every other breath.* ❑ *The child was so grateful that she was thanking me with every breath.*

with flying colors łatwo i wspaniale. ❑ *John passed his geometry test with flying colors.* ❑ *Sally qualified for the race with flying colors.*

within an inch of one's life bardzo blisko utraty życia; ocierając się o śmierć. (Klisza.) ❑ *The accident frightened me within an inch of my life.* ❑ *When Mary was seriously ill in the hospital, she came within an inch of her life.*

with no strings attached AND **without any strings attached** bezwarunkowo; bez żadnych zobowiązań. ❑ *My parents gave me a computer without any strings attached.* ❑ *I want this only if there are no strings attached.*

with one hand tied behind one's back AND **with both hands tied behind one's back** bardzo łatwo. (Klisza.) ❑ *I could put an end to this argument with one hand tied behind my back.* ❑ *John could do this job with both hands tied behind his back.*

without any strings attached Patrz pod *with no strings attached.*

without batting an eye nie okazując strachu ani żadnej innej reakcji; bez mrugnięcia okiem. (Klisza.) ❏ *I knew I had insulted her, but she turned to me and asked me to leave without batting an eye.* ❏ *Right in the middle of the speech – without batting an eye – the speaker walked off the stage.*

without further ado bez słowa więcej. (Klisza. Wyrażenie nadużywane w publicznych wystąpieniach.) ❏ *And without further ado, I would like to introduce Mr. Bill Franklin!* ❏ *The time has come to leave, so without further ado, good evening and good-bye.*

wit's end, at one's Patrz *at one's wit's end.*

wolf in sheep's clothing coś groźnego przebranego za coś miłego. (Klisza.) ❏ *Beware of the police chief. He seems polite, but he's a wolf in sheep's clothing.* ❏ *This proposal seems harmless enough, but I think it's a wolf in sheep's clothing.*

woods, out of the Patrz *out of the woods.*

word, go back on one's Patrz *go back on one's word.*

word go, from the Patrz *from the word go.*

word of mouth, by Patrz *by word of mouth.*

words stick in one's throat, have one's Patrz *have one's words stick in one's throat.*

work like a horse pracować bardzo ciężko. (Klisza.) ❏ *I've been working like a horse all day, and I'm tired.* ❏ *I'm too old to work like a horse. I'd prefer to relax more.*

work one's fingers to the bone pracować bardzo ciężko. (Klisza.) ❏ *I worked my fingers to the bone so you children could*

have everything you needed. Now look at the way you treat me!
❏ *I spent the day working my fingers to the bone, and now I want to relax.*

work out for the best skończyć się w najlepszy możliwy sposób.
❏ *Don't worry. Things will work out for the best.* ❏ *It seems bad now, but it'll work out for the best.*

world, in the Patrz *in the world.*

world of one's own, in a Patrz *in a world of one's own.*

world, out of this Patrz *out of this world.*

worst comes to worst, if Patrz *if worst comes to worst.*

worth its weight in gold bardzo cenny. (Klisza.) ❏ *This book is worth its weight in gold.* ❏ *Oh, Bill. You're wonderful. You're worth your weight in gold.*

worth one's salt wart swojego zarobku. (Klisza.) ❏ *Tom doesn't work very hard, and he's just barely worth his salt, but he's very easy to get along with.* ❏ *I think he's more than worth his salt. He's a good worker.*

wrack and ruin, go to Patrz *go to wrack and ruin.*

wrong, in the Patrz *in the wrong.*

wrong track, on the Patrz *on the wrong track.*

X

X marks the spot to dokładnie to miejsce. (Klisza. Może być użyte dosłownie, kiedy ktoś pisze *X*, żeby oznaczyć właściwe miejsce.) ❏ *This is where the rock struck my car – X marks the spot.*
❏ *Now, please move that table over here. Yes, right here – X
marks the spot.*

Y

year in, year out rok po roku, przez cały długi rok. ❑ *I seem to have hay fever year in, year out. I never get over it.* ❑ *John wears the same old suit, year in, year out.*

You can say that again! AND **You said it!** To prawda.; Masz rację. (Słowo *that* jest zaakcentowane.) ❑ MARY: *It sure is hot today.* JANE: *You can say that again!* ❑ BILL: *This cake is yummy!* BOB: *You said it!*

You can't take it with you. Powinieneś cieszyć się pieniędzmi teraz, bo ci się nie przydadzą, jak umrzesz. (Klisza.) ❑ *My uncle is a wealthy miser. I keep telling him, "You can't take it with you."* ❑ *If you have money, you should make out a will. You can't take it with you, you know!*

You can't teach an old dog new tricks. przysłowie mówiące, że starzy ludzie nie potrafią nauczyć się niczego nowego. (Używane również dosłownie w odniesieniu do psów.) ❑ *"Of course I can learn," bellowed Uncle John. "Who says you can't teach an old dog new tricks?"* ❑ *I'm sorry. I can't seem to learn to do it right. Oh, well. You can't teach an old dog new tricks.*

Your guess is as good as mine. Twoja odpowiedź prawdopo-dobnie będzie tak samo poprawna jak moja. ❑ *I don't know where the scissors are. Your guess is as good as mine.* ❑ *Your guess is as good as mine as to when the train will arrive.*

You said it! Patrz pod *You can say that again!*

Z

zero in on something   skoncentrować się na czymś. ❏ *"Now,"*
said Mr. Smith, "I would like to zero in on another important
point." ❏ Mary is very good about zeroing in on the most
important and helpful ideas.